FUNDAMENTALS OF HEALTH INSURANCE

PART B

The Health Insurance Association of America
Washington, DC 20004-1109

©1997 by the Health Insurance Association of America
All rights reserved. Published 1997
Printed in the United States of America

ISBN 1-879143-38-0

TABLE OF CONTENTS

FIGURES, TABLES, AND EXHIBITS v
FOREWORD... vii
PREFACE ix
ACKNOWLEDGMENTS xi
ABOUT THE AUTHORS xiii

Chapter 1
MANAGING THE COST OF HEALTH CARE 1

Chapter 2
POLICY ISSUE, RENEWAL, AND SERVICE 35

Chapter 3
CLAIM ADMINISTRATION... 67

Chapter 4
PRICING HEALTH INSURANCE PRODUCTS 101

Chapter 5
GOVERNMENT REGULATION.. 137

Chapter 6
FRAUD AND ABUSE 173

Appendix A
UNFAIR LIFE, ACCIDENT AND HEALTH CLAIMS SETTLEMENT
PRACTICES MODEL REGULATION...................................... 203

Appendix B
UNFAIR TRADE PRACTICES ACT 207

SUGGESTED READINGS 221

GLOSSARY 225

INDEX.. 263

FIGURES, TABLES, AND EXHIBITS

CHAPTER 1
Figures
Figure 1.1....... Consumer Price Index: All Items and Medical Care Items, 1969–1995
Figure 1.2....... National Health Expenditures as a Percent of Gross Domestic Production, 1969–2000

CHAPTER 3
Exhibits
Exhibit 3.1...... Uniform Billing Form
Exhibit 3.2...... Health Insurance Claim Form

CHAPTER 4
Tables
Table 4.1........ Examples of Blended Manual/Experience Rating
Table 4.2........ Effect of Different Premium Structures
Table 4.3a ...... New Cost: Hospital Charge
Table 4.3b ...... New Cost: Surgeon's Charge
Table 4.4........ Example of Loss Ratio Formula

CHAPTER 6
Tables
Table 6.1........ Fraud versus Abuse
Table 6.2........ Fraud against Health Insurance Companies, by Type
Table 6.3........ Federal Government Fraud Control, by Agency

FOREWORD

The HIAA Insurance Education Program aims to be the leader in providing the highest quality educational material and service to the health insurance industry and other related health care fields.

To accomplish this mission, the Program seeks to fulfill the following goals:

1. Provide a tool for use by member company personnel to enhance quality and efficiency of services to the public;
2. Provide a career development vehicle for employees and other health care industry personnel; and
3. Further general understanding of the role and contribution of the health insurance industry to the financing, administration, and delivery of health care services.

The Insurance Education Program provides the following services:

1. A comprehensive course of study in Fundamentals of Health Insurance, Long-Term Care Insurance, Disability Income Insurance, Managed Care, and Health Care Fraud;
2. Certification by examination of educational achievement for all courses;
3. Programs to recognize accomplishment in the industry and academic communities through course evaluation and certification, which enables participants to obtain academic or continuing education credits; and
4. Development of educational, instructional, training, and informational materials related to the health insurance and health care industries.

PREFACE

Fundamentals of Health Insurance: Part A and *Fundamentals of Health Insurance: Part B* introduce students to the basic concepts and socioeconomic aspects of group and individual health insurance.

Previously, the HIAA Insurance Education Program had separated group and individual health insurance into two different courses of study. The HIAA's revised program, as reflected in the new texts, addresses group and individual insurance within the same course of study. The restructured program allows for ensuing courses to parallel insurance company trends toward specialization in one or more product lines.

Other HIAA books in the curriculum provide students the opportunity to delve more deeply into specialized product lines, such as medical expense, managed care, specialized or supplemental medical expense, disability income, and long-term care insurance, and into issues of industrywide concern, such as health care fraud and abuse.

Health insurance is the term used to define a broad array of coverages for payment of benefits as a result of sickness or injury. Although all of the above coverages are discussed to some degree in this book, more attention is given to medical expense insurance and disability income insurance because so many millions of Americans have these coverages.

The contents of this book are educational, not a statement of policy. The views expressed or suggested in this and all other HIAA textbooks are those of the contributing authors or editors. They are not necessarily the opinions of the HIAA or of its member companies.

ACKNOWLEDGMENTS

Chapter 1: Managing the Cost of Health Care
Martin Rosenbaum
Great-West Life & Annuity Insurance Company

Chapter 2: Policy Issue, Renewal, and Service
Julie Clopper-Smith
The Principal Financial Group

Chapter 3: Claim Administration
Nancy Eckrich
Trustmark Insurance Company

Chapter 4: Pricing Health Insurance Products
Alex Bagby
American Fidelity Assurance Company

Chapter 5: Government Regulation
Donald W. Kress
Healthsource Provident Administrators, Inc.

Chapter 6: Fraud and Abuse
Terry Lowe
State Farm Mutual Automobile Insurance Company

Reviewers
Bruce Boyd
Bruce Boyd Associates

Marianne Miller
Health Insurance Association of America

Editor
Jane J. Stein
The Stein Group

ABOUT THE AUTHORS . . .

Alex Bagby is currently an officer and manager for American Fidelity Assurance Company. As assistant vice president and manager of individual health products, his numerous responsibilities include the design, development, and compliance of the company's portfolio of individual health policies. Bagby's background includes a degree in statistical mathematics, and he is affiliated with several professional actuarial associations.

Julie L. Clopper-Smith oversees several underwriting and administrative teams at The Principal Financial Group, where she works as a coordinator in small group life and health insurance. Before beginning her career in the insurance industry, Clopper-Smith taught mathematics and computer science. She has completed numerous education courses with the Health Insurance Association of America and the Life Management Institute.

Nancy M. Eckrich is a vice president of individual major medical and disability claims for Trustmark Insurance Company. She has been an active participant in of the Chicago Claim Association and the Midwest Claim Conference. For several years, Eckrich has served on the Midwest Claim conference planning committee, and, in 1997, she will become general chairperson for the conference.

Donald W. Kress has years of experience as an insurance underwriter and manager in group financial underwriting on a national level. He is currently vice president of legislative and industry affairs for Healthsource Provident Administrators, Inc. and, for the past eight years, has managed federal and state compliance activities. Kress has also served as chair of the Health Insurance Association of America's Insurance Education Committee.

Terry R. Lowe has enjoyed a 20-year career in the health insurance industry with particular emphasis in the area of claims. Currently, he is superintendent of training for State Farm Insurance Companies' life and health claims and is chair of the Health Insurance Association of America's Insurance Education Curriculum Subcommittee. Lowe has written and edited numerous health insurance industry publications.

Martin Rosenbaum has spent 22 years in the employee benefits division of the insurance industry. As a vice president of employee benefits products for Great-West Life & Annuity, he is responsible for product development in group life, health, disability, and managed care. Other responsibilities include pricing and financial reporting, as well as marketing communications and claim policy and audit. Rosenbaum is a member of several professional associations.

Chapter 1

MANAGING THE COST OF HEALTH CARE

1 *Introduction*
5 *Cost Containment Through Benefit Plan Design*
14 *Payment Controls*
17 *Utilization Review*
23 *Case Management*
26 *Managed Care*
30 *Prevention and Education Services*
31 *Emerging Trends*
32 *Summary*
33 *Key Terms*

■ Introduction

Health care costs in the United States are increasing at an alarming rate, outdistancing other indices such as the consumer price index (CPI) and the gross domestic product (GDP) to which they are generally compared. From 1990 through 1995 the CPI for the economy as a whole rose an average of only 3.1 percent annually while the price index for medical care items was twice that level at 6.2 percent. (Figure 1.1)

During the same time, national health expenditures as a percent of GDP increased from 12.6 percent in 1990 to more than 14 percent in 1995, and are projected to reach nearly 16 percent by the year 2000. (Figure 1.2) These more recent rates of increase in health care costs are in addition to the significant annual rates of increase experienced throughout the previous decades.

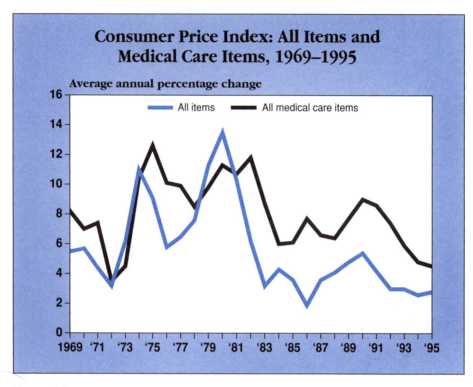

Figure 1.1
SOURCE: U.S. Department of Labor, Bureau of Labor Statistics, CPI detailed report, various issues.

Many employers have found that the cost of providing health coverage for their employees has taken an ever increasing percentage of their pretax profits. One way for employers to reduce costs is by limiting coverage or implementing other programs that provide more cost-effective forms of health care.

Individual purchasers of health insurance also share the burden of increasing costs, and their premiums have risen dramatically over the past several years. These higher costs have adversely affected individual purchasers as well as small businesses that provide coverage to employees through individual policies.

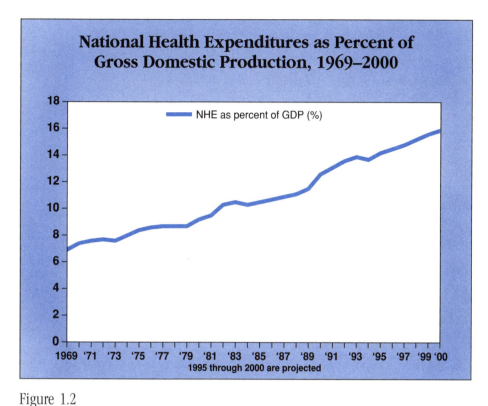

Figure 1.2

SOURCES: U.S. Department of Health and Human Services, Health Care Financing Administration, U.S. Department of Commerce, Survey of Current Business, various issues.

Government programs have also been hard hit. The expenditures for Medicare have increased from $74.1 billion in 1986 to $159.3 billion in 1994. Payments to Medicaid recipients have increased even more rapidly over the same period, rising from $41.1 billion to $107.9 billion.

There are many factors contributing to the rise in health care costs. (See page 4.) Probably the greatest concern resulting from these costs is that more people will be unable to obtain necessary medical treatment either because they cannot afford it through either government or private sector insurance programs or because government health programs for the needy and the elderly will become more restrictive.

Causes of Rising Health Care Costs

There are numerous reasons that health care costs in the United States have risen dramatically. The major ones are:

- inappropriate or nonexistent incentives for providers and consumers to utilize the health care system efficiently;
- lack of coordination and integration in the management of chronic conditions or serious diseases or trauma;
- regulatory barriers to cost containment;
- unrealistic public expectations of the health care system, coupled with lack of individual responsibility for maintaining a healthy life-style;
- proliferation of new, expensive technologies with unproven benefits;
- a shift to chronic, long-term care services necessitated by an increasingly aging population and other demographic changes;
- cost shifting by health care providers from Medicare and Medicaid to privately insured patients to compensate for revenue lost either because of lower fees paid by government or uncompensated care costs by those unable to pay;
- an excess of health care resources in certain geographic areas;
- the practice of defensive medicine, in which excessive and unnecessary services are delivered because of the fear of malpractice suits;
- fraud and waste; and
- insufficient data to determine the best and most cost-effective course of treatment.

Most Americans agree that some reform or change in the health care system is necessary. While the health care reform debate continues in Congress and state legislatures, the private sector has been in the forefront in initiating efforts to manage health care costs. This chapter discusses the industry's major cost containment activities for medical expense insurance. Most of them apply to group and individual plans; it is noted where they apply to group plans only. The HIAA Insurance Education curriculum includes a two-part course on managed care.

■ Cost Containment Through Benefit Plan Design

Insurers have taken an active role in cost containment efforts through modification and design of benefit plans. Policy language and the structure of benefits are being modeled so that insureds use benefits more cost effectively. In addition, claim review techniques can help to minimize billing errors and payment for ineligible services. Four ways that insurers contain costs through benefit plan design are cost sharing, maximum reimbursement levels, employee contributions, and coordination of benefits.

Cost Sharing

Cost-sharing provisions in benefit plans require insureds to pay a portion of their medical expenses through deductibles, coinsurance, and copayment.

Deductibles

Deductibles are the amount of covered expenses that must be incurred and paid by the insured before benefits become payable by the insurer. Under most group plans, deductibles shift costs from employers to employees; in individual plans, they shift costs from the insurer to the insured. They also encourage insureds to seek less expensive health care.

Variations of the deductible principle include:

- separate individual deductibles;
- maximum family deductibles; and
- per cause or occurrence deductibles (usually for hospital coverage).

FUNDAMENTALS OF HEALTH INSURANCE: PART B

There are several types of deductibles:

- **Flat Deductible.** A specified dollar sum that must be paid for each person or for each family. An example of a flat deductible is $100 per person per year or $300 per family per year.
- **Percentage Deductible.** A percentage of annualized salary absorbed by the insured. The percentage is usually small, with a calendar-year maximum. A common requirement is 1 percent of annualized gross salary, with a $1,000 maximum.
- **Benefits-Related Deductible.** A certain amount of specific benefits absorbed by the insured before insurance begins. For example, the policy may not pay for the first day of room and board charges for each confinement.
- **Threshold Corridor Deductible.** A specific dollar amount of out-of-pocket expenses absorbed by the insured after payment of benefits under a basic plan and before major medical coverage begins to provide benefits.
- **Sliding or Variable Deductible.** The deductible amount is the greater of that amount stated in the policy (e.g., $500) or the aggregate amount of benefits paid by all other insurance for the particular claim. This form of deductible incorporates a cost-sharing measure as well as protection against overinsurance by the policyholder.

The trend in deductibles is to increase the flat and percentage deductibles.

Coinsurance/Copayment

Coinsurance requires insureds to pay a percent of costs after the deductible is met. For example, insureds may be required to pay 20 or 25 percent of all eligible charges until they incur a fixed amount of expenses (commonly from $500 up to $2,500). Thereafter, the insurance company pays 100 percent of all covered charges. Some companies reduce the coinsurance percentage if the insured uses certain preferred providers or obtains a second surgical opinion when surgery is recommended.

A copayment is a flat dollar amount per type of service (e.g., $10 for an office visit). This method of coinsurance typically is used by managed care plans such as health maintenance organizations (HMOs) and preferred provider organizations (PPOs).

By requiring insureds to pay a portion of the cost of their health care, coinsurance reduces employer costs in group plans and insurer costs in individual plans. It also is designed to make insureds more cost-effective purchasers of health care services.

Many plans have a coinsurance limit or out-of-pocket maximum that eliminates coinsurance for the balance of the calendar year after the insured has paid a fixed amount of expenses (e.g., $1,000, $1,500, or $2,500). This feature is designed to protect the insured financially in the event of catastrophic illness.

Maximum Reimbursement Levels

Many plans contain a maximum amount payable for certain benefits. The insured absorbs the remainder of the cost. For example, a plan may have a maximum amount available for dental benefits.

Employee Contributions

Most employees share the cost of employer-sponsored health plans with their employers through premium contributions. Contributions generally are a flat-dollar amount per month but also may be a percentage of a person's salary. Contributions usually vary based on whether a person selects single or family coverage. If multiple plans such as high- and low-benefit options are offered, the employer contribution often is based on the low-benefit option plan.

Financial Incentive Programs

Some group plans give cash awards to insureds for reducing their medical care costs and for practicing preventive medicine. The awards go to employees whose claims are eliminated or reduced below a specified dollar amount on an annual basis.

The following are examples of different approaches to financial incentive programs:

- A special account set up for each employee for a certain amount (typically $300 to $500) is used to pay the deductible and coinsurance for all claims during the year.
- An account is established as above, but the dollars are used to pay for benefits rather than for the deductible and coinsurance. This method maintains the cost-sharing concept that is lost in the first approach. Any balance remaining at the end of the year and paid to the employee under either of the above approaches is subject to personal income tax under current law.
- Some plans award a paid day off from work for employees who do not receive annual benefit payments in excess of a certain dollar amount. The amounts are small and vary with family size—for example, $75 for a single employee or $200 for a family.
- In 1996 Congress responded to significant public enthusiasm for medical savings accounts by authorizing, on a limited demonstration basis, tax preferences for medical savings accounts (MSAs) coupled with high-deductible health coverage. The higher deductible will, presumably, cause individuals to seek and use health care more prudently, thereby reducing the delivery of medically unnecessary care. Funds in the medical savings account are used to pay for the insured's medical expenses, and account balances may be rolled over from year to year.

Coordination of benefits. Overinsurance is insurance that pays benefits in excess of actual loss. It is caused by duplicate coverages. Overinsurance is costly to insurers, employers, and individual insureds, and it can result in overutilization of services.

Coordination of benefits (COB) is the method designed by the insurance industry to ensure that a covered person does not recover more than the actual medical expenses when more than one policy provides benefits. One insurance company is designated the primary carrier, based on National Association of Insurance Commissioners (NAIC) guidelines. The plans that are determined not to be the primary plan determine responsibility for payment under various NAIC alternatives so that total payments from all plans do not exceed actual medical expenses. Coordination of benefits is used primarily in group insurance contracts, but it also is found in individual plans. For more information on coordination of benefits see Chapter 3: Claim Administration.

Cost-Effective Alternatives

Initial approaches to health care cost containment focused on savings opportunities within the limits of the benefits covered. Increasingly, group and individual plans have been modified to cover the costs of less expensive treatments or services, some of which were not previously covered. Insurers also have established financial incentives to encourage insureds not to use hospital emergency rooms for nonemergency care and to follow other cost-effective alternative procedures. Examples of cost-effective alternatives offered by group and individual health insurers are preadmission testing, outpatient surgery, ambulatory care, birthing centers, skilled nursing facilities, home health care, alcohol and drug treatment facilities, and hospice care.

Preadmission Testing

Certain tests are conducted as part of any hospital stay to determine the appropriate course of treatment for a patient. The purpose of preadmission testing is to help contain hospital costs by reducing the number of in-hospital patient days by having the necessary X-rays, laboratory tests, and examinations conducted on an outpatient basis prior to a scheduled hospital admission.

Preadmission testing is not an outpatient diagnostic benefit program; rather, it is an inpatient benefit that may prevent a longer, or in some cases unnecessary, hospital confinement.

The advantage of preadmission testing for the patient is that medical treatment can begin immediately upon hospital admission; otherwise, the patient is admitted a day or two ahead of time for tests and waits for the results before treatment begins. Some insurance plans assess a charge against benefits for insureds who do not have testing done prior to admission. This charge is a flat-dollar amount (e.g., $200) or the cost of one day's hospital stay.

Emergency Room Treatment

To discourage the unnecessary use of expensive hospital emergency rooms instead of a doctor's office, insurers have added a deductible (e.g., $50) for emergency room use. A second approach is to increase an insured's coinsurance for the cost of the emergency room. In either case, the insured pays increased out-of-pocket costs when visiting a hospital emergency room unnecessarily. If a visit to an emergency room results in a hospital admission, the additional deductible or coinsurance is waived.

Weekend Admissions

Hospitals, like any businesses, reduce their activities on weekends. Not many surgeries are performed and fewer tests are ordered. In many cases, a patient admitted on Friday does not receive treatment until Monday and is discharged at the same time as a patient admitted that same Monday.

However, the patient admitted on Friday spends three extra days in the hospital, which adds considerably to the bill. For this reason, when an elective (nonemergency) admission to a hospital takes place on Friday or Saturday, many insurers either do not provide any benefits or charge an additional substantial deductible (e.g., $250). If a weekend admission is necessary, as in the case of childbirth or a life-threatening or potentially disabling emergency, the weekend days are reimbursed.

Outpatient Surgery

New surgical techniques and anesthetics that allow a quick recovery have made it possible for doctors to perform many surgeries safely on an outpatient basis. Outpatient surgery is performed at a hospital outpatient unit, a freestanding surgical center, or a doctor's office. The cost of surgery is reduced by avoiding expensive hospital room and board charges. Outpatient surgery often is reimbursed at 100 percent of the allowable charge.

Ambulatory Care

A significant portion of the diagnosis and treatment provided to hospital inpatients can be given more economically on an ambulatory basis when appropriate facilities and adequately trained personnel are available. Many communities have hospitals with expanded outpatient departments and emergency services to provide ambulatory care, including diagnosis, treatment, and rehabilitation. Insurers are structuring plans to encourage patients to utilize ambulatory care services.

Birthing Centers

Many insurers provide incentives to maternity patients to use birthing centers by waiving the deductible and/or coinsurance. These centers are a popular, cost-effective alternative to hospitalization for low-risk deliveries and postpartum newborn care.

Most birthing centers are owned and operated by obstetricians or nurse-midwives who have a business relationship with an acute care facility. They usually are situated close to a full-service hospital, allowing easy transport if complications occur during childbirth. A center operated by a nurse-midwife has specialty physicians available if a need for them should arise. Because of the popularity of birthing centers, hospitals are establishing them within their own walls.

Progressive Care

In progressive care, patients proceed through various levels of care as dictated by their health condition. The levels include intensive care, normal acute inpatient hospital care, confinement in a skilled nursing facility requiring limited medical attention, and home health care. Progressive care does not necessarily have to begin with a hospital confinement. Progressive care allows insurers to provide coverage for less costly alternatives to hospitalization without sacrificing quality of care for insureds.

Skilled Nursing Facilities

Skilled nursing care, most often furnished in a skilled nursing facility (SNF), is performed by or under the supervision of registered nurses or a physician. Skilled nursing facility coverage may include room and board charges, registered nursing services, physical therapy, prescription drugs, supplies, and equipment. Intermediate care and self-care may or may not be covered, and custodial care generally is not covered. The per-day charge in a skilled nursing facility is lower than a hospital's daily room and board charge.

Home Health Care

Health care services are provided to a patient at home by a home health care agency. These services include:

- part-time or intermittent nursing care provided under the supervision of a registered nurse;
- physical therapy, occupational therapy, and speech therapy;
- medication and laboratory services; and
- part-time or intermittent services of a home health aide.

Physician decisions to use home health care benefits are based on factors such as the family's ability to assist in providing care and the patient's desire to be at home. Home health care programs are appropriate for some chronically ill or disabled persons, for persons convalescing from heart attacks or strokes, and for orthopedic cases; traditionally, persons with these conditions would have recuperated in the hospital. In addition, patients requiring oxygen therapy, those with spinal cord injuries or respiratory illnesses, and those in the last stages of a terminal illness may receive home health care. Home health care usually provides supportive care at costs considerably less than hospital confinements and in an atmosphere that is often far more desirable for the patient. Home therapy has become more sophisticated with the advent of improved technology such as home dialysis.

Alcohol and Drug Treatment Facilities

Many benefit plans cover the expenses of approved treatment facilities for individuals recovering from alcohol and chemical dependency. In addition to providing detoxification services, these facilities offer counseling and workshops that help patients confront and deal with their dependency. More cost effective than a hospital stay, alcohol and drug treatment facilities have demonstrated some success in assisting patients with alcohol and drug problems.

Hospice Care

Hospice care is aimed at providing terminally ill patients (those whose life expectancy is six months or less) with an alternative to traditional modes of treatment. Hospice emphasizes palliative care (medical relief of pain rather than curative care), attention to emotional needs, and assistance to patients and families in coping with death.

Four basic principles distinguish hospice from the traditional health care system:

- The patient and family, not the patient alone, are considered the unit of care.
- A multidisciplinary team, which may include a physician, nurse, home health aide, social worker, psychiatrist, psychologist, clergy, and trained volunteers, as well as family members, is used to assess the physical, psychological, and spiritual needs of the patient and family, develop an overall plan of care, and provide coordinated care.
- Pain and collateral symptoms associated with the terminal illness are controlled, but no heroic efforts are made to cure the patient.
- Bereavement follow-up is provided to family members to help them with the grieving process.

Hospice care is less costly than care provided in the typical hospital setting. The terminally ill patient in hospice care may at some point, however, need to or choose to be admitted to a hospital.

■ Payment Controls

There are several ways of containing health care costs through payment controls. Most of these approaches are used by group and individual plans, including hospital billing audits, paying only reasonable and customary charges, and controlling administrative expenses. In addition, group plans can save by negotiating provider price discounts and providing financial incentive programs for employees and their families.

Hospital Billing Audits

Many insurers have hospital bills audited by their own staff or independent companies that specialize in this service. Audits are performed to determine whether services or supplies were actually delivered and whether charges were correct. The audit report indicates undercharges and overcharges by each hospital department. All overcharges usually are discussed with the patient accounts department by the auditor prior to reporting to the insurer. Most insurers pay the hospital based on the auditor's findings, whether it is over or under the original bill.

Many hospitals self-audit a certain percentage of bills to catch errors before insurance claims are filed or to uncover faulty billing practices. In addition, some insurers encourage insureds to audit their own bills; if errors are found, the insurance company will pay the insured part of the savings realized.

Some companies automatically audit all bills over a certain amount (e.g., $20,000). Other companies prescreen bills over certain amounts to determine whether an audit is indicated. In general, about $2 in overcharges are saved for every $1 spent for auditing.

Eligible Charge Limits and Reasonable and Customary Charges

Insurers typically pay hospital and physician benefits based on a determination of an eligible charge limit. The provider charge for service, if at or below the eligible charge limit, is the amount against which deductibles and coinsurance provisions are applied. If a doctor charges the patient an amount in excess of what is recognized as the eligible amount, the doctor may bill the patient for the difference.

For example, an insurance contract may state that the eligible charge limit is the lesser of three calculations:

- the physician's actual charge;
- the physician's usual charge, which is based on an analysis of the physician's billed charges during a period of time for the same or similar procedures or services; or
- the reasonable and customary charge for the procedure or service in the geographic area.

A reasonable and customary charge is a charge amount limit determined by the insurer, group policy holder, employer, or administrator to fairly represent or be consistent with amounts charged by similar health care providers for identical or similar procedures or services in a geographic area.

Controlling Administrative Expenses

The cost of administrative expenses is factored into the cost of health insurance premiums. Administrative expenses are particularly significant in individual and small group benefit programs. Insurers want to keep these expenses to a minimum because of:

- policyholder resistance to higher premiums;
- competition among insurers to provide the most insurance for the lowest premium; and
- pressures from regulatory authorities.

Marketing, underwriting, and claims administration account for a substantial portion of administrative expenses.

Marketing Expenses

Aside from benefit payments, acquisition and issue expenses of new business are the costliest expenses incurred by insurers. These expenses generally are in excess of the first-year premium for individual health insurance. (They are far less than the cost of the first-year premium for group plans.) Whether or not expected persistency is maintained can mean the difference between profit and loss for an insurer in a particular line of business.

Marketing representatives have the greatest control over the persistency of business. If the agent or group representative has received proper training and has made the initial sale properly, then occasional personal contact should enable him or her to reinforce the insured's recognition of the need for continuance of the coverage. Personal contact by an agent will not only help conserve the existing coverage but will allow the agent to keep abreast of changes that would suggest a need for updating the insured's insurance program. It is important that the company's marketing representative thoroughly understand the coverage he or she sells so that it meets a prospective insured's need.

Underwriting Expenses

The process of underwriting health insurance applications is becoming more costly to insurers because of increasing salaries, rising overhead expenses, and higher costs for medical examinations, attending physicians' statements, and inspection reports.

Underwriting expenses for group insurance drops dramatically as the size of the group increases. This is because the underwriting process focuses on the attributes of the group as a whole, and employees and dependents are not usually underwritten individually.

An efficient and time-saving application processing system is necessary for any cost reduction in underwriting administration. Delays and additional costs can be eliminated or reduced substantially by proper initial handling of applications.

Claims Expenses

To reduce costs associated with health claims, many insurers have the majority of routine claims handled by associate claim examiners. These

MANAGING THE COST OF HEALTH CARE

examiners need less training and experience in claim handling than senior claim examiners. This leaves a smaller number of claims with complex problems to be handled by the experienced claim personnel.

Computerized systems for processing claims have increased efficiencies and reduced administrative costs. Examples are electronic transmission of claims, automatic calculation of benefits, and automatic payment of claims.

■ Utilization Review

Utilization review was designed to reduce unnecessary hospital admissions and to control inpatient lengths of stay through prospective and retrospective analyses of records. The principles have been expanded to cover other forms of care. Utilization review is used by group and individual health plans.

Prospective Review

Prospective review programs, which are designed to determine the need for health care services before they are provided, concentrate primarily on managing the use of in-hospital services. There also are prospective review programs for skilled nursing care facilities (SNFs), surgery, and certain outpatient services.

Inpatient Utilization Review

Inpatient utilization review is designed to reduce the incidence of unnecessary or inappropriate hospitalization. Through established guidelines, insurers review cases for appropriate admissions, hospital lengths of stay, and course and quality of treatment. Guidelines are based on age, sex, and diagnosis. The review process is done either by an independent review organization or by an insurer's in-house program.

Hospital utilization is reviewed on a preadmission, concurrent, continued stay, and discharge planning basis.

17

Preadmission certification. The preadmission certification process requires an insured to obtain an authorization in advance from the review program for an elective or nonemergency hospitalization. Qualified health care professionals perform the review and authorize an inpatient stay and the proposed treatment plan. This review results in an assurance that the proposed treatment is customary for the diagnosis and that opportunities for treatment in a more cost-effective setting (such as a skilled nursing facility, outpatient surgical facility, hospice, or the home) have been identified. Most of the preadmission review programs also require a second opinion before certain surgical procedures can be done.

If the criteria for inpatient hospitalization are not met, the review organization refers the request to an appropriate medical specialist for further evaluation and recommendation of approval or denial of certification. The review organization gives prompt written notice of certification, or lack of it, to the hospital, physician, patient, and pertinent claim office of the insurer.

If insureds do not have hospitalizations preauthorized, most group health plans either will not pay or will pay a reduced amount of the benefit. Three common options are:

- denying for any days of hospital confinement not certified as medically necessary;
- reducing the coinsurance rate for any days of hospital confinement not certified as medically necessary; and
- reducing by a flat-dollar amount the cost of any hospital confinement or extension not certified as medically necessary.

Concurrent review. Concurrent review takes place on-site when a patient is confined to a hospital. The concept involves determining whether treatment and continued inpatient care during a patient's hospitalization are necessary and appropriate. Since concurrent review can lead to a shortened length of stay, it has a great potential to reduce costs. Concurrent review usually is carried out by a nurse coordinator who reviews a patient's chart immediately following admission and at suitable subsequent intervals for the following:

MANAGING THE COST OF HEALTH CARE

- to assign an initial length of stay, if not already done, and assess the medical need for any extensions;
- to assess the treatment program and efficacy of the care being given; and
- to abstract data for retrospective quality assessment in comparison with medical care criteria.

The nurse coordinator can authorize care that falls within predetermined, explicit quality and length-of-stay guidelines. These guidelines are based on common practice and experience. Within 24 hours of each admission, the nurse coordinator initiates a thorough review for a patient. Using diagnosis-specific criteria or general quality guidelines, the process begins with an initial chart review to determine the need for admission. If the chart does not clearly show the needed information, the nurse coordinator requests clarification from the attending physician.

Next, the appropriateness of the level of care is determined. Potential levels of care include intensive, acute, extended or rehabilitative, supportive, ambulatory, coordinated home health, and hospice care.

The nurse coordinator also assigns a diagnosis-specific length-of-stay range during the initial review. The length-of-stay range may be defined within a minimum that represents the median length of stay determined necessary to ensure quality care and a maximum that represents a limit on the nurse coordinator's independent authority to extend the stay. Medical advisory review is necessary for an extension of stay beyond this maximum.

The date representing the minimum length of stay is noted on the patient's chart. On that date the patient's length of stay is reviewed again, and the nurse coordinator, after looking at the patient's chart, may assign a new review date.

Continued-stay review. Continued-stay review is an off-site medical review conducted during the insured's hospitalization. It is based on telephone conversations between the nurse coordinator and the attending physician, hospital utilization review staff, or discharge planning staff. Telephone contacts are made at designated intervals consistent with the patient's condition until discharge occurs. Using established medical criteria and length-of-stay norms, the reviewer determines the medical necessity and appropriateness of both the treatment plan and length of impatient stay. The purpose of continued-stay review is to ensure that only patients with a medical need for hospitalization are certified to remain as inpatients and that the treatment plan is customary for the diagnosis.

Discharge planning. Discharge planning should occur as early as possible in a patient's hospital stay. For patients who have not fully recovered but who do not require the acute care of a hospital, arrangements may be made for continuing care in a less costly setting, such as a skilled nursing facility. Discharge planning ensures that the patient receives the proper care in the most appropriate setting after a hospital stay.

Extended Care Facility Review

As admissions to and lengths of stay in acute care hospitals have decreased, utilization of skilled nursing facilities has increased. Also, because of advances in medical technology, many more people survive severe accidents and illnesses but then face months of care and rehabilitation.

Extended care facility review manages and reduces long-term health care expenses in two ways:

- by working with discharge planning programs to identify patients in acute care hospitals who can successfully be transferred to an appropriate, less costly skilled nursing facility; and

- by providing preadmission review and continued stay review for admissions to skilled nursing homes.

As with hospitalization review, the extended care facility review process uses established guidelines to determine coverage, conformance with medical criteria of norms, length of stay, and appropriateness of the facility. If the case is approved, the patient is admitted, a length of stay is assigned, and the review program monitors the patient's progress and the appropriateness of the placement. If the patient does not meet established extended care facility guidelines, the review program may try to direct the case to a more appropriate facility, such as an intermediate, custodial, or home health care setting.

Surgical Review

Since surgery is a high-cost, sometimes elective procedure, insurers use several methods to assess its appropriateness. Many group and individual plans require that insureds obtain a second surgical opinion for certain nonemergency surgical procedures, especially those where medical treatments may be just as or more effective. A second surgical opinion is a prospective screening process that relies on a consulting physician's or surgeon's evaluation of the need for inpatient and outpatient surgery that another surgeon has recommended. While one doctor may recommend surgery, another may recommend other alternatives.

The potential for cost savings in a second opinion program lies primarily in the following areas:

- surgeries not confirmed and not performed;
- surgeries performed on an ambulatory rather than an inpatient basis as initially recommended; and
- general reduction in surgical claims due to physician awareness of the program (the sentinel effect).

Second opinion programs also encourage physicians to justify their recommendations for surgery, strengthen patient confidence by reducing anxieties, and disclose alternatives that may avoid or postpone surgery and its cost.

Assistant Surgeon Review

Fees for assistant surgeons are one of the health care industry's fastest growing expenses. Scheduling an assistant surgeon can add significantly to the cost of a surgical procedure. However, an assistant surgeon is not needed in all cases where one is recommended.

An assistant surgeon review helps eliminate such unnecessary fees by monitoring the use of assistant surgeons to make sure that the cost is incurred only when medically appropriate. If the request meets accepted medical criteria, authorization for the assistant surgeon is discussed and negotiated between the assistant surgeon review service and the attending physician.

Ambulatory Surgery Facility Review

Many surgical procedures are performed on an ambulatory basis in a surgicenter, clinic, hospital outpatient department, or doctor's office. While the cost of such surgery is typically much lower than when performed in a hospital, there are still a number of costs and other variables that should be controlled for maximum cost efficiency. The objective of ambulatory surgery facility review is to see that the patient receives only surgical care that is necessary.

Retrospective Review

A retrospective review program determines the appropriateness of the care that has been provided and the extent to which health care costs should be reimbursed. This mechanism can create substantial economic incentive for changing patterns of care.

The retrospective review of claims allows an insurer or group policyholder to establish a utilization profile for use in monitoring trends. Included in such a profile would be diagnoses, the kinds of prices of medical services purchased by each insured, where they were provided, and the portion paid by the insurer. Action can then be taken in excessively high-cost areas.

Outpatient Utilization Review

With the shift of services to the outpatient setting, insurers have developed prospective and retrospective reviews for care delivered there. The procedures are similar to those for inpatient review.

Prospective outpatient certification review for certain high-cost, high-frequency procedures requires the patient or doctor to call the administrator prior to getting a particular medical service. The administrator reviews the request based upon the patient's diagnosis and the appropriateness of the prescribed treatment or test. The administrator either approves the treatment or recommends alternative approaches.

In a retrospective review of outpatient utilization, appropriate treatments for a given diagnosis in terms of tests required, office visits permitted, and so forth, are established. As claims are received, they are reviewed against these treatment guidelines. Any treatment that does not fall within the guidelines must be justified by the physicians or it may be declined.

■ Case Management

Case management is a planned approach to providing services or treatments to an insured with a serious medical problem. It is aimed at managing costs and promoting more effective interventions to meet patient needs. Long-term or catastrophic illnesses can account for as much as 40 percent of an insurer's annual claim dollars; case management was designed to control those costs.

Case management makes benefits available for appropriate and cost-effective health care services, including alternatives to hospitalization. For example, a patient may be reimbursed for having a full- or part-time nurse at home. Home health care services are less expensive than inpatient treatment and often are more beneficial to the patient.

Case Management Needs

Catastrophic illness or injury can result from a sudden, unanticipated acute event or chronic medical or degenerative disorder. These conditions usually are associated with extensive use of medical resources and high benefit payments over a long period of time. Illnesses and injuries most appropriate for case management include amputations, multiple fractures, major head traumas, high-risk infants, severe burns, spinal cord injuries, severe strokes, acquired immunodeficiency syndrome (AIDS), amyotrophic lateral sclerosis (ALS), Crohn's disease, multiple sclerosis, anorexia nervosa/bulimia, severe rheumatoid arthritis, substance abuse, and selected psychiatric conditions.

Case Management Process

Case management is designed to identify catastrophic illness or injury cases as early as possible—even before the first hospital admission. Preadmission review, concurrent review, and continued-stay review programs are excellent ways for insurers to identify cases that would benefit from case management.

In some companies, all claims for certain conditions (such as the ones listed above) are referred to case management. Individual claims above $10,000 or aggregate claims above $25,000 for one covered person also are usually referred to case management. Insureds, their families, employers, and medical care providers can alert the insurer about a potential case management patient.

Case management, which usually is voluntary, stresses the importance of involving the patient and his or her family in the treatment program. The patient is kept informed at each step of treatment and rehabilitation and is advised of his or her options. If the patient does not wish to be treated under the care management program, he or she can continue to receive the benefits available under the regular provisions of the group health plan.

Rehabilitation Management

Rehabilitation is one form of case management. It is both a process and a goal in which the insurer assumes an active management role. The long-range goal of rehabilitation is to restore a disabled individual as nearly as possible to a state of good health, independence, and predisability functioning. This is achieved by providing cost-effective medical treatment alternatives to the insured, in addition to other assistance with the usual activities of daily life.

There are two basic kinds of rehabilitation services: medical rehabilitation and vocational rehabilitation.

- Medical rehabilitation concentrates on treatment and procedures designed to reduce the physical effects of disability.
- Vocational rehabilitation, which is the primary objective of insurance in the disability area, furnishes services designed to enable disabled persons to become self-sufficient and to return to work.

There is no clear boundary between these two rehabilitation services, and both may be practiced to some extent at all points on the continuum of disability, impairment, and recovery. Medical rehabilitation is generally thought of as being of most importance immediately after the acute phase of an illness, and vocational rehabilitation as being of most importance after impairment and functional limitations have been minimized with the help of medical rehabilitation.

Benefits of Rehabilitation

Insurers benefit from offering rehabilitation services because such services reduce their financial liability. This occurs when an insured returns to work either full or part time, or when effective medical management stems the progression of a disability. The savings are achieved by eliminating or reducing benefit payments and by reducing reserves. A rehabilitation program also enhances an insurer's competitive position. Ideally, it minimizes disability durations and medical costs and, consequently, loss ratios, which can favorably affect future premium rates.

For an employer offering group disability insurance, an effective rehabilitation program can reduce or eliminate disability benefit payments and promote cost-effective medical management, all of which may contribute to maintaining or reducing premiums. It also can help return a highly trained and valuable employee to work. In addition, a rehabilitation program is an attractive component of an employee benefits package.

Managed Care

Managed care is a system of health care delivery that integrates the financing and delivery of health care services. It began in the 1930s, when the first prepaid group practices were established to improve access to quality health care and to provide preventive health care services. The early prepaid group practices were the forerunners of HMOs.

During the past decade, the health care system has evolved at a pace that few expected, largely in response to the ever-rising cost of care. The most visible change is the explosion in the number of managed care organizations (MCOs). Although there can be significant variations among different plans, most MCOs have the following common elements:

- arrangements with selected providers to furnish a comprehensive set of health care services to enrollees;
- explicit standards for selection of health care providers;
- formal programs for ongoing quality assurance and utilization review; and
- financial incentives for enrollees to use providers and procedures covered by the MCO.

Managed care is available mostly through group plans, and currently about two-thirds of people eligible for employer-sponsored health plans receive care through an MCO.

Types of Managed Care Organizations

The are many ways to structure MCOs, and as managed care matures, variations on existing systems are emerging. The most common MCOs are HMOs and preferred provider organizations (PPOs). Other new forms of MCOs are exclusive provider organizations (EPOs), point-of-service (POS) plans, carve-outs, integrated delivery systems, and centers of excellence.

Health Maintenance Organizations (HMOs)

Although HMO delivery systems take many forms, all provide a defined, comprehensive set of health benefits on a prepaid basis to a voluntarily enrolled population. The prepayment is determined in advance and depends on the number of enrolled members. HMOs often use a primary care physician as a gatekeeper or manager to coordinate the care of enrollees to maximize efficiency and effectiveness in the delivery of care.

There are four basic types of HMOs:

- In a staff model HMO, physicians practice solely as employees and are usually paid a salary.
- A group model HMO pays a physician group a negotiated, per capita rate, which the group in turn distributes among individual physicians in a variety of ways.
- In an independent practice association (IPA), the managed care plan contracts with a separate IPA composed of individual physicians in independent practice or with independent physicians. These physicians provide services to an HMO's enrollees at a negotiated rate per capita, a flat retainer, or a negotiated fee-for-service rate. Physicians maintain their own offices and also see non-HMO patients on a fee-for-service basis while contracting with one or more HMOs.
- A network model HMO contracts with both a group, perhaps one or more, and with an IPA or with individual physicians. There is a fixed monthly fee per enrollee.

Preferred Provider Organizations (PPOs)

PPOs offer consumers more flexibility than HMOs because they give consumers greater freedom in choosing providers. At the same time, PPOs try to achieve savings by directing patients to providers who are committed to cost-effective delivery of care.

PPOs are financing and delivery systems that combine features of standard fee-for-service indemnity plans and HMOs. They were developed during the 1980s. Typically organized by insurers but sometimes by providers or others, PPOs have contracts with networks or panels of providers that agree to provide medical services and to be paid according to a negotiated fee schedule. Individuals enrolled in a PPO can get care from a nonaffiliated provider, but that option carries a financial penalty, usually an increased coinsurance amount.

Exclusive Provider Organizations (EPOs)

Exclusive provider organizations are the strictest form of PPOs. Services rendered by nonaffiliated providers are not reimbursed, so people belonging to an EPO must receive their care from affiliated providers or pay the entire cost themselves. Providers typically are reimbursed on a fee-for-service basis according to a negotiated discount or fee schedule.

Point-of-Service (POS) Plans

Point-of-service plans, sometimes called HMO-PPO hybrids or open-ended HMOs, combine characteristics of HMOs and PPOs. POS plans use a network of participating providers under contract. Enrollees choose a primary care physician, who controls referrals for medical specialists. If an enrollee receives care from a POS provider, the enrollee pays little or nothing out-of-pocket as in an HMO and does not file claims. Care provided by out-of-plan providers is reimbursed, but enrollees must pay higher coinsurance amounts. The basis of provider reimbursement may be fee-for-service or capitation for in-plan physicians. However, there are usually financial incentives for these providers to avoid overutilization.

Specialty Managed Care Arrangements (Carve-Outs)

As managed care has evolved, several areas of health care delivery have been singled or carved out for individual management. Behavioral health, prescription drugs, and dental services are three areas often managed as carve-outs. Many MCOs and traditional insurers have found it difficult to control costs in these areas. In response to that problem, the new specialty managed care providers function much as HMOs do.

Integrated Delivery Systems

Integrated delivery systems bring all the components of health care delivery—such as physicians, hospitals, clinics, home health care, long-term care facilities, and pharmacies—into a single entity. This form of MCO has some capacity to take on financial risk, but usually an integrated delivery system contracts out for services it does not want or cannot develop itself, such as reinsurance for high-cost cases or claims payment administration. Integrated delivery systems are organized by physicians and hospitals.

Centers of Excellence

Some group health insurance plans contract with a select number of institutions to perform high-cost procedures such as heart, liver, kidney, and bone marrow transplants. The facilities where these highly complex procedures are performed are called centers of excellence.

Insurers use a number of different criteria to establish a facility as a center of excellence, such as the transplant team's training, transplant performance (including number of transplants performed and outcomes), and the institution's relative efficiency. In addition, geographic location is considered in terms of being able to service insureds' needs.

Care at centers of excellence is attractive to patients and group policyholders because:

- The patient receives a higher level of benefits than would otherwise be provided. For example, deductibles, coinsurance, or copayments often are waived, and patient travel expenses are reimbursed.
- Employers can expect savings because of negotiated discounts with the institution, plus additional savings from better patient outcomes (e.g., fewer infections and complications).

Insurers have extended this concept to other treatments and procedures, such as coronary by-pass surgery and cancer treatment. By contracting with local or regional facilities, insurers may be able to bring the center of excellence approach to a wider array of medical services.

Insurer Response to Managed Care

Traditional fee-for-service health plans have adopted several managed care techniques for cost containment for employers and other purchasers of insurance. The most common managed care features in a fee-for-service plan are:

- utilization review;
- use of specialty organizations to manage utilization; and
- case management of high-cost chronic or catastrophic cases.

Managed indemnity plans are not MCOs and do not have a contracted network of providers.

Recognizing the need to respond to the growing managed care movement, many insurers entered the managed care market during the merger and growth period of the mid-1980s. Because PPOs do not require the significant start-up investment that HMOs demand, insurers became more heavily committed to this model, which more closely resembles traditional indemnity insurance.

As the insurance industry came to recognize that traditional indemnity insurance was losing market share to prepaid health plans, it responded by investing in many forms of managed care, including HMOs, PPOs, and EPOs.

■ Prevention and Education Services

Health education and promotion are two insurance industry and employer efforts to encourage healthy life-styles, discourage risk-associated behavior, and educate individuals about health care and appropriate use of services. The public has become increasingly aware of the impact of smoking, excessive drinking, uncontrolled hypertension, lack of exercise, and poor diet on the incidence of disease and injury. People have begun to assume more responsibility for their own health with the understanding that changes in life-style can significantly reduce risk factors associated with premature death and disability.

Some insurance companies and employers have developed wellness or health promotion programs to encourage insureds and employees to improve the quality of their health. While these programs vary considerably, some of the popular components are:

- smoking cessation;
- hypertension recognition and control;
- stress management;
- nutrition and weight control;
- exercise and fitness;
- alcohol and drug abuse control;
- cancer risk reduction;
- cardiopulmonary resuscitation (CPR) training;
- accident risk reduction;
- blood pressure screening;
- emergency medicine;
- glaucoma screening;
- prudent utilization of medical care benefits;
- life-style counseling;
- self-care training; and
- family counseling.

Wellness programs attempt to integrate the concepts of disease prevention and life-style modification with the more traditional practice of treating diseases after they occur. The expectation is that such a program will benefit not only employees and their families but also the employer by a decrease in health care costs, absenteeism, and turnover and an increase in employee morale and productivity.

■ Emerging Trends

Recent statistics show a slowing of the rate of increase in national health care spending. In 1995, spending on health care increased only

4.5 percent. While still higher than the rate of inflation in the overall national economy, it is the lowest rate of increase in three decades. It is much too early to declare victory over health care cost increases, but this development may serve as a validation of the combined impact of private and public programs to better manage the rising cost of health care.

Congress has debated sweeping health care reforms to make insurance more affordable and available. Although such broad proposals have not been enacted, Congress has begun to pass gradual reform measures. Many analysts believe that reform of the health care system will continue to be incremental at the state and federal levels.

To this end, the health insurance industry supports legislation to:

- simplify the administration of health care;
- reduce health care fraud;
- reform medical liability rules;
- limit punitive damages;
- support managed care by eliminating federal and state laws that impede competition;
- extend full health insurance tax deduction to the self-employed;
- establish tax-advantaged medical savings accounts;
- reduce the cost-shift from Medicare and Medicaid and encourage expanded managed care enrollment;
- encourage the coordination of medical benefits provided under primary medical coverage and automobile medical coverage;
- implement technology assessment; and
- encourage individual responsibility, wellness, disease prevention, and early intervention.

■ Summary

Private sector and government health benefit programs have successfully provided financial access to health care services for the vast majority of Americans. However, the disproportionate increase in health care costs over the last three decades is jeopardizing these programs. Indeed, solutions to the problems of the uninsured have become even more elusive.

All participants in the delivery and financing of health care services have a responsibility to assist in making the necessary changes to manage costs by building on the best features of the current system. Insurers have undertaken many efforts both singly and in combination to contain costs. The most significant change in recent years is the development of managed care organizations as a vehicle to provide cost-effective health care services. Managed care integrates many cost containment features that were developed by traditional health benefits plans.

Despite the effectiveness of the efforts to manage health care costs, a number of cost-related health policy issues regarding access and affordability will continue to challenge private sector health benefit programs.

■ Key Terms

Administrative expenses
Alcohol and drug treatment facilities
Ambulatory care
Ambulatory surgery facility review
Assistant surgeon review
Benefit plan design
Birthing centers
Carve-outs
Case management
Centers of excellence
Claims
Coinsurance
Concurrent review
Consumer price index (CPI)
Continued-stay review
Coordination of benefits (COB)
Copayment
Cost sharing
Deductibles
Discharge planning
Duplicate coverage
Emergency room treatment
Employee contributions
Exclusive provider organization (EPO)
Extended care facility review
Financial incentive programs
Flat deductible
Gross domestic product (GDP)
Health maintenance organization (HMO)
Home health care
Hospice care
Hospital billing audits
Inpatient utilization review
Integrated delivery systems
Managed care
Managed care indemnity plans
Managed care organization (MCO)
National health expenditures
Negotiated discounts

Outpatient surgery
Outpatient utilization review
Overinsurance
Percentage deductible
Point-of-service (POS) plan
Preadmission certification
Preadmission testing
Preferred provider organization (PPO)
Premium
Progressive care
Prospective review
Reasonable and customary charges
Rehabilitation
Retrospective review
Skilled nursing facility (SNF)
Sliding (variable) deductible
Specialty managed care arrangements
Surgical review
Threshold corridor deductible
Utilization review
Weekend admissions
Wellness program

Chapter 2

POLICY ISSUE, RENEWAL, AND SERVICE

35 *Introduction*
35 *Policy Issue*
42 *Installation for Group Policies*
43 *Continuing Administration*
57 *Renewal Activities*
61 *Third-Party Administration*
62 *Auditing Self-Administered Policyholders*
64 *Emerging Trends*
65 *Summary*
66 *Key Terms*

■ Introduction

The various functions involved in issuing new group or individual policies and providing for their ongoing administration are important in the health insurance operation. How and where a particular insurer accomplishes these functions may vary, depending on its size and organizational structure. The proper administration of health insurance requires the continuous and cooperative efforts of field- and home-office personnel. Also essential to the smooth working of the administrative process for a group insurance plan is the cooperation of the policyholder. Typically the policyholder is involved in the day-to-day details of administering the group plan.

This chapter discusses the processes for issue, renewal, and administration of group plans and individual health insurance policies.

■ Policy Issue

Issuing and administering a group plan or individual policy begins with completion of the application. There are two stages: preissue and issue.

The procedures followed by group and individual health insurers differ in detail for both stages.

Preissue Procedures for Group Health Insurance

The group representative starts the preissue process as soon as the sale is completed. The process begins with obtaining the application and ends with submitting the entire group plan (also called the case).

Obtaining the Application

Applications for group insurance are completed in the field and signed by the prospective policyholder. The group representative completes a worksheet, which is accompanied by an application that contains the detailed data necessary for underwriting consideration and issue. Typically, the application and/or worksheet include:

- types of coverage requested;
- benefit amounts requested;
- legal name of the policyholder;
- location of the policyholder as well as any other locations at which employees are to be insured, including employees of any affiliated or subsidiary organizations;
- effective date of the policy;
- classes of employees eligible to participate and their classification for insurance purposes;
- method of premium payment and how much of the total cost will be assumed by the policyholder and/or employees;
- type of administration and method of paying claims; and
- the producer to whom commissions are to be paid.

Securing an Initial Premium Deposit

Most insurers require an initial premium deposit with the application. The group representative is responsible for collecting this deposit, which normally is equal to one month's premium based on the estimated premium rates for the plan.

Preparing Announcement Literature

Prior to enrollment of the group, the policyholder usually distributes announcement material—often a form letter—to describe the plan in simple, nontechnical language to the firm's employees. A typical announcement letter:

- details the employer's plan and its proposed effective date;
- states the eligibility requirements;
- broadly describes the benefits to be provided;
- states the amount of each employee's contribution; and
- encourages all eligible employees to enroll.

Enrolling Employees

The next preissue step is enrolling eligible employees. The key to successful enrollment is the attitude and extent of the policyholder's involvement. Employers select a time and place when the greatest number of employees can be contacted, and announce the proposed meeting to employees. The insurer's representative (the agent, broker, or group representative) usually handles the enrollment with the policyholder's managerial or supervisory personnel.

Enrollment forms. Enrollment forms provide the necessary data for calculating final rates, computing the initial premium, issuing certificates of coverage, and preparing a coverage record for each participant in the group plan. The information contained in the enrollment forms includes such items as an employee's name, insurance classification, date of birth, occupation, sex, annual earnings, spouse's date of birth, eligible dependents to be covered, and the name of the beneficiary (if the plan includes life and accidental death and dismemberment insurance).

The enrollment form also includes a statement signed by the employee that authorizes the policyholder to deduct from his or her wages the portion of the cost the employee will contribute, and acknowledges that the signer understands the statement. If the plan offers a choice of coverages, the employee's selection also appears on the enrollment form.

Waiver of coverage. Most insurers ask employees who reject participation in a group plan to sign a waiver or refusal-of-coverage card. This waiver serves as evidence that the employee was given an opportunity to participate in the plan but refused.

Submitting the Case

At the conclusion of the enrollment, the group representative examines all items—application for group insurance, initial premium deposit, announcement letter, and enrollment forms—for accuracy and completeness. These items are sent to the home or regional office for final underwriting and issue of the policy.

Issue Procedures for Group Health Insurance

The issue of a group insurance policy involves six steps.

Reviewing the Application

The insurer's home office reviews the application to make sure that it is complete and that it meets the insurer's underwriting requirements. The application also must meet the legal requirements for the state in which the contract is to be issued. The home office obtains any missing information from the group representative. After careful review, the insurer sends the new policyholder a letter that acknowledges the insurer's acceptance of the group.

Preparing a Case Summary Record

Following acceptance, the insurer usually prepares a case summary record (sometimes referred to as an abstract, policy abstract, history card, specification sheet, or digest). The record contains information

POLICY ISSUE, RENEWAL, AND SERVICE

used for issuing the case and calculating the premium rates; for preparing the master policy, the employees' certificates, and the policyholder's administration manual; and for the continuing administration of the plan. The record also contains information regarding the benefits, which is needed for processing claims.

Preparing the Master Policy and Employee Certificate

The master policy and employee certificates are prepared according to the information on the case summary record. Although insurers use model policy and certificate wording as a guide, they develop wording tailored to the specific requirements of the case if the policy or certificates require special language. The terms and provisions of the policy must be acceptable to the insurance department of the state in which the policy is to be issued.

Master policy. The master policy—the legal instrument that contains the insuring clause between the insurer and the group policyholder—includes the following:

- coverages provided;
- eligibility requirements;
- level of benefits; and
- conditions for termination of individual employee benefits or of the policy.

Employee certificates. Each insured employee usually receives a certificate of insurance coverage. These certificates do not constitute a legal contract between the insurer and the employee, but they do outline the benefits and other provisions of the master policy that apply to the insureds.

Two formats are most common in certificates. In one format, the size, style, terminology, and face page of the certificate are similar to a master policy form. The second format is a combined certificate-booklet. It is written in less formal terminology than a policy and has an attachable page or sticker to personalize and validate the booklet as a certificate.

39

Many insurance companies have switched to the certificate-booklet concept.

Distributing Identification Cards

Most insurance companies supply identification cards (also known as information cards) to insured employees, although no statute requires furnishing such cards. The identification card provides the employee (and his or her insured family members) with evidence of coverage that can be presented to providers of medical care. Insurers use three types of identification cards. The first and most common is simply an information card providing brief details of the benefits. The second type certifies (or guarantees) coverages, with certain limitations. The third type of card is used less often, but is likely to become popular as the technology becomes more available. This card allows a provider's office (hospital, doctor, and so forth) to electronically read the benefits of the individual and to confirm not only the benefits covered but also deductibles that have been met.

Calculating Initial Premium Rates

If the case is to be rated using standard rates from the insurer's premium manual (manual rates), which are unadjusted for group-specific historic claim experience, the data for calculation of initial premium rates are taken from information on the enrollment cards. These calculated initial premium rates are compared with the estimated premium rates quoted in the proposal. Any substantial difference between the two rates is brought immediately to the attention of the group representative for explanation to the policyholder. The agreed-upon premium rates then are incorporated into the premium billing system for use in preparing the policyholder's premium statements.

Preparing Premium Statements

As a final step in the issue process, the administrative unit responsible for billing prepares the statement for a group's initial premium.

POLICY ISSUE, RENEWAL, AND SERVICE

Preissue Procedures for Individual Health Insurance

The preissue process for individual health insurance begins in the field when the agent closes the sale by recording the prospective insured's answers on the application. The applicant verifies the information, signs the application, and, in most cases, pays the initial premium. Usually the application is screened in a field office for completeness and accuracy.

When the application is received by the insurer, a separate administrative, new business, or policy issue unit typically establishes the underwriting file. The preissue process includes calculating rates and commission, ordering underwriting forms, and setting up records.

Issue Procedures for Individual Health Insurance

An application for individual health insurance that is approved as applied for usually goes through the issue process quickly. However, this process can be complicated by differing legal requirements of the various states. Every policy must comply with all the laws and regulations of the state of issue—normally the state in which the insured lives. An insurer that operates in a number of states must be able to produce a variety of individual forms and also ensure their correct use.

Many states require provisions that must be either incorporated in the policy or attached to it as a rider or amendment. A policy with exclusion riders, extra premiums, or modifications of benefits requires additional care so that the policy is issued exactly as approved by the underwriter.

Automation, with its capacity for revision and printing, has made the issue process more efficient. Since policy issue is mainly a time- and service-oriented function, day-to-day reliability of the issue system is essential.

41

■ Installation for Group Policies

Installation is the process of assisting a group policyholder set up the administrative practices that are essential to the proper handling of all initial and ongoing administrative activities of the plan. When the group policy, certificates, and other case materials have been prepared by the home office, they usually are mailed according to the group representative's instructions. They may go to the policyholder directly or to the group representative for delivery. Bulk items, such as certificates and forms, ordinarily are sent directly to the policyholder. The administration manual, master policy, and initial premium billing normally are mailed to the group representative, who delivers them to the policyholder. The group representative checks the materials for accuracy and completeness before making installation arrangements with the group policyholder.

Role of Group Representatives and Agents

Group representatives and/or agents are the insurer's liaison with the policyholder. They meet with the policyholder to explain various documents and procedures and to keep the insurer aware of policyholder requirements and expectations.

When installing the plan, the group representative or agent normally meets with the plan administrator—the individual designated by the policyholder to run the insurance plan—and reviews the administrative materials with this person. This review acquaints the administrator with the policy provisions that are relevant to daily administration, the forms, the system for maintaining employee insurance records, and the claim procedures. The group representative also sets up the filing system for enrollment cards and records.

The group representative or agent instructs the policyholder's administrator about the purpose of each administrative and claim form and how to complete it, and acquaints the policyholder with the time requirements for filing claims. Except for claim forms, little—if any—standardization exists among insurance companies in the design or use of administrative forms. The characteristics of the forms are determined mainly by the insurer's own organizational system and requirements.

Finally, the policy is reviewed during the installation to make sure that its provisions are those requested in the application. Many insurance companies require acknowledgment—usually by a countersignature by the policyholder—that the policy provisions are satisfactory and that the master policy has been accepted. Personal data in the certificates of insurance for the original group also are checked for accuracy, and arrangements are made for the distribution of the certificates to the employees.

■ Continuing Administration

After a group plan or individual policy has been sold, underwritten, issued, and installed, the insurer's concern is with the administration of the policy. The administration of an insurance policy is a continuing process involving billing, handling inquiries and complaints, premium payment, changes in coverages, and updating of insureds' records. Many group policyholders assume some of the administrative duties.

Insurer-Policyholder Shared Administration

The degree to which a group policyholder is involved in administrative functions determines whether the plan is self-administered or insurer-administered. A minority of insurers administer all their group business; most have some self-administered cases. Factors determining whether a policyholder is self-administered include the number of persons insured, price, and the capability of its personnel to assume administration of the plan. Large groups are more likely to have a full-time insurance staff to handle administrative details.

Insurance Company Administration

When done by the insurer, the continuing administration of the group plan is a joint function of both the insurer and the policyholder. The policyholder initiates various procedures by submitting forms and reports to the insurer.

The insurer, however, conducts principal activities and maintains a complete ongoing record of each employee insured under the plan. The insurer also establishes records for new entrants, deletes the records of terminated employees, and makes the necessary adjustments for various changes.

When the policyholder sends the enrollment cards of new employees to the insurer, the dates of employment and eligibility are reviewed. If the plan is noncontributory, the insurer accepts all eligible applicants. Their participation in the plan becomes effective immediately after the completion of the probationary period, subject to actively-at-work requirements. If the plan is contributory, some employees will choose not to enroll. As a rule, the names of those who choose not to participate (and who complete a waiver to that effect) are not transmitted to the insurer, and the refusal forms (waiver cards) are retained by the administrator.

Certificates. At one time, insurers delivered all certificates to new employees as they became insured. Some insurers still follow this practice, but three other methods are now more common:

- Insurers furnish the policyholder with a supply of certificates that have no face or validation page. When an individual is added to the plan, the insurance company completes the face or validation page and sends it to the policyholder. The policyholder attaches this to the body of the certificate or the booklet and delivers it to the employee.
- The policyholder affixes a sticker to validate the certificate.
- Instead of personalizing the certificates, the employees receive booklets that indicate they are insured if they meet the conditions explained in the booklet.

Accounting and record keeping. The insurer computes the amount of the premium and sends a bill to the policyholder. The policyholder reviews the bill to ensure that it reflects all transactions that previously have been reported to the insurer. Any unreported items, such as changes in names or insurance classification, are sent promptly to the insurer.

Self-Administration

A policyholder that administers its group plan—a process sometimes called self-accounting—maintains the only individual records of the employees insured. The self-accounting policyholder also performs such functions as:

- enrolling employees;
- issuing certificates;
- arranging for evidence of insurability;
- preparing monthly premium statements on the insurer's forms; and
- processing claims, in some cases. (For more information about claims see Chapter 3: Claim Administration.)

The insurer maintains only a record of the total number of employees insured and total amounts of insurance in force—information obtained from the policyholder's premium statements. If there are unusual administrative issues that are not covered in the policyholder's administration manual, the policyholder submits these to the insurer for handling or guidance.

Group Premium Billing, Accounting, and Collection

Premium billing, accounting, and collection involve the processing of monetary transactions. The more these systems can be integrated, the more likely the policyholder will be satisfied. Integration that includes automated updating of eligibility, billing, coverages, and so forth provides up-to-the-minute accuracy of multiple databases.

Group Premium Billing

Insurers commonly calculate premiums by coverage, class, and age bands.

- The coverage method applies the rate against the base, which may be either the number of persons insured or the total amount of insurance in force. Common practice combines certain coverages, such as medical and dental, and determines the premium rates and the number of lives.

- The class method determines a composite of the per-coverage rates for each insurance class and applies them against the number of employees in the classification. The bill may list individual employees.
- The age-band method uses a per-person premium based on the age of the insured—ages less than 25, 25-29, 30-34, 35-39, . . . 60-64, and 65 and over.

Specialized coverages, such as group short- or long-term disability, may use other types of billing methods. The premium charged may be based on a percentage of the policyholder's payroll for the persons covered. Benefits are based on a percentage of the person's salary.

Whatever the method used, insurers total the premiums and credit the policyholder's previous premium payment to arrive at the balance of any premium due. They also use different billing arrangements, depending on who administers the plan.

The insurer generally uses one of three types of billing for group cases it administers: list, exception, or level.

- With list billing, a list of all insured employees and the premium for each is sent to the policyholder each month.
- Exception billing is a variation of list billing that shows the beginning lives and volume, lists only those employees whose coverage or status has changed during the month, and then shows the closing total that determines the final premium due.
- Level or equal installment billing computes a premium at the beginning of each policy year; the policyholder is billed for this amount on each premium due date during the policy year. The level method is not commonly used because it works well only if the number of insureds in the group is stable.

When a policyholder administers a plan, the insurer prepares a bill for the initial premium. All subsequent premiums are computed and reported by the policyholder on forms the insurer provides. Some insurers provide a starter or skeleton bill each month showing the prior

POLICY ISSUE, RENEWAL, AND SERVICE

month's totals and request the policyholder to update it for changes that have occurred.

The insurer prepares premium statements on insurer-administered cases for each premium due, using as a due date either any day of the month or a particular day as a common due date for all policies. With the common due date, if a plan becomes effective on the tenth of the month and the insurer does all billing as of the first day of each month, the first premium statement would be prorated from the tenth through the end of the month.

To simplify the billing process for both insurer- and self-administered cases, premium charges for individual participants usually begin on the premium due date of each month and end on the last day of the billing month.

For example, if premiums for a group are due on the first of each month, the premium charge for a new entrant whose insurance is effective on March 12 begins April 1; no charge is made for coverage provided during the 20-day period between the effective date of coverage—March 12—and the monthly premium due date—April 1. Assuming that premiums are due on April 1, the charge for an employee who leaves the group on March 12 will cease March 31. There is no premium refund for the interval between the termination date and the end of the billing month.

As an alternative method, the insurer may design the eligibility provision to allow employees to become insured only on the premium due date.

The insurer prepares and mails the premium statement in advance of the due date. A statement for a premium due on the first of a month might be prepared on the 20th day of the preceding month and mailed within the next day or two. The 20th day, in this example, would be referred to as the billing date or the billing calculation date. The insurance company must receive reports of changes in participation, benefits, and coverage several days before the billing date to include them in the most current premium statement.

47

Only changes completely processed by the billing date can be included in determining the amount of premium due. Changes that are completed after the statements have been prepared are not reflected in the premium until the next amount due is calculated. However, the adjustments are retroactive, and the policyholder is charged or credited accordingly. Many insurers establish a limit on the retroactive period, such as the last policy anniversary or 12 months.

Group Premium Payments

Group insurance premiums usually are mailed by policyholders either directly to the insurer or to a lock box. With a lock-box arrangement, the insurer enters into agreements with banks located in areas of the greatest concentration of its group business, authorizing those banks to have access to assigned post-office boxes. Throughout the day the bank collects all mail in the post office's lock box, depositing the premium payments to the insurer's account, and each day sending to the insurer a list of all checks deposited and a statement of the total amount credited to its account.

The advantages of lock-box arrangements include:

- almost immediate availability of funds for insurer investment, which improves cash flow and increases investment interest earned;
- faster collection of premium remittances; and
- lower clerical costs by relieving the insurer of the work involved in receiving, endorsing, and depositing checks in payment of premiums.

Another remittance method used by some insurers, particularly on small group business, is the use of preauthorized checks (PACs). By this method the policyholder's bank account is used to pay the group premiums. The PAC policyholder gets the same type of premium statement from the insurer as other policyholders. However, instead of showing an amount due, the statement usually indicates that a preauthorized check has been drawn, so no further premium payment is owed. Statements on PAC business are mailed from three to six days before the transaction is to occur. If the policyholder has a low bank balance, this

POLICY ISSUE, RENEWAL, AND SERVICE

method allows time for the account to be replenished. Experience indicates that the persistency can be substantially better with the PAC methods than in cases where the policyholder remits directly by check.

Many of the largest policyholders are moving to the use of electronic funds transfer (EFT). This billing arrangement works much the same as the PAC, except that the policyholder has the option of having the billed amount automatically transferred to the insurer, or the policyholder may initiate this transfer each month. The issue seems to be who has access to these premium dollars. The policyholder may transfer these dollars on the last day of the grace period, thereby retaining its cash until the last possible moment.

Group Premium Accounting

All premium remittances, whether received directly by the insurer or through a lock box or EFT, are credited promptly to the policyholder's account. For each policyholder, premiums generally are allocated by line of coverage and accumulated monthly by policy. Total premiums collected from all policyholders are accumulated by line of coverage for the calendar year. For premium-tax purposes, the insurer maintains a record of the amount of premiums allocated in each state (and in counties and cities, where required). Division is made, in some instances, on the basis of first-year premiums, renewal premiums, and line of coverage.

Group Premium Collection

A group policy usually permits a 31-day grace period for the payment of premiums. Rather than automatically cancel the policy if the premium is not received by the 31st day of the grace period, the insurer makes an effort to secure payment of the premium. If its attempts are not successful, the insurer sends a formal cancellation notice to the policyholder. This notice usually is sent sometime between the 31st day and the 60th day after the due date of the premium in default. Claims incurred after the end of the grace period are not paid unless the policy is reinstated. In most instances, the insurance company reinstates the policy when the overdue premium is paid.

49

It is possible for an insurer to cancel a policy if the number of participants falls below the minimum specified in the policy. Usually in such cases, the insurer gives notification of the decision to cancel or terminate in advance of the termination date. Termination also may occur at the request of the policyholder.

Legislation in some states has caused insurers to review formerly liberal lapse and reinstatement practices. In effect, these laws say that if an insurer acts as though it considers the case to be in force, the insurer may become liable for claims beyond those contemplated in the contract.

Individual Premium Billing and Collection

Individual Premium Billing

The four most common modes of premium payment for individual insurance policies are monthly, quarterly, semi-annually, and annually. Premiums paid annually are lower than those paid by other modes. Because of interest factors and increased billing and collection costs, the more frequent the premium payment, the higher the premium.

Although the insurer generally does not have a contractual obligation to let the insured know when a premium payment is due, as a practical matter it is sensible to do so. Without a systematic method of billing for premiums due, a collection effort would be chaotic at best, and policy lapses would be extremely high. The two most common types of billing are direct and automatic bank payments.

Direct billing. Direct billing is the most traditional type of billing method. It involves sending a premium statement to the insured as notification in advance that a premium is due. The biggest drawbacks to direct billing are the relatively high incidence of lapses and the high administrative costs of the more frequent modes, especially monthly. This experience has led some insurers to make direct monthly (and sometimes quarterly) billing unavailable.

Automatic bank payments. Individual health insurance premiums also are paid by preauthorized checks in much the same way as group health insurance premiums. (See page 48.)

POLICY ISSUE, RENEWAL, AND SERVICE

Individual Premium Collection

All individual health insurance policies are required to have grace period and reinstatement provisions. The grace period provision allows the insured 31 days to pay a premium after its due date. The insurer may allow shorter grace periods when premiums are paid weekly or monthly. The grace period protects an insured with a temporary budget problem or one who simply has failed to mail the premium on time. If the premium is not paid before the end of the grace period, the policy lapses.

The reinstatement provision sets forth the following procedures for putting a lapsed policy back in force:

- If the insurer accepts a premium payment after the expiration of the grace period without requiring a reinstatement application, the policy is automatically reinstated.
- If the insurer does require an application for reinstatement and issues a receipt for the money sent with it, the insurer has 45 days to determine whether it wishes to reinstate the policy. If the insurer does not notify the policyholder of its disapproval within 45 days, the policy is automatically reinstated on the 45th day following the date of receipt of the application and payment.

Handling Inquiries and Complaints

Consumerism is an important factor for businesses that deal with the public, and the health insurance industry is no exception. Accordingly, most insurance companies have units set up to handle inquiries and complaints from group policyholders and individual insureds.

Inquiries

Group policyholders and individual insureds rely on getting information from the administrative unit that handles policyholder inquiries. Typical requests are for:

- explanation of policy language and policy rights;
- premium status of policies;

- information regarding additional coverage;
- reduction of benefits;
- change of premium mode;
- policy reinstatement; and
- addition of new family members.

Complaints

Consumer complaints can occur under a variety of circumstances, but for a health insurer they are most common in the areas of claim administration, underwriting, and sales. In claim situations, complaining insureds usually believe they have not been compensated adequately for a loss. Underwriting complaints commonly involve a dispute as to the individual's insurability. Improper methods used by a salesperson are typically the basis for sales complaints. #36

In a competitive environment, goodwill is one of an insurer's primary concerns. Most insurers, therefore, put great emphasis on resolving consumer complaints promptly and fairly. In addition, an important regulatory function of state insurance departments is to make sure that consumers are given fair treatment. Complaints usually are handled by the consumer division of the state insurance department. Many state insurance departments require insurers to maintain a complaint register. #37 This register includes the identification, handling, and disposition of consumer complaints. It may be used by states for judging unfair trade practices.

Processing Changes

Group Insureds' Changes

There are many administrative activities that result from changes in the composition of a group or of an employee's status within the group. Handling these activities in a timely, efficient, and accurate manner enables the insurer to maintain a high standard of policyholder service.

New enrollments. Each new employee's insurance record begins with the completion of the enrollment form. When the insurer administers the plan, the form may be either the completed card or a computer record. The coverage and benefit amounts for employees insured under a self-administered plan usually are recorded directly on their enrollment cards and are kept by the group policyholder.

Employers ordinarily enroll employees in the group plan when they are hired; coverage becomes effective upon completion of the waiting period. Evidence of insurability is not required for these timely entrants. If an employee enrolls more than 31 days after he or she is initially eligible, that employee is a late entrant and must furnish evidence of insurability acceptable to the insurer. Some insurers use an automatic three-months' deferral of the effective date instead of evidence of insurability for late entrants.

Employee terminations. The names of those who leave the group or otherwise become ineligible for the group plan are reported to the insurance company either individually as the terminations occur or collectively at weekly or monthly intervals. An employee may withdraw from a contributory plan by informing the administrator of the intention to discontinue coverage. The customary practice in this situation is to have withdrawing employees sign a statement indicating that they no longer authorize their employer to deduct insurance premiums from their paycheck. In reporting a termination, the administrator furnishes the exact date of termination and the reason for discontinuance of the insurance. This voluntary cancellation automatically cancels dependent coverage.

Dependent benefit changes. After an employee becomes a participant in the group plan, the insurance premium may be adjusted by either adding or discontinuing coverage for dependents. If the insurance is noncontributory, this coverage automatically begins with the first eligible dependent; it is deleted only when the employee is no longer a member of the group or no longer has qualified dependents.

Under a contributory plan, coverage for dependents is optional and provided upon the written request of the employee. In the past, insurers ordinarily would require evidence of the dependents' insurability if the request for coverage had not been made within 31 days of the date that the employee's dependents are eligible for insurance. The Health Insurance Portability and Accountability Act (HIPAA) of 1996 requires insurers to accept eligible employees who apply late, but allows insurers to impose longer pre-existing condition exclusions (up to 18 months rather than the maximum of 12 months for employees who enroll in a timely manner).

Dependent coverage terminates when an employee no longer is eligible for insurance and when an employee no longer has eligible dependents. In addition, an employee may discontinue dependent insurance at any time by signing a revocation of the agreement to make the required contributions for the premium.

Under the HIPAA, health insurance policies covering the insured and spouse or the insured and at least one child must provide that a child born while the policy is in force is eligible to be enrolled. The child generally is covered for the policy benefits without cost from birth until the next premium due date. However, the insurer must be notified to add the child to the coverage sometime prior to the next premium due date. Thereafter, coverage is continued subject to the payment of additional premium, if any.

New family members generally are added, if they qualify, through the usual application process. These include the spouse, spouse's children by a former marriage, family members not included at the time of issue, and any newborn child.

Termination of coverage occurs for a number of reasons. A dependent child's coverage usually ceases because the dependent's marriage, employment, or attainment of the maximum age allowed by the policy for dependent child coverage results in the ending of dependence on the insured. Adult coverage may terminate at a maximum age limit, at eligibility for Medicare coverage, or through legal separation or divorce. The coverage of handicapped children is not terminated solely because of age, provided they remain dependent on the insured and otherwise remain eligible.

Group Plan Changes

The administrative activities involved in processing group plan changes are similar to those required for issuance of a new case. The insurer underwrites plan changes, develops needed announcement literature, and enrolls new employees, if necessary (e.g., if adding a new subsidiary to the plan).

For a major plan change, the group representative or agent carefully reviews the revised plan and new installation material or procedures with the policyholder. A plan change normally requires amendments rather than reissuance of the group policy. New certificates may be issued for some changes; for others, certificate riders are sufficient.

Rate assessment also is involved. When adding a new coverage, insurers will calculate initial premium rates. If the change involves only existing coverage, premium rates for that particular coverage usually are recalculated. When the new rates are available, the insurer prepares new premium statements.

The insurer revises the administration manual, or replaces it completely, to reflect plan changes. New supplies, if required, are assembled for the policyholder.

Individual Policy Changes

A change in occupation or employment almost always requires a review and possible change in a person's individual insurance program. An increase in salary may result in the need to increase an amount of disability income coverage. Added family responsibilities may have an effect on the need for additional disability income or medical expense insurance. Health coverages must be updated regularly to keep pace both with changes in an insured's life and with the changing nature and cost of medical care.

The insured should be made aware of these needs on an ongoing basis rather than having to discover at the time of a claim that he or she is inadequately covered. A good agent keeps clients aware of their changing needs and offers sound insurance advice. The insurer, too, must have a flexible program that is able to meet the ever-changing needs of its policyholders.

Increases on existing policies. Increasing the benefits of an existing policy usually is more beneficial to both the insured and the insurer than issuing additional policies. For the insured, it usually is cheaper; for the insurer, it helps eliminate duplicate coverage and thus reduces claim costs in reimbursement-type coverages. For example, if the insurer issues two separate insurance contracts, each reimbursing from the first dollar of expense, the result will be duplicate coverage ($2 of benefit for each $1 of expense). In addition, two policies require separate maintenance and administration.

Underwriting changes in coverage. The underwriting requirements for an increase in coverage vary depending on the amount of the increase, the nature of the coverage, and the practices of the insurer. The common procedure is to require a new completed application with up-to-date medical history. Although the insurer should have a history of any claims paid under the policy, changes in insurability may have occurred that are unknown to the insured. Such changes could affect the underwriting decision. If the increase in risk is small (e.g., changing to a shorter elimination period before benefits are payable on a disability income policy), a limited special application form may be used.

A decrease in benefits usually requires only some type of formal request from the insured—either a specially prepared form or a signed request from the insured. In most cases, an insurer will process a decrease request without question.

Dependent benefit changes. The addition of new family members usually is accomplished by the use of a rider or amendment sent to the insured for attachment to the policy. Eligibility and notification requirements are much the same for group policies, as are the reasons for termination of dependent coverage.

When a dependent leaves a family group because of marriage or reaching the maximum age, the agent should attempt to write a separate policy to continue the coverage for this individual. Coverage for the former dependent usually can be arranged with little or no underwriting. The coverage may be considered merely a transfer from one policy to another with a change to the proper adult premium at the attained age.

POLICY ISSUE, RENEWAL, AND SERVICE

Many family policies provide a conversion privilege when children reach the maximum age and have not obtained other coverage through employment, marriage, or some other sources. The family policy is endorsed for termination of coverage, and a new policy is issued to the child at adult rates.

Other increases or decreases in coverage. An increase in coverage is any type of change that increases the risk assumed by the insurance company. Examples of increases in coverage include:

- increase in the dollar amount of a benefit;
- reduction in a deductible amount;
- reduction in the elimination period;
- increase in a benefit period; and
- addition of a type of benefit not previously applied for or available under the policy.

Most increases require completion of an application and are subject to current underwriting limits and satisfactory evidence of insurability. Others may be granted automatically under an option such as a guaranteed insurability option.

A decrease in coverage is any type of change that reduces the risk assumed by the insurer. Examples of decreases include:

- dollar reduction in a benefit amount;
- increase in a deductible amount;
- increase in the length of the elimination period; and
- elimination of a supplementary benefit no longer needed.

A decrease usually requires only a signed request from the insured.

■ Renewal Activities

Each year upon a policy's renewal, a certain amount of administrative, underwriting, and actuarial work must be performed. The role of administrative personnel in renewal generally consists of compiling the data

57

on premiums, claims, commissions, taxes, and other expenses that are needed by the underwriting and actuarial personnel for renewal rating, federal and state disclosure act purposes, and experience refunds.

Renewal Underwriting

Premium, claim, and commission data usually are provided automatically from the insurer's administrative system. For group renewals, certain employee data are requested from the policyholder. An employee's current earnings, for example, may be required before short- or long-term disability benefits for the next policy year can be determined. On a self-administered case, even more information is furnished by the policyholder because the insurer has no employee records available from which certain data, such as age, sex, and earnings distribution, can be taken. The information needed for an individual policy renewal is in the insurer's records.

The same factors that were significant in accepting a group initially also are important at each renewal to help the insurer establish a renewal rate level based on an accurate projection of anticipated claims and expenses. Major changes in the plan of benefits, employee characteristics, participation levels, methods of funding, and managed care arrangements are examples of changes that require close scrutiny by the underwriter. Changes in group size and employee mix resulting from the downsizing of a company, severe economic conditions, or the buying and selling of large operations also must be considered.

Insurers are aware that some group policyholders and individual insureds may terminate their policies because of the increase in cost to them associated with renewal underwriting. Nevertheless, some form of renewal underwriting is necessary for adequate control of the insurer's claim experience. The degree of renewal underwriting that may take place is limited by the renewability provision of the policy.

Insurer Actions for Renewal

The HIPAA requires insurers to renew group and individual medical expense insurance policies, except in a few specified circumstances such as nonpayment of premiums. For other types of insurance, there are specific actions that insurers can take in the renewal process, which are discussed in the following section. For definitions of the basic renewal provisions see Chapter 4: Health Insurance Contract in *Fundamentals of Health Insurance: Part A.*

Optionally Renewable Policies

When policies renewable at the option of the insurer were first developed, they could be canceled during the policy term by either the insurer or the insured with an appropriate refund of premium. Later policies reserved to the insurer the right to nonrenew a policy on any premium due date or the policy anniversary date, but not to cancel between these dates.

The insurer may choose to modify an optionally renewable policy rather than to nonrenew. The modification may be:

- an exclusion endorsement or special-class premium because of a given physical impairment;
- an increase in the basic premium because of a change to a more hazardous occupation; or
- an increase in elimination periods to avoid small, repetitious claims.

The insurer must give a policyholder written notice that the coverage will terminate in accordance with the renewal provision unless the insured agrees to the changes requested. Insurers usually prepare an agreement that must be signed by the policyholder before the renewal premium is accepted.

Although many reasons exist for the nonrenewal of policies, some insurers follow the practice of limiting the nonrenewal of policies to those involving:

- fraud;
- a moral hazard;
- overinsurance;
- discontinuing a class of business;

- submission of false claims; or
- malingering on a claim.

In some states, insurers are not permitted to nonrenew an individual policy solely because of deterioration of the insured's health between the issue date and the renewal date of a policy. (The HIPAA prohibits nonrenewal of individual medical expense policies solely because of deterioration of an insured's health.)

Nonrenewable for Stated-Reasons-Only Policies

Some health insurance policies are nonrenewable only for stated reasons, such as when a policyholder ceases to be employed or when an insurer is having adverse experience on a particular type of policy form as a whole. These policies generally are handled on the same basis as optionally renewable policies, except for the limitations in the policy on the insurer's right to nonrenew.

Guaranteed Renewable Policies

The renewal underwriting of a guaranteed renewable policy is limited to the rescission of the policy during the contestable period or refusal to accept an application for reinstatement. When the insurer discovers a material misrepresentation within the contestable period, the policy may be rescinded if the omission on the application materially affected the risk, and the insurer would not have issued the policy had the correct information been known. The insurer may refuse to reinstate a policy in accordance with its current underwriting practices.

Guaranteed renewable coverages may be subject to premium rate changes if the insurer has had to pay out more in claims than it expected. Such premium changes cannot be made on an individual policy basis, but only on a block of individual policies within a given class. Classes must be defined in broad categories such as age, sex, and occupation.

POLICY ISSUE, RENEWAL, AND SERVICE

Noncancellable Policies

Except for periodic review of the experience on a given block of business for continued marketing, the renewal underwriting of noncancellable coverage is limited to the rescission of contracts during the contestable period for material misrepresentation on the application and refusal to reinstate a lapsed policy. Since the coverage must be renewed to the stated age at the stipulated premium, the only other action that can be taken is to discontinue further sale of the particular policy form.

Renewal Notice

Most states require advance notification of at least 30 days for any increase in premium charges, changes in plan design, or plans to nonrenew. Typically, an insurer will send a letter to the policyholder explaining any rate increase, along with an offer of alternate plan designs that may be available at a lower cost. Copies of this letter also will be sent to the group representative or agent to assist in planning how to retain the customer for another year.

■ Third-Party Administration

Administration of group cases by third-party administrators (TPAs) often is desirable from the standpoint of the policyholder because of the complexities and special requirements involved. Since some group plans are national or international in scope, the policyholder's office is not always equipped with either the necessary staff or the expertise to perform the administrative function at a reasonable cost.

Insurers have assumed the role of a third-party administrator on a number of self-insured or partially insured plans. The services offered by these insurers range from only the claim payment function to complete administration of the plan. A third-party administrator does not have to be an insurance company, but because of their experience, insurers often are in a favorable position when negotiating fees for these administrative services. The administration fee is usually a direct charge, and no commissions are paid. To handle this third-party administration, some insurers have created a separate organizational unit that concentrates on this specialized activity.

Claim Services Only

Insurers initially offered claim services only (CSO) to very large clients, but now offer it to medium-sized groups as well. The insurer provides only the claim processing function for medical expense coverages, basing its fee for this service on the number of claims processed.

Administrative Services Only (ASO)

In administrative-services-only business, the insurance company as administrator does not bear the risk of insurance. Rather, the employer bears this risk. However, generally the same processes (enrollment, billing, distribution of information regarding the plan, and so forth) must be handled whether or not the business is insured. There are two notable differences in the plan itself: there is no traditional contract, and the document detailing the plan is not required to meet the standards of state insurance departments. (It may have to meet other requirements, such as those under the Employee Retirement Income Security Act.)

Administrative services only is available for medical and dental coverages. Some insurers also offer it for disability income coverage. Like claim services only, administrative services only was originally offered only to very large clients, but now is also available to medium-sized groups. Some insurers estimate the cost of providing the services and add a margin for profit. The resulting figure may be expressed to the client as a flat charge per claim processed, as a charge per employee in the plan, as a percentage of claims paid, or as a combination of these methods.

■ Auditing Self-Administered Policyholders

Most insurance companies have their own internal general auditing staff whose major responsibility is to audit periodically home office departmental operations, agency offices, and branch offices.

POLICY ISSUE, RENEWAL, AND SERVICE

The primary objectives in auditing are to verify financial records and accounts and to uncover fraud. Auditing of group insurance, however, is concerned most frequently with self-administered policyholders. Its two main objectives are:

- to review the policyholder's procedures and controls and educate those handling the administration of the plan in correct procedures; and

- to examine the policyholder's records to determine whether all eligible people are enrolled properly and to make sure that premiums are being paid on all persons who are insured under the plan.

Insurers differ on the issue of whether to audit self-administered cases. Assuming the case has been installed properly, some insurers feel the cost involved exceeds any possible benefits, particularly if the experience has been satisfactory. Others feel that a definite need exists to audit self-administered business and that the cost is justified. Perhaps one of the most important influences on whether an insurer establishes an audit program is the attitude of the state insurance department examiners. In recent years, state examiners have been paying more attention to self-administered group business and are asking insurers who are not conducting an audit to establish an audit program to protect the rights of covered persons.

There are two kinds of audit: an internal audit and an external audit.

Internal Audit

Internal auditing involves checks of all incoming premium statements from self-administered policyholders at the insurer's home office by group administration personnel. If an error is detected, they correspond with the administrator, outline the nature of the error, and inform the administrator of the proper way to correct it. When the audit is completed, the appropriate information from the premium statements is entered on the master records in the insurer's administrative system.

63

External Audit

Most insurers make it a practice to visit policyholders who are self-administered. During such a visit, the external part of the auditing function is done by a trained auditor under a formal type of audit program. Under this program some insurers have delegated full responsibility to group personnel; others have placed it under the overall charge of their general auditor or comptroller.

The audit is aimed at two principal areas: the policyholder's records, to determine whether they properly reflect the insurer's risk on the case and the terms of the case, and the policyholder's administrative procedures, to determine their adequacy and how well the administrator is performing them.

In a typical audit, the auditor might be expected to:

- review the employer's payroll records to verify such data as eligibility, benefits, and income;
- manually check the enrollment cards to determine if they are being completed properly;
- make a count of the number of cards and volume in force to determine whether these balance with the latest premium statement and, if not, make the necessary corrections;
- check the eligibility of employees and dependents and, in cases that are contributory, verify that evidence of insurability is used when necessary;
- determine, by means of spot checks, if any claims were paid on employees or dependents who were ineligible for benefits; and
- spend whatever time may be necessary in reviewing administrative procedures with the person involved.

■ Emerging Trends

Legislation being passed on the state and federal levels is having an increasing impact on the processes and procedures of insurance companies. The issue and ongoing administration of group and individual health insurance policies are no exceptions. For example, many states now require the use of group enrollment, individual application, medical evidence, and waiver of coverage forms specific for their state. This is costly for insurers, especially those operating in many states.

In addition, many states have open enrollment requirements on small employer plans that allow those individuals who were previously unable or unwilling to obtain group coverage to enter the plan without supplying medical evidence. Insurers have had to establish notification and enrollment procedures to accommodate these one-time or annual open enrollments.

Another trend deals with the increased use of technology to help the insurer operate more efficiently and cost effectively. Innovations such as electronic mail (e-mail) and automated voice response systems (AVRS) make it easy and quick for the home office and field personnel to communicate with each other and with their customers. Technologies such as optical scanning of documents and pen-based computing are beginning to integrate and speed up the enrollment and issue processes for some companies.

As consumers become more technologically sophisticated, the demand for high-tech, efficient approaches to doing business will continue to grow. Those insurers who stay on the cutting edge of this growing technology will position themselves competitively in the marketplace.

■ Summary

The issue and continuation in force of group and individual insurance policies is a complex process involving a number of operating areas of the insurance company. Efficiency, cost-effective procedures, and cooperative interaction among the different company functions result in a smooth administrative operation. Insurers also consider a number of matters—legal, supervisory, and statistical—that relate to administrative aspects of the ongoing administration of an insurance policy. It is mainly through these administrative services to policyholders that an insurer serves the public and creates a favorable corporate and industry image.

FUNDAMENTALS OF HEALTH INSURANCE: PART B

■ Key Terms

Administrative services only (ASO)
Age-band billing
Application
Audit
Automatic bank payment
Case
Case summary record
Certificate-booklet
Claims services only (CSO)
Class billing
Complaint register
Coverage billing
Direct billing
Electronic funds transfer (EFT)
Enrollment
Enrollment form
Exception billing
Grace period
Guaranteed renewable policy
Identification card
Initial premium deposit
Installation
Issue
Lapse
Late entrant
List billing
Level billing
Lock-box arrangement
Master policy
Noncancellable policy
Nonrenewable for stated-reasons-only policy
Optionally renewable policy
Plan administrator
Preauthorized check (PAC)
Preissue
Premium statement
Reinstatement
Renewal underwriting
Self-administration
Service fee
Third-party administrator (TPA)
Timely entrant

Chapter 3

CLAIM ADMINISTRATION

67 *Introduction*
68 *Organizational Structure*
71 *Methods of Claim Administration*
73 *Claim Documentation*
80 *Claim Processing*
88 *Claim Investigation*
90 *Claim Payment Process*
92 *Customer Service*
92 *Controlling Claim Costs*
97 *Technology in Claim Processing*
98 *Emerging Trends*
99 *Summary*
99 *Key Terms*

■ Introduction

The claim function of a health insurance company is the means by which it fulfills contractual promises to provide financial protection in the event the insured incurs a covered loss. Claim administration is the process of:

- gathering facts relating to illness or injury;
- comparing them with the insurance contract; and
- determining the benefits payable to the insured.

The primary objective of claim administration is to pay all valid and appropriate claims promptly, courteously, and fully to the extent of the policy. The second objective is to accumulate and make available claim data for accounting, statistical, analytical, and research purposes. Such

FUNDAMENTALS OF HEALTH INSURANCE: PART B

data are essential for pricing, financial control, and long-range planning. To accomplish both objectives, the insurance company utilizes claim processing systems as well as accounting, data analysis, and reporting systems.

The insurance industry traditionally has used the terms *claims, claim department,* and *claim administration* to describe the process by which benefits are paid to insureds. While a claim is the means by which an insured declares a loss and provides the necessary proof, the insurance company receiving claims literally provides benefits, giving rise to an increasing use of the terms *benefits, benefits department,* and *benefits administration* to describe the process.

This chapter focuses on claim documentation, investigation, and payment procedures for group and individual medical expense insurance and disability insurance.

■ Organizational Structure

The claim function may be conducted from the insurer's home office or through field claim offices. Group carriers also allow self-administration and third-party administration.

Home Office Claim Administration

Home office claim administration is attractive to insurers because it promotes:

- prompt, efficient, and consistent claim handling because of the concentration of claim personnel in one location and the availability of professional personnel, such as doctors and attorneys;
- easy notification of claim staff of changes affecting payment of claims and of new forms of coverage; and
- simplified training of new claim personnel.

Claim administration from the home office of an insurer usually is organized in one of two ways: a single department that handles all claims or

68

CLAIM ADMINISTRATION

separate claim departments for group health insurance and for individual health insurance.

Single Department Organization

The single claim department operates under one executive who often consults with the executives of other departments, such as underwriting and marketing. In this type of administrative organization, it is possible to maintain greater consistency in claim administration for all product lines because experience can be transmitted swiftly and easily from one line to another. Below the managerial level, there is likely to be a considerable amount of work specialization. Medical expense claims, for example, involve different considerations than disability claims.

Product Line Organization

Under the separate product claim department type of organization, the claim department management is responsible to and takes direction from the management of the product line it serves. There is a sense of identification with the product line that enables greater flexibility and adaptability in handling claim problems peculiar to it.

Field Office Claim Administration

Claim administration in a field office, sometimes referred to as geographic organization, uses essentially the same claim processing methods as home office administration. Because of shortened lines of communication between the field office and the group policyholder or local insured, there usually is greater opportunity for personalized service than when all claims are paid from the home office.

The number and location of field claim offices set up by an insurer depend on the geographic distribution of its policyholders and insured population, the type of business the insurer writes, and the competitive need for local claim service. The degree of authority exercised by a field office usually is proportionate to the volume of claims it handles.

69

Self-Administration

Policyholder or self-administration of claims is a method by which the group policyholder processes certain claims instead of sending them to the insurance company. It is used exclusively by group carriers.

Self-administration of claims usually is limited to short-term disability income benefits and basic hospital, surgical, and medical expense benefits. Some group insurance companies also permit policyholder administration of dental and major medical claims. Most, however, exclude long-term disability income benefits because of the complexities involved and the large benefit amounts at risk.

General Procedures

The usual method of paying self-administered claims is by drafts drawn by the policyholder. Accordingly, policyholder administration of claims is commonly referred to as a policyholder draft or draft book system.

A draft is a form of check, but there are important differences between the two. A check always is payable on demand and must be drawn on account with sufficient funds on deposit. In contrast, no funds have to be on deposit to cover a draft until after it arrives at the insurance company for acceptance. Funds then are deposited by the insurance company to cover payment of the draft. Drafts allow a delayed deposit. The policyholder is given a supply of drafts and the authority to pay claims. Generally, copies of policyholder-issued drafts are sent daily to the insurance company. Some insurers may require that the claim form and associated documentation be included with the draft copies.

The personnel responsible for claim processing are selected by the group policyholder; the insurer exercises no direct control over the selection or supervision of such personnel. Because it is in the best interests of the insurer to make sure that people processing the claims are competent and adequately trained, insurance company representatives usually assist in the training.

The insurer usually gives the group policyholder that administers its claims a lower premium rate or a lower claim administration charge in its dividend or experience refund formula.

Third-Party Administration

Another method of claim administration is claim processing by a third party. As with the draft book system, the third party is given a supply of drafts and the authority to pay claims with insurance company funds. Union welfare plans, multiple employer groups, and association groups usually are the policyholders that use third-party administrators. Some small individual carriers also use third-party administrators when they no longer can economically process their claims.

■ Methods of Claim Administration

There are two major ways that insurers handle the claim process: a direct submission to the insurer and, for group insurance only, submission by the policyholder.

Direct Submission

Under the direct submission method, the insured is provided with claim forms and instructions on how to submit claims. The insured sends all claims directly to the insurance company. The insurer maintains the coverage data on insured individuals and verifies coverage at the time the claims are submitted. The insurer then makes payment of the claim directly to the insured or, if benefits are assigned, to the provider.

Insureds can file claims through the claim-kit approach or the card-only approach.

Claim-Kit Approach

Under the claim-kit approach, each insured is provided with a claim kit that includes claim forms requiring completion only by the insured and

71

provider. For the group carrier, this means the policyholder has no responsibility for claim form completion. The claim kit also contains instructions on how to complete the form and submit the claim.

The kits usually contain an identification card that outlines the benefits available and refers the provider to the insurer for verification that the claimant is insured. Insurers determine claimant eligibility from their records.

When an insured person is admitted to a hospital, the hospital generally verifies eligibility for benefits directly with the insurer. Sometimes the policyholder of a group contract may be contacted because the insurance identification card contains its name. Depending on the provisions of the particular plan or policy, an assignment of benefits may or may not be necessary to pay benefits directly to the provider of medical care.

The claim-kit approach was developed initially for use by large groups. Its success has led some insurers to extend this approach to smaller groups of under 100 lives and to individual insureds.

Card-Only Approach

The identification card–only approach to direct submission of claims differs significantly from the claim-kit approach. Each insured is provided with a card that identifies him or her as insured for the benefits summarized on the card. The card may indicate that benefits can be paid directly to the provider by the insurer, and providers often accept the card as an assurance that benefits are available. No claim forms are required, and the provider of medical care submits bills directly to the insurer with sufficient identification, itemization, and other information necessary to permit payment.

The card-only approach works best with a large, centrally located employer whose employment population is stable and whose group plan provides broad medical expense benefits with few limitations and exceptions. Individual carriers also are experimenting with this approach.

CLAIM ADMINISTRATION

Policyholder Submission

Instead of having employees submit claims directly to the insurance company for verification of coverage, some group policyholders prefer to conduct this function. Although this approach is less popular than direct submission, it is still used by some small and mid-sized employers. The steps of policyholder submission are as follows:

- The claimant notifies the policyholder of a claim.
- The policyholder verifies that the person is an eligible member of the group plan and that coverage is in force.
- The policyholder furnishes the claimant with claim forms, along with instructions for completion.
- When the completed claim forms are received from the insured person, the policyholder reviews them for completeness, certifies that the person is eligible for coverage, and sends the claim to the insurer.
- The insurer processes the claim and, except for benefits assigned to providers of service, payments are sent to the policyholder for delivery to the insured. In lieu of sending payments to the employer, payments may be sent directly to the insured.

■ Claim Documentation

Before an insurer can pay a claim, notice of claim, proof of loss, and status of coverage must be documented.

Notice of Claim

The notice of claim provision contained in all group and individual health insurance policies specifies that the insured must give the insurer written notice of claim for any loss covered by the policy—typically within 20 days after the occurrence or commencement of the loss or as soon thereafter as is reasonably possible.

Some insurers provide a form for notice of claim with each new policy. As claims occur and notice is furnished to the insurer, the insurer sends

73

a new notice of claim form to the insured. The requirement for notifying the insurer of a claim is fulfilled when notice is given to the insurer at the home office or to any authorized representative of the insurer.

The insured's notice of claim alerts the insurer that a loss may have been sustained and that forms for filing proof of loss are needed by the insured. In addition, it permits the insurer to begin the preliminary work of assembling the claim file and determining the policy status.

Proof of Loss

For hospital or medical expense benefits, written proof of loss must be furnished within 90 days of the date of the loss. For disability benefits, the insured must furnish written proof of loss within 90 days after the termination of the period for which the insurer is liable. Failure to furnish proof of loss within the required time will not invalidate a claim, provided proof is furnished as soon as reasonably possible.

Claim Forms

Proof of loss usually is submitted on claim forms supplied by the insurer. The purpose of claim forms is to establish the facts concerning a loss so that it can be evaluated and the insurer's liability determined. Claim forms include a claimant's or insured's statement and an attending physician's statement; in some instances, a hospital statement is required in addition to or in lieu of the attending physician's statement. Some hospitals or physicians associated with large clinics submit their own form instead of the one provided by the insurer. As long as the form contains the right information, it will be accepted by most insurers.

Uniform, simplified claim forms for group and individual carriers have been developed for use by hospitals and physicians. The most important of these forms are the following two:

- Uniform Billing UB-92 (HCFA-1450) is the form used for submitting bills from hospitals and other institutional health care providers. It provides summary billing information, such as charges for health services provided to the patient, diagnoses, medical procedures, and payer information. It provides a summary of the patient's account and other information. The form has been adopted by Medicare and Medicaid, and is accepted by the majority of third-party payers for billings from hospitals. It is designed to be flexible and to accommodate the needs of both the payer and the provider. (Exhibit 3.1.)

- Health Insurance Claim (HCFA-1500) is the form used for submitting claims for medical care and treatment and medical supplies. The HCFA-1500 form includes information such as who the insured's payer(s) are, diagnoses, procedures, services or supplies, and charges for health services. It has been approved by the American Medical Association in an effort to reduce and simplify insurance paperwork for health care providers. Many states have enacted legislation mandating acceptance of these forms, and others are expected to follow suit. (Exhibit 3.2.)

Status of Coverage

Before processing a claim, insurers need to determine the status of coverage of the claimant.

Effective Date of Coverage

A loss that occurs before the effective date of coverage will not be covered. The date and the conditions under which coverage becomes effective initially are determined by the language of the policy and the application.

Date of coverage for group health insurance. For group claims, it is necessary to review whether the group's policy was in force at the time of loss and whether the employee's or dependent's coverage was in force at the time of loss. Both levels need to be reviewed before paying a claim.

Date of coverage for individual health insurance. For individual claims, if a claimant applied for a policy but did not pay a premium at the time, the insurer, as a general rule, incurs no liability. If the applicant/claimant pays a premium at the time of application, a conditional receipt usually is given. In addition to being a receipt for the premium

Exhibit 3.1
Uniform Billing Form

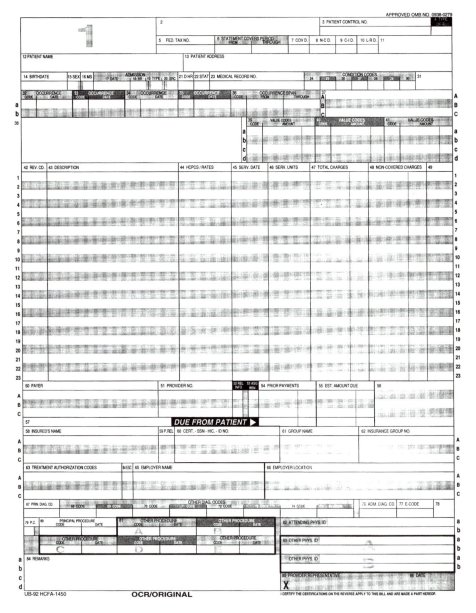

Exhibit 3.2
Health Insurance Claim Form

PLEASE
DO NOT
STAPLE
IN THIS
AREA

APPROVED OMB-0938-0008

CARRIER

PICA

HEALTH INSURANCE CLAIM FORM

PICA

1. MEDICARE (Medicare #) MEDICAID (Medicaid #) CHAMPUS (Sponsor's SSN) CHAMPVA (VA File #) GROUP HEALTH PLAN (SSN or ID) FECA BLK LUNG (SSN) OTHER (ID)

1a. INSURED'S I.D. NUMBER (FOR PROGRAM IN ITEM 1)

2. PATIENT'S NAME (Last Name, First Name, Middle Initial)

3. PATIENT'S BIRTH DATE MM DD YY SEX M F

4. INSURED'S NAME (Last Name, First Name, Middle Initial)

5. PATIENT'S ADDRESS (No., Street)

6. PATIENT RELATIONSHIP TO INSURED Self Spouse Child Other

7. INSURED'S ADDRESS (No., Street)

CITY STATE

8. PATIENT STATUS Single Married Other

CITY STATE

ZIP CODE TELEPHONE (Include Area Code) ( )

Employed Full-Time Student Part-Time Student

ZIP CODE TELEPHONE (INCLUDE AREA CODE) ( )

9. OTHER INSURED'S NAME (Last Name, First Name, Middle Initial)

10. IS PATIENT'S CONDITION RELATED TO:

11. INSURED'S POLICY GROUP OR FECA NUMBER

a. OTHER INSURED'S POLICY OR GROUP NUMBER

a. EMPLOYMENT? (CURRENT OR PREVIOUS) YES NO

a. INSURED'S DATE OF BIRTH MM DD YY SEX M F

b. OTHER INSURED'S DATE OF BIRTH MM DD YY SEX M F

b. AUTO ACCIDENT? PLACE (State) YES NO

b. EMPLOYER'S NAME OR SCHOOL NAME

c. EMPLOYER'S NAME OR SCHOOL NAME

c. OTHER ACCIDENT? YES NO

c. INSURANCE PLAN NAME OR PROGRAM NAME

d. INSURANCE PLAN NAME OR PROGRAM NAME

10d. RESERVED FOR LOCAL USE

d. IS THERE ANOTHER HEALTH BENEFIT PLAN? YES NO *If yes,* return to and complete item 9 a-d.

READ BACK OF FORM BEFORE COMPLETING & SIGNING THIS FORM.

12. PATIENT'S OR AUTHORIZED PERSON'S SIGNATURE I authorize the release of any medical or other information necessary to process this claim. I also request payment of government benefits either to myself or to the party who accepts assignment below.

SIGNED DATE

13. INSURED'S OR AUTHORIZED PERSON'S SIGNATURE I authorize payment of medical benefits to the undersigned physician or supplier for services described below.

SIGNED

PATIENT AND INSURED INFORMATION

14. DATE OF CURRENT: MM DD YY ILLNESS (First symptom) OR INJURY (Accident) OR PREGNANCY(LMP)

15. IF PATIENT HAS HAD SAME OR SIMILAR ILLNESS. GIVE FIRST DATE MM DD YY

16. DATES PATIENT UNABLE TO WORK IN CURRENT OCCUPATION FROM MM DD YY TO MM DD YY

17. NAME OF REFERRING PHYSICIAN OR OTHER SOURCE

17a. I.D. NUMBER OF REFERRING PHYSICIAN

18. HOSPITALIZATION DATES RELATED TO CURRENT SERVICES FROM MM DD YY TO MM DD YY

19. RESERVED FOR LOCAL USE

20. OUTSIDE LAB? YES NO $ CHARGES

21. DIAGNOSIS OR NATURE OF ILLNESS OR INJURY. (RELATE ITEMS 1,2,3 OR 4 TO ITEM 24E BY LINE)

1. ___ . __

3. ___ . __

2. ___ . __

4. ___ . __

22. MEDICAID RESUBMISSION CODE ORIGINAL REF. NO.

23. PRIOR AUTHORIZATION NUMBER

24. A DATE(S) OF SERVICE From MM DD YY To MM DD YY	B Place of Service	C Type of Service	D PROCEDURES, SERVICES, OR SUPPLIES (Explain Unusual Circumstances) CPT/HCPCS MODIFIER	E DIAGNOSIS CODE	F $ CHARGES	G DAYS OR UNITS	H EPSDT Family Plan	I EMG	J COB	K RESERVED FOR LOCAL USE
1										
2										
3										
4										
5										
6										

25. FEDERAL TAX I.D. NUMBER SSN EIN

26. PATIENT'S ACCOUNT NO.

27. ACCEPT ASSIGNMENT? (For govt. claims, see back) YES NO

28. TOTAL CHARGE $

29. AMOUNT PAID $

30. BALANCE DUE $

31. SIGNATURE OF PHYSICIAN OR SUPPLIER INCLUDING DEGREES OR CREDENTIALS (I certify that the statements on the reverse apply to this bill and are made a part thereof.)

SIGNED DATE

32. NAME AND ADDRESS OF FACILITY WHERE SERVICES WERE RENDERED (If other than home or office)

33. PHYSICIAN'S, SUPPLIER'S BILLING NAME, ADDRESS, ZIP CODE & PHONE #

PIN# GRP#

PHYSICIAN OR SUPPLIER INFORMATION

(APPROVED BY AMA COUNCIL ON MEDICAL SERVICE 8/88)

PLEASE PRINT OR TYPE

FORM HCFA-1500 (U2) (12-90)
FORM OWCP-1500 FORM RRB-1500

paid, it is an agreement that the coverage applied for will be effective as of the date of the application or medical examination (if one is required), whichever is later. Some courts have ruled that, regardless of the intent, conditional receipts provide interim coverage subject to later rejection of the application by the insurer.

Status of the Policy

For benefits to be payable under a group or individual plan, a covered loss must occur while the policy is in force. Therefore, records must be available to establish the date when premiums are paid, and a determination must be made as to whether the loss occurred while the policy was in force. The policy is considered to be in force during the grace period.

Reinstatement for group health insurance. A group policy usually permits a 31-day grace period for the payment of premium. The policy ordinarily is not canceled automatically if the premium is not received by the 31st day of the grace period. Rather, the insurance company makes an effort to secure payment of the premium. If payment is not received, a formal cancellation notice is sent to the policyholder. Losses incurred after the end of the grace period are not paid unless the policy is reinstated. In most instances, the insurance company reinstates the policy when the overdue premium is paid. Claims that were received in the lapsed period would then be paid.

Reinstatement for individual health insurance. If an individual policy lapses and is later reinstated, a loss that occurred during the lapsed period would not be covered. The Uniform Policy Provision Law used by individual health insurers specifies that a reinstated policy shall cover only loss resulting from accidental injury sustained after the date of the reinstatement and such sickness as may begin more than ten days after that date. Some insurers liberalize this provision and cover sickness that begins any time after the date of reinstatement.

An insured who wishes to reinstate a lapsed policy may be required to complete an application for reinstatement that asks for answers to questions concerning the health history of those persons insured under the policy. If a claim that applies to the reinstatement application occurs within the contestable period (generally two years), and if material misrepresentation in the application for reinstatement is found, the insurer may rescind the reinstated policy and refund all premiums paid since the reinstatement date.

Onset of the Condition

The claim form or proof of loss usually establishes when an injury occurred for group and individual plans. If there is any suspicion that loss beginning during the contestable period might actually have been caused by an injury that occurred before the effective date of coverage, the question can usually be resolved by an investigation.

Determining with certainty the onset of a sickness is sometimes more difficult than determining injury. Many conditions begin with vague symptoms that the individual may ignore. Some people may treat themselves for a while before they seek medical attention. Exact dates are not noted or are forgotten. An insurer could not rely on such information to determine when a sickness was contracted or when it began. The test is when the condition first manifested itself—generally considered as when medical treatment and advice were first sought. If the individual delayed seeking medical attention, the condition would be considered to have manifested itself at the time when the symptoms were of such degree as to cause an ordinarily prudent person to seek diagnosis, care, or treatment.

Validity of the Policy

Although infrequent for a claim submitted during the contestable period, there are instances when the group and individual insurers wish to contest the validity of the policy because of material misrepresentation in the application for the policy.

If the condition misrepresented was such that a policy would not have been offered under any circumstances, the insurer can seek rescission of the policy. If the condition misrepresented was such that the insurer would have offered a policy with an exclusion rider or at an additional premium, the insurer may offer to reform the existing policy retroactively, effective to its date of issue. If the reformation is not acceptable to the insured, the insurer can seek to rescind the policy.

After two years (three years in some states) from the issue date of the policy, the insurer may not contest the validity of the policy because of misstatements made in the application.

Benefits to the Proper Payee

To discharge effectively their liability for a given claim, group and individual insurers must pay the benefits to the proper person, usually the insured. Insurers also must consider any assignment of benefits or authorizations that the insured has made to pay doctors, hospitals, or creditors.

■ Claim Processing

Insurers have specific methods for handling various types of insurance claims.

Medical Expense Claims

The policies under which basic medical expenses and major medical expenses are covered are characterized by wide variations in benefit provisions. Before a claim examiner can issue the benefit payable, the examiner must determine what services or supplies have been provided and whether they are covered under the particular policy involved before calculating the amount of the benefit payable, if any, for the expenses incurred.

Hospital Expenses

In examining hospital expense claims, the patient's diagnosis, age, and sex are important factors in evaluating the necessity for and the reasonableness of the types and costs of services and whether the length of stay is appropriate or of excessive duration. Statistical norms have been developed that define the average or customary length of stay for common conditions. For hospital stays in excess of these norms, it may be necessary to contact the hospital or the attending physician for additional information.

Professional Expenses

Included under medical expense insurance are claims in which benefits are payable for professional services such as doctors' visits in or out of the hospital, diagnostic X-rays, laboratory examinations, and radiation therapy. Unless there is indication of abuse, the examination of these claims generally is straightforward, as long as the expense was incurred for diagnosis or treatment of a nonoccupational injury or sickness and meets all the other provisions of the policy. Benefit formulas and schedules contained in the policy are used to calculate basic medical expense benefits.

Major Medical Claims

When a major medical claim is submitted, the information on the claim form may be supplemented by itemized bills for the services or supplies provided. Because the bills may be from many different sources, each bill has to be reviewed to determine whether it pertains to the patient and the condition reported on the claim form. This is important because the policy may have a pre-existing conditions limitation.

Establishing a Benefit Period

Generally speaking, the requirements for establishing a benefit period are satisfied if covered medical expenses sufficient to meet the required deductible amount are incurred within the period prescribed in the policy. Group contracts are normally paid on a calendar-year basis. Individual major medical policies have two basic types: benefits are payable on either a per-condition or a calendar-year basis. Covered expenses incurred throughout the benefit period will be payable. Any expenses incurred after the benefit period has expired will not be payable, unless the requirements for a new benefit period are satisfied.

The claim examiner arranges all charges in chronological order to determine whether the requirements have been met for establishing a benefit period within the required length of time or whether the charges were all incurred in the same calendar year. If benefits are payable on a per-cause basis, the examiner determines whether all charges were for the same or related conditions. If the conditions for establishing a benefit period have not been satisfied, the claim should be denied with an appropriate explanation.

Reasonable and Customary Charge Limits

In reviewing a medical claim, primary consideration is given to the necessity of services and supplies and the eligible charge limit, which is frequently based on a determination of reasonable and customary charges.

Consideration also may be given to concurrent conditions and complications, the experience and professional specialty of the physician, and the insured's economic status. For example, if a surgical claim does not contain sufficient information to justify the fee charged, a copy of the operative report describing the surgery performed is secured, or the surgeon is contacted for additional details to determine whether there were any complications that would justify a higher fee. If a mutually satisfactory adjustment of the fee cannot be reached between the surgeon and the insurer, the claim may be referred to a medical society peer review committee.

Reasonable and customary charge limits for the same procedure or service are not uniform among insurers, group policyholders, employers, administrators, and other claims paying organizations. The variation arises from the benefit payment levels desired and the differences in databases that use differing methodologies, data collection periods, and geographic areas (see Chapter 1: Managing the Cost of Health Care).

The HIAA produces a database of claim charge information known as the Prevailing Healthcare Charges System (PHCS). PHCS data, available to qualified subscribing organizations, is widely used by insurers and other payers to make their own determination of reasonable and customary charge limits. The PHCS database collects charges from claims for surgical, anesthesia, medical, dental, and hospital services, as well as equipment, drugs, and supplies. The reports produced semi-annually display charges by geographic area, by procedure code, and by mean, mode, and 8 percentiles (varying from the 50th to the 95th). Companies may also use their own claims experience to develop statistics to determine reasonable and customary charge limits.

Group Disability Income Claims

Employers provide short-term and long-term disability income insurance to partially replace the income of employees who are unable to work because of sickness or accident. Short-term disability (STD) insurance provides income benefits for varying durations (anywhere from six months to two years from the date of disability). Long-term disability (LTD) insurance provides income benefits for an extended period after an employee has been disabled for a specified period of time.

Short-Term Disability Income Claims

Proof of loss is furnished on a claim form that includes the insured's statement of the disability, a statement by the attending physician, and a statement by the employer indicating the date and reason for cessation of active work. Prompt filing of these claims is very important, and preferably should be done as soon as the benefit waiting period has been completed. Once the insured has returned to work, little opportunity exists for control and effective investigation.

A claim is compared to expected disability norms for the same or similar conditions. If the attending physician's estimate of the duration of disability seems unduly long in relation to the nature of the disability, or if there is any reason to question the information furnished, the claim examiner can request additional information from the attending physician or ask the insured to undergo a physical examination by one of the insurer's consulting physicians.

After a claim has been approved, the weekly benefit is paid until either the insured recovers or receives the maximum benefits allowed under the group plan. Arrangements also are made for a periodic review of the claim to ensure that total disability continues and that the insured remains under a physician's care. Supplementary reports from the attending physician may be requested at reasonable intervals for these purposes.

Recent federal legislation requires insurers to give claimants the option of having income taxes deducted from their disability benefits. The insurer is responsible for reporting and remitting such taxes to the federal government.

Another federal law mandates that insurers withhold the employee's portion of Social Security taxes from the benefits paid during the first six months of disability. Social Security taxes are withheld only with respect to the portion of the disability benefit attributable to the employer's premium contribution. If the employer pays 60 percent of the premium, for example, then only 60 percent of the benefit is taxable. The insurer must pay the taxes to the government and advise the policyholder of the amounts remitted.

Long-Term Disability Income Claims

Because of the long benefit periods and the high amount of monthly benefit available (as much as $5,000 to $10,000), a single LTD income claim can represent a large potential liability. Consequently, these claims must be given closer scrutiny than their short-term counterparts even though the processing is similar in many respects.

Assessing LTD claims differs from assessing short-term claims in certain aspects. First, under LTD policies, income from other sources usually is taken into account in determining the monthly benefits payable to the insureds; this may not occur in STD. A second difference lies in the greater potential for malingering when long-term benefits are available. The high level of benefits provided by LTD income insurance may act to

CLAIM ADMINISTRATION

curtail an insured's desire to work, especially if the person has no job to return to or is only a few years from retirement.

Evidence of insurability and pre-existing condition exclusions also may be factors in LTD coverages. Evidence of insurability sometimes is a prerequisite for LTD insurance. For claims arising during the contestable period, therefore, the insured's application for insurance is examined carefully and investigated to determine if there has been a material misrepresentation concerning a prior physical impairment or medical treatment, or if there was nondisclosure of material facts. A misrepresentation is material if the insurer would have rejected the application or accepted it on other terms if these facts had been known.

Investigation also may be necessary if there is a pre-existing condition exclusion in the policy. In general, if the investigation confirms that the disability resulted from an injury or disease that was sustained or contracted prior to the effective date of insurance, the claim is denied.

LTD benefits have the same federal tax requirements as do STD benefits.

Credit Health Claims

Credit health claims are a special type of disability claim. Credit health insurance provides payment on the balance of a loan if the debtor becomes disabled. A debtor generally is considered to be totally disabled when that person is prevented, as a result of an accident or sickness, from engaging in any occupation for wage or profit.

Benefits are payable to the creditor in the amount of the debtor's monthly installments and are continued as long as the debtor is totally disabled, but not beyond the point at which the debt is canceled or its maturity date is reached. Because of the absence of an employee-employer relationship, the early detection of abuse or malingering is more difficult and, therefore, a particularly important claim payment consideration.

85

Common Claim Provisions for Group and Individual Disability Income Insurance

- *The claimant must be under the regular care of a legally qualified physician.* The determination of whether or not total disability exists most often is based on the attending physician's reported evaluation. If the information supplied by the physician is inadequate to permit the claim examiner to make a judgment, a telephone call or a letter to the physician's office may be necessary to obtain additional information or to clarify certain points. When there has been treatment by several physicians, the insurer may need to obtain statements from each physician.

- *An insurer can require the claimant to be examined by a physician it selects.* Courts have held that the right of examination is a reasonable one. An insured's refusal to submit to an examination during a pending claim may delay the insured's right to payment until the insured consents to an examination.

- *A policy exclusion may prevent payment of benefits.* Even though an insured has sustained a loss because of injury or sickness, the claim may be denied because of a policy exclusion. Common exclusions are disabilities resulting from self-inflicted injuries or attempted suicide, occurring during the commission or attempted commission of a criminal offense, and resulting from nervous or mental conditions if the condition does not involve a period of hospital confinement.

- *An insurer may consider rehabilitation when a claimant is unable to return to work.* The National Council on Rehabilitation defines rehabilitation as "the restoration of the handicapped [person] to the maximum physical, mental, social, vocational, and economic usefulness for which [he or she is] capable." The cases best suited to rehabilitation are those in which the disability is expected to be of a long duration, the claimant is well below the normal retirement age, and background and education suggest that, with proper motivation, the claimant can be retrained for other work. Although insurers generally handle rehabilitation administratively, some insurers do define it in their policies.

CLAIM ADMINISTRATION

Individual Disability Income Claims

Individual carriers offer disability coverage to individuals to replace their income if they are unable to work because of sickness or accident. Policy provisions and different kinds of disability affect claims for disability income benefits.

Total Disability as it Relates to Occupation

The most common types of definitions of total disability in disability policies are:

- the own occupation disability provision, which requires that to be eligible for benefits the insured be unable to perform the duties of his or her own occupation; and
- the any occupation provision, which requires that to be eligible for benefits the insured must be unable to perform the duties of any occupation for which that person is reasonably fitted by education, training, or experience.

Distinction Between Injury and Sickness

The distinction between injury and sickness is an important claim consideration. Some individual policies provide benefits only when disability is the result of accidental bodily injury. Policies that cover injury and sickness may contain shorter elimination periods and longer maximum benefit periods for disability that is due to injury.

Partial Disability

The payment of partial disability benefits is designed to encourage the insured to make an effort to return to work without penalty. Benefits are payable if the insured meets the total disability definition and either is unable to work full-time or is prevented from performing one or more important occupational duties. In many cases, the insured actually has returned to full-time work but is limited in the activities he or she is able to perform. The tendency is for partial disability claims to run for the maximum period provided by the policy for this benefit (usually no more than six months).

87

Recurrent Disability

When evaluating individual claims involving recurrent periods of disability, the insurer must determine whether the later period of disability should be considered a new claim or a continuation of the earlier period of disability. This determination is not always easy to make.

If total disability is due to injury and the insured has returned to work, disability is considered to have ended. If later problems resulting from the original injury cause another period of loss, disability is considered as being due to sickness unless the recurrence began within the period for considering disability as being due to injury. If the insured tried to work but was unable to continue, the later period is considered a continuation of the original claim. What constitutes a return to work and how long a period should be considered are matters that must be based on the facts of the individual case and the contract language.

Residual Disability

Residual or permanent partial disability is a concept based on reduction of earnings. The residual benefit pays a percentage of the total disability benefit equal to the percentage of earnings lost due to disability. As the condition improves and the percentage of lost income decreases, the percentage of the total disability benefit also decreases.

The claim examiner closely follows residual disability claims to prevent possible abuse. Since a percentage of prior earnings determines benefit amounts, the claim examiner must obtain accurate information regarding the insured's earnings before the disability began and the insured's income while the disability continues. In addition, the claim examiner must monitor the insured's medical condition to determine if he or she is indeed unable to work full time.

■ Claim Investigation

Claim investigations are required most often for:

CLAIM ADMINISTRATION

- losses that occur during the contestable period;
- disability income claims that are questionable as to the extent or duration of the disability; or
- questionable hospital claims.

Investigative Report

The extent of the investigation varies with the type of claim, the nature and amount of information required, and the difficulty in obtaining it. The insurer must have relevant factual information. Therefore, the investigative report plays an important part in an insurer's legal defense should a suit become necessary. Ways of investigating claims vary among companies, but usually involve home office claim personnel, independent insurance adjusters, commercial inspection companies, or field claim personnel who are home office employees but located in field offices.

Often the investigation consists of writing a letter to the hospital or to the attending physician. Such letters must be accompanied by properly executed authorizations, indicating the insured's permission for the doctor or hospital to release this information. It may be possible to clear up doubtful areas by a telephone call to the attending physician. In such cases, it is usually wise to write the physician in advance, enclosing an authorization and indicating when the call may be made so that the doctor will have the patient's record readily available.

Monitoring Self- and Third-Party Administered Plans

Self-administered and third-party administered groups normally have authority to process claims where there is no question about contractual liability. Many group insurers require that questionable or doubtful claims be referred to them for review and advice on proper processing. Also, the group insurer has auditing procedures to see that claims are being properly paid. The three general types of audits are described below. In addition, managed care programs may assist in assessing appropriateness of services through their focus on utilization of health care resources.

Large Amount Audit

Some group insurers require that claims in excess of a certain amount be referred to them for approval before payment is made.

Random Sample Audit

With this type of audit, the administrator sends the insurer a random sample of closed claim files for review to determine whether proper claim practices and procedures are being followed.

On-Site Audit

With this type of audit, an insurance company representative randomly reviews closed and active files in the administrator's office. This is helpful in determining:

- the attitudes of the people processing claims;
- whether they have a proper understanding of benefits; and
- whether the claims are being processed in a manner consistent with the claim practices and procedures of the insurance company.

Indications of Claim Fraud

Claim fraud involves a deliberate attempt by claimants to obtain benefits to which they are not entitled. It may take many forms. For example, the claimant may provide the insurer with false information as part of the claim proofs, such as claiming to be totally disabled when he or she is actually working. Claim fraud also might consist of altering information contained on the attending physician's statement, submitting bogus bills on hospital or medical expense claims, or staging phony accidents. For more information on fraud, see Chapter 6: Fraud and Abuse.

■ Claim Payment Process

Most claims are processed and paid, but after a review of the benefits allowed under the policy or an investigative report, some are denied.

CLAIM ADMINISTRATION

Paying the Claim

When a group or individual claim has been approved, there are several steps in paying it.

- First, the amount of the benefit to be paid is calculated in accordance with the provisions of the policy, taking into consideration schedules, deductibles, or benefit formulas.
- The next step is to determine to whom the benefits are to be paid. Generally this will be the insured or the medical provider. If a claim involves periodic payments, a payment schedule is established.
- Insurers are required to submit federal income tax forms for all providers receiving payments of medical claims totaling over $600 in a calendar year. This reporting consists of sending form Medical-1099 to the Internal Revenue Service and the provider who has received payments.

Denial of Claims

Some claims are denied because the claimant is not eligible for the benefits stated in the policy, although this doesn't happen often. When a decision to deny a claim is made for whatever reason, the claimant always receives an explanation of the denial.

Grounds for denial of claims are:

- the claimant's loss not being covered; and
- fraud and misrepresentation.

Most denials of health claims occur because the insurance was not in force at the time of service or the policy did not cover the service. Some exclusion riders remain in effect permanently and some for only a specified period. Under disability income benefit plans, including credit health insurance, the most frequent cause of denial is that the insured is not found to be disabled to the extent required by the policy.

■ Customer Service

Claim administration provides an opportunity for group and individual carriers to build a rapport with their insureds. The claim department often is the only contact an insured has with an insurer. The insured's opinion of the insurance company reflects the effectiveness of the claim department in satisfying claimant expectations.

Telephone Inquiries

Most insurance companies recognize the importance of being accessible to their insureds and offer toll-free phone lines for the insured to contact the claim department. In addition, some companies go a step further and have a dedicated unit for claim customer service. The dedicated unit is staffed by permanent customer service representatives or claim examiners who rotate in for a specified time frame. An insured's degree of satisfaction with the insurer is quite often the direct result of customer service dealings with the claim department. The first opportunity to serve the insured usually is when he or she contacts the claim department to find out whether the policy covers a certain expense.

Written Communication

The claim department sends a written explanation of benefits (EOBs) to the insured for each claim filed. If a claim is not covered under the policy, a copy of a letter explaining the reason for the denial may be sent to the policyholder in the case of a group plan or to the agent for individual insurance. If the insured assigned benefits to a medical provider, the provider also may receive a copy of the letter.

■ Controlling Claim Costs

Most insurers make claim cost control an integral part of the claim examination process. The basic cost control methods used by health insurers are covered in Chapter 1: Managing the Cost of Health Care. The ones that relate specifically to claims are discussed here.

CLAIM ADMINISTRATION

Coordination of Benefits (COB)

Coordination of benefits is a process by which two or more insurers, insuring the same person for the same or similar health insurance benefits, limit the total benefits received to an amount not exceeding the actual amount of allowable health care expenses incurred. COB is utilized primarily in group insurance contracts but also is seen in some individual policies.

COB was developed because of the rapid increase in duplicate coverage or overinsurance. Overinsurance occurs when a person is covered under two or more health care plans and may collect total benefits that exceed actual loss. Possible sources of overinsurance are:

- Both husband and wife are employed and eligible for group health coverage, and each covers the other as a dependent.
- A person is employed in two jobs, both of which provide group health insurance coverage.
- A salaried or professional person who has group health insurance coverage with an employer also has an association group plan.
- A person has two individual health plans.

COB works by applying established rules. The plan that pays benefits first is determined by using order of benefit determination rules. The order may differ from state to state, but the standard and custom within the group and individual insurance industry is to follow NAIC guidelines and model language to facilitate consistent claim administration.

Order of Benefit Determination Rules

The primary plan pays benefits up to its limit, as it would in the absence of any complicating factor. The secondary plan pays the difference between the primary insurer's benefits and the total incurred allowable expenses (historically 100 percent of allowable expenses) up to the secondary insurer's limit. Reimbursing up to 100 percent of allowable expenses is one of the three approaches allowed by the NAIC Model Regulation, as discussed below.

93

The first point to be determined is which plan is primary. According to the NAIC guidelines, if only one plan has a COB provision, the plan without the COB provision pays its benefits first and the plan with a COB provision would then coordinate its benefits with the benefits paid by the other plan.

When both plans have a COB provision, the order of benefit determination generally is as follows:

- **Nondependent/Dependent.** The benefits of the plan that covers the person as an employee, member, or subscriber (that is, other than as a dependent) are determined before those of the plan that covers the person as a dependent.

- **Dependent Child/Parents Not Separated or Divorced.** The benefits of the plan of the parent whose birthday falls earlier in a year are determined before those of the plan of the parent whose birthday falls later in that year. If both parents have the same birthday, the benefits of the plan that covered one parent longer are determined before those of the plan that covered the other parent for a shorter period of time.

- **Dependent Child/Parents Separated or Divorced.** If two or more plans cover a person as a dependent child of separated or divorced parents, benefits for the child are determined in this order: the plan of the parent with custody of the child; then, the plan of the spouse of the parent with custody of the child; and finally, the plan of the parent not having custody of the child.

Determination of Secondary Plan's Payment

Historically, COB provisions allowed the reimbursement of 100 percent of allowable expenses. In other words, the secondary plan paid the difference between the primary insurer's payment and total allowable expenses.

The current NAIC model COB regulation allows three alternative approaches to be used. The first is the traditional approach discussed above (referred to as the "Total Allowable Expense" approach, Alternative 1, or informally as COB). The second alternative limits the total

CLAIM ADMINISTRATION

combined payment from both plans to no less than 80 percent of allowable expenses (the "Total Allowable Expenses with Coinsurance" approach or Alternative 2). The third alternative allows the secondary plan to pay the difference between what it would have paid if it had been primary and what the primary plan has paid. This has the effect of limiting total reimbursement to the level that would be provided by the richer of the two plans in the absence of other coverage (the "Maintenance of Benefits (MOB)" approach or Alternative 3).

COB and HMOs

Coordination of benefits with HMOs occurs in the same manner as benefits with traditional insurance plans. One area of difficulty is that of determining value of service in HMOs. One way that insurers do this is to base the cost of HMO services on the reasonable and customary charges for the geographic area in which it is located.

Impact of COB

Depending on the method of calculation, the use of coordination of benefits can save approximately 3 to 8 percent in claim payments that would otherwise have been made. The MOB approach produces the largest savings and is becoming more popular as employers look for cost savings. Even though there is a certain amount of extra work in determining duplicate coverage, COB savings more than offset the additional administrative costs.

Analysis of Claims by Claim Personnel

A number of techniques are used to assist claim personnel in administering a claim cost control program.

Screening Guides

Most companies have developed guides for claim examiners to use when analyzing claims. Data for such guides come from various sources, such as recognized health care professional groups, agencies of the federal government, professional publications, and the insurer's own claim

95

payment data. These guides provide information such as the average period of disability for various causes, and the expected utilization parameters, treatment protocols, and hospital length of stay of a particular diagnosis.

Using these guides, claim personnel can determine which claims should be reviewed more closely. This does not necessarily mean that there is anything improper about the claim. Rather, it means that the established parameters have been exceeded and is a signal to the insurers to see which claim cost control measures should be taken.

Medical Consultants

An effective means of controlling claim costs as well as maintaining sound relations with the medical and dental professions is the use of medical consultants. These consultants provide assistance in identifying areas of abuse and overutilization, and guidance on claims requiring investigation.

Auditing Hospital Bill Charges

Hospital bills are routinely scanned for accuracy by claim examiners through the use of predetermined criteria. For example, bills in excess of $10,000 are routinely audited by the insurer to verify that the charges on the bill are accurate and that the services were actually provided to the patient.

Analysis of Claim Experience

An analysis and review of claim experience may indicate trends that result in unsatisfactory claim ratios. A continuous record of the experience of each group policyholder or block of individual insureds is useful in establishing the existence of unfavorable trends. Poor claim experience is the signal for a more detailed study of the group or block of individual insureds to determine whether certain elements, such as misuse of benefits or poor policy design, are causing the unsatisfactory claim record. After the causes are identified, recommendations can be made to the policyholder for correcting abuses or for making contract changes that will prevent future problems.

CLAIM ADMINISTRATION

Technology in Claim Processing

Technology has had a tremendous impact in the area of claim administration. Claim administration lends itself well to high-volume transaction processing and rule-based decision making—two characteristics that play directly to the strengths of automation and technology. Today most insurers have fully computerized the claim process.

Imaging System

Imaging technology is the process of taking a likeness of a paper document using specialized equipment. This likeness is indexed and stored electronically for recovery at a later date. Imaging technology has made it possible to administer claims in a paperless environment. Documents are viewed on a computer screen and the same document can be seen simultaneously on multiple screens. Imaging has improved data availability and accessibility, which are critical factors in claims processing.

Scanning System

Scanning technology is the process of extracting data from a paper document and creating usable electronic data. The primary goal of scanning is to replace data entry. Scanning technology has made the automation of paper claims a reality. Using specially adapted hardware and software, standardized forms are scanned into the computer system. The system extracts the variable information and recognizes and converts the characters into usable pieces of data that are fed into the claim administration system. Scanning technology also provides a preaudit function by editing the data from paper claims and directing the exceptions appropriately.

Electronic Claims Processing

Electronic claims processing allows for the complete adjudication of a claim without manual intervention. The process begins by taking in electronic claim data by some means of telecommunication or storage

97

medium. The system then applies this electronic data against a predetermined rule set. Based on these rules, the claim is adjudicated, paid, or denied. This automated process includes the production of explanation of benefits, checks, and letters without any interaction with an examiner.

Fraud Detection Software

Fraud detection software identifies certain situations that may be at high risk for fraud. By applying its predetermined rule set against large volumes of data, the system can be an effective way of prescreening and identifying instances of potential abuse.

Expert Disability System

An expert disability system is a computerized aid to determine disability durations. This system analyzes data such as diagnosis, age, and occupation and determines, based on its predetermined rule set, an estimated length of disability.

Automated Repetitive Payment System

An automated repetitive payment system is used when a disability case has been reviewed and a set benefit has been determined as payable at regular intervals for a set period of time. This system automatically produces a payment to the claimant for the determined amount at the appropriate interval for the set length of time. When the set length of time expires, the case needs to be reviewed again.

■ Emerging Trends

Claim administration is taking place in an atmosphere of change and rapid advances in health care technology and information management systems. New approaches in underwriting and marketing health insurance have added to the complexity of the claim administration process. Demands also exist to control rising claim costs. Other changes that

CLAIM ADMINISTRATION

affect and will continue to affect claim administration are insurance department rulings, federal and state legislation, and the expectations of the insured population.

■ Summary

The claim function in health insurance plays a vital role in the performance and operations of the insurer. It requires knowledge of the benefit structure of group and individual plans and coordination with other departments in the insurance company to ensure that all appropriate claims are paid. Today's claim department needs to have up-to-date computerized systems, well-informed personnel, and the ability to be flexible in a rapidly changing environment.

■ Key Terms

Assignment of benefits
Benefit period
Claim administration
Claim cost control
Claim denial
Claim department
Claim documentation
Claim forms
Claim investigation
Claim kit
Conditional receipt
Contestable period
Coordination of benefits (COB)
Credit health claim
Customer service
Direct submission
Disability income claim
Draft book system
Effective date of coverage
Exclusion rider
Explanation of benefits (EOB)
Field office administration
Fraud
Grace period
Home office administration
Identification card
Investigative report
Large amount audit
Material misrepresentation
Notice of claim
On-site audit
Partial disability
Policyholder submission
Proof of loss
Random sample audit
Reasonable and customary charges
Recurrent disability
Rescission
Residual disability
Self-administration
Third-party administration
Total disability

Chapter 4

PRICING HEALTH INSURANCE PRODUCTS

101 *Introduction*
102 *Principles of Pricing Insurance Products*
103 *Components of the Premium Rate*
111 *Factors that Influence Premium Rates*
116 *Rating Classes and Structures*
121 *Development of Premium Rates*
130 *Experience Monitoring and Rate Review*
134 *Emerging Trends*
135 *Summary*
135 *Key Terms*

■ Introduction

Before an insurer can market its contracts, it must decide the price of the coverage it wishes to offer. Each insurance contract has a price, called a premium rate. The premium rate is the amount of money that the insured pays to the insurer for the coverage promised in the contract. Premiums usually are paid monthly, but may be paid less frequently, such as semi-annually or annually.

The task of developing premium rates for a contract is assigned to the insurer's actuary. The actuary must consider many factors to ensure that the premium rate is both adequate and reasonable.

This chapter summarizes the principles and factors on which premium rates for group and individual health insurance contracts are based. It should be noted that state insurance laws frequently define allowed or disallowed rating procedures. While the HIPAA of 1996 does not address rating directly, it will have a significant impact on pricing small group and individual medical expense products.

Principles of Pricing Insurance Products

The insurer's pricing objective is to write business at profitable rates. To help ensure this, health insurers consider the following four principles when developing premium rates: adequacy, reasonableness, equity, and competitiveness.

Adequacy

Premium rates must be adequate to cover the costs of benefits, acquisition and administrative expenses, and taxes. In addition, they must provide for higher-than-expected claims and for the insurer's profit. If premium rates are inadequate, the insurer will lose money on the coverage. If losses are large enough, the insurer may become insolvent and thus unable to fulfill the promises in its contracts. Insurers sometimes are required to file rate schedules with their state insurance department.

Reasonableness

Premium rates must be considered reasonable in relation to the benefits promised. A certain portion of premiums should be returned to policyholders as benefits. If too much of the premium is used for expenses and profit, benefits will not be considered a reasonable portion of the premium. Many states require the insurer to certify that benefits are reasonable in relation to the total premium charged for a line of coverage. Some states require that rates be developed to achieve a specific loss ratio (ratio of claims cost to premium income).

Equity

Premium rates must be fair among the various classes of policyholders. To be equitable, a premium rate structure charges each policyholder a rate reflecting the expected cost of providing insurance coverage. If two policyholders present the insurer with the same risk in terms of anticipated claims and expenses, they should pay the same premiums. If the risk differs, the premiums should relate to the degree of risk.

For example, the cost of medical care is greater in certain areas of the country than in others. Thus, major medical premiums often vary according to the geographic area in which the group or individual resides.

Practically every state has laws against unfair discrimination in insurance transactions. Even if not governed by ethical principles or law, equity is necessary for practical business reasons.

Competitiveness

It is important for premium rates to be competitive in the market where the insurance is sold. If premium rates are set too high, the product will not sell well. If the premium rates are set too low, it could indicate a flaw in pricing assumptions, which could attract an unacceptable number of poor risks. The product may sell well, but may not be profitable.

■ Components of the Premium Rate

The basic components of the gross premium rate for health insurance are expressed as follows:

Premium = Claims + Reserves + Expenses + Margin + Profit − Investment Income

Claim Costs

The largest component of the gross premium rate is the cost of benefits, sometimes referred to as claim cost or expected claims. For group insurance, the expected claim cost is the portion of the premium necessary to fund those claims that the group is expected to incur during the rating period. The actuary must estimate what the group's experience will be during the period in which the rates will apply. The group actuary usually studies past claims experience from one of three sources:

- the past experience of the insurer's group insurance business;
- past experience of the group itself; or
- data from intercompany studies.

For individual insurance, the claim cost is the amount anticipated as necessary to pay the benefits covered by the policy. The difference between individual and group claim costs is that individual claim costs are not based on the experience of a particular group. The claim costs for individual contracts are estimated by projecting the morbidity of individual policyholders as a whole.

Concept of Morbidity

Both group and individual health insurance use the concept of morbidity in estimating claim costs. The measurement of morbidity considers two elements: frequency and severity.

Frequency is defined as the number of occurrences of an insured event. For example, assume that for a given age and sex, the average frequency of hospitalization is 10 percent. This means that there will be ten hospital confinements a year for every 100 persons insured.

Severity is defined as the average size of each loss. For example, assume further that the average hospital stay is eight days. For each $1 of daily hospital benefit, the average claim would be $8. The estimated annual claim cost would be the frequency multiplied by the severity. For a policy that provided a daily hospital confinement benefit of $200, the claim cost would be calculated as follows:

Morbidity as a Factor of Claim Cost

Benefit		Frequency		Severity		Claim Cost
$200	×	10%	×	$8	=	$160

PRICING HEALTH INSURANCE PRODUCTS

Sources of Morbidity Statistics

The actuary has several sources of information to assist in predicting future claim costs. The best source is the insurer's own morbidity experience from similar coverages issued previously. For group insurance, this experience comes from groups with similar demographics or from the past experience of the group being rated. For individual insurance, experience from similar policy forms with similar benefits is used. Other sources must be used if the insurer has not marketed enough contracts with a particular benefit to have statistically reliable data available for each benefit.

Intercompany studies on group insurance are published periodically in the *Transactions of the Society of Actuaries*. The Society of Actuaries also publishes studies of experience data contributed by a number of the larger writers of individual health insurance as well as claim studies done by individual actuaries. Some insurers work with actuarial consulting firms that have specific expertise and experience data for a particular product.

Relevant statistics are available from other professional organizations. The National Safety Council annually publishes "Accident Facts," which is useful in studying the relative incidence of on-the-job injuries. The American Cancer Society annually publishes "Cancer Facts and Figures," which is useful in studying the incidence of cancer. Other valuable statistics relevant to the cost of claims may be found in government reports on experience under Social Security and Medicare plans.

Credibility of Statistics

Credibility refers to the statistical reliability of the data being considered. To be credible, the data must be derived from a sample that is large enough to be representative of the individuals or groups with a given type of coverage. As the size of the sample increases, the data become more credible and more reliable in projecting the cost of future claims.

FUNDAMENTALS OF HEALTH INSURANCE: PART B

In group insurance, the credibility of the group's experience determines the degree to which an insurer uses that data as a basis for predicting future claims.

In individual insurance, the credibility of the sample data depends in part on the frequency of claims and the average size of claims. Claim costs associated with low frequency claims or claims that have a large fluctuation in average size require larger samples to be credible. Examples of these claims are long-term disability and specified disease claims. Conversely, claim costs associated with relatively high frequency claims and claims with more stable claim sizes require smaller samples. Examples of these claims are doctors' office visits, preventive care, and prescription drugs.

Reserves

The reserve fund, which is used to pay outstanding claims, is another component of the premium structure. When an insurer evaluates claim experience, it cannot just look at the paid claim experience alone because this would not reflect the claims incurred but not yet paid. There are two basic types of reserves established on health insurance products: claim reserves and policy reserves.

Claim Reserves

Claims are seldom paid at the time they are incurred. When a valid claim is incurred, the insurer recognizes this liability by setting up a claim reserve to pay the claim once the proper claim forms have been submitted and claim investigation has been completed. There are two types of claim reserve: the incurred but not reported (IBNR) claim reserve and the pending claim reserve.

- IBNR claim reserves are established to fund claims that have been incurred but have not yet been reported to the insurer. It may take the insured several days or even weeks to accumulate the necessary information to report a claim.

- Pending claim reserves are established to fund claims that have been reported but not yet paid or are in the process of being paid. It takes

Policy Reserves

Another type of reserve that is necessary on certain types of contracts is the policy reserve, also called the active life reserve. This is particularly important in individual health insurance contracts where insurers use a level premium structure, even on coverages where morbidity increases significantly by age. The premium collected in the earlier policy years will be more than sufficient to cover the cost of claims and expenses, but in later policy years the claim costs alone may exceed the premium. The excess premium collected in the earlier policy years is set aside in a reserve fund to pay for the higher claims incurred in the later years of the policy when the premium alone is not sufficient to cover these claims. This reserve fund is called the policy reserve.

Expense of Operation

The next largest component of the premium rate is the insurer's expense of operation. Insurers frequently divide expenses into five categories: sales compensation expenses, acquisition expenses, maintenance expenses, general overhead, and taxes.

Sales Compensation Expenses

This broad category includes all expenses associated with the solicitation of new business. For group insurance, this can include association fees that are paid when an association endorses a particular product. Some companies include advertising expenses in this category because the goal of advertising is the sale of new business.

A sales compensation expense for both group and individual health insurance is the agent commission, which usually is figured as a percentage of the gross premium. First-year compensation typically is higher than renewal compensation because the insurer uses a high-low commission scale that pays more in the first year or pays bonuses based on the agent's production of new business.

Acquisition Expenses

Expenses associated with the acquisition and processing of new business are called home office acquisition expenses. Underwriting expenses include the salaries of the home office underwriting staff, medical examinations, attending physicians' reports, and inspection reports. These expenses arise not only from policies approved and issued but also from rejected applications and from approved policies not taken by applicants. Once an application is approved, there are additional expenses, such as the cost of issuing the contracts and establishing records.

Group insurance has the expense of the group underwriter. The group underwriter analyzes the group's experience and demographics to develop a competitive premium rate.

Maintenance Expenses

Expenses incurred to keep business in force and to pay claims are called maintenance expenses. They include the cost of maintaining records, billing and collecting premiums, paying claims, compiling and analyzing statistics, calculating liabilities and reserves, making policy changes, and providing customer service. Claim expenses include claim investigation, corresponding with medical providers, utilization review, and issuing claim checks.

General Overhead

In addition to the expenses already mentioned, each policy must cover its share of the general overhead expenses. These expenses vary but generally include corporate salaries, occupancy of the premises, office furniture and equipment, recruiting, and training. Some companies include product development costs in general overhead expenses.

Taxes

Individual states levy a premium tax. The tax can be a percentage of gross premiums paid or premiums net of dividends.

PRICING HEALTH INSURANCE PRODUCTS

Methods of Allocating Expenses

Insurers allocate expenses in various ways when they develop premium rates. Three widely used ways of allocating expenses are as a percent of premium, per policy, and as a percent of claims.

As a percent of premium. Expenses that vary as premiums vary are best allocated as a percent of premium. Sales compensation expenses and premium taxes fall into this category.

Per policy. Expenses that are roughly the same regardless of the size of the policy often are allocated on a per policy basis. The home office acquisition expenses of underwriting and issuing policies fall into this category. For example, the cost of issuing a hospital indemnity policy should be the same regardless of whether the indemnity amount was $100 per day or $500 per day. The total expenses in this category are divided by the number of policies issued to determine the cost allocated to each policy issued. Most maintenance costs also are allocated on a per policy basis.

As a percent of claims. Some companies allocate claim administration expenses as a percent of claims paid because these expenses may vary based on the number or dollar amount of claims processed.

Contingency Margins and Profit

Two additional components of the premium rate are contingency margins and profit. Although these represent different concepts, they often are considered together. If adverse contingencies occur, profits will be smaller than anticipated. Conversely, if there are favorable developments, profits can be larger.

Contingency Margins

None of the factors that go into the computation of premium rates can be predicted with perfect accuracy. Therefore, the insurer usually includes a protective financial margin in the premium rate in case higher than expected claims result. This protective financial margin is called a contingency margin or a morbidity fluctuation margin.

Profit

Stock companies have a responsibility to make to make a profit for their stockholders. Although mutual companies have no stockholders, they must maintain an adequate level of surplus similar to stock companies. The insurer's surplus of assets over liabilities assures policyholders that their claims will be honored even if there are periods when an insurer's current costs exceed current income. The size of the surplus determines, to some extent, how much business the insurer may write. It is also a measure of the financial strength and stability of the insurer. Once a mutual company's surplus reaches a desired level, any excess amounts can be returned to the policyholders as dividends. Profit margins are incorporated into the premium:

- as a percent of premium;
- as a percent per year;
- by including margin in one or more of the premium components; and
- as a rate of return on capital invested to sell and administer the policy.

Investment Income

The interest earned on cash flow and funds held in reserve is called investment income. Investment income provides an additional source of income for the insurer and is the final component of the premium rate. Investment income can be added to premium income as a source of funds to meet the insurer's obligations. The greater the investment income, the lower the premium needs to be. Investment income is greater on long-term reserves such as policy reserves. Claim reserves generally are more short term in nature and earn only modest amounts of investment income.

On group products, investment income often is used to offset the amount of contingency or fluctuation margin needed to protect against higher-than-anticipated claims experience. The more investment income expected, the lower the margin for contingencies.

■ Factors that Influence Premium Rates

The primary determinants of the level of the premium rate are the type and level of benefits promised in the contract. However, there are many other factors that influence the premium rate. Most of these factors are similar for group and individual insurance, but a few are different.

Overall Plan Design

The specific benefit provisions in group and individual plans can have a dramatic impact on utilization of medical services. Deductibles and coinsurance also can influence the level of claims. For example, a high deductible and 20 percent coinsurance could deter insureds from seeking treatment for minor illnesses because they will have to pay the initial costs themselves.

Age/Sex Distributions

Age is a factor in developing rates for group and individual health insurance premium rates. Health insurance experience reflects differences in claim frequency and claim severity among different age groups. A 50-year-old person is more likely to experience a long illness than a 30-year-old person. In the case of maternity coverages, the reverse is true; maternity claim frequency decreases as women advance beyond age 30.

Sex also is an important factor in developing premiums for group and individual products. Health care coverages, in general, show higher claim costs for women than for men (exclusive of the impact of maternity claims). Various studies have shown that women under age 65 require hospitalization more often and have more surgery, medical treatment, and dental services than men. The expected claim costs of an all-male group would be considerably less than for a comparable group in which the proportion of women was 75 percent of the total. Some states prohibit or limit rating based on individual age and/or sex.

Income/Occupation Classes

Medical and dental claim costs tend to be higher for persons with higher incomes. Physicians' charges sometimes are influenced by a patient's ability to pay. Also, persons in higher income brackets often seek more frequent or extensive medical and dental care.

In recent years, there has been a leveling of medical care charges among persons in different earnings brackets. This is due in large part to the general availability of medical expense insurance and federal programs such as Medicare that reimburse providers of medical care without consideration of the income of the patient. As dental expense insurance becomes more widely available, a similar leveling of charges may occur there, too.

Income is a significant factor in long-term disability insurance, since the monthly indemnity is calculated as a percent of salary. Occupation also is a key factor in disability insurance, and many occupations carry a greater risk for accidental injury and disability.

Geographic Location

Charges for health care services vary widely by geographic location. For example, large cities on the West Coast have a different pattern and a much higher level of charges for health care than do most cities in the southeastern part of the United States. These variations in claim costs result from differences in the cost of living, in the availability and organization of health care facilities, and in the general attitude of insured individuals, employers, and physicians toward the use of hospitals and medical care facilities.

Trends in Medical Care, the Economy, and Inflation

Over the years there has been a consistent upward trend in medical care claim costs experienced by insured and self-insured group plans

PRICING HEALTH INSURANCE PRODUCTS

and individual plans. These rising claim costs are associated with increases in medical care charges and utilization of services, improved treatment, and an aging population.

Other economic factors that influence premium rates are fluctuating interest rates, which affect the amount of investment income that can be earned on reserve funds and rising administrative costs due to inflation.

Group Participation Level

Many group products are offered on a voluntary basis, and employees can choose the ones that meet their needs. For example, an employee can choose to fund medical costs through an HMO, PPO, or a traditional comprehensive plan. For some coverage, there is only one product available, and the alternative would be to have no coverage. This is commonly seen in voluntary disability programs where employees can choose whether to have disability coverage or no coverage at all.

Participation level is an important factor in the development of premium rates. If the participation is low, there is a greater chance for adverse selection, or antiselection. Antiselection indicates that the group's experience is expected to be worse than the overall population because of a larger proportion of people with unhealthy risks selecting coverage. The greater the participation level, the greater the chance that there will be sufficient healthy lives insured to compensate for antiselection. Many companies vary premium rates on voluntary products based on participation level.

Individual Underwriting

An individual health insurance policy usually is not issued to a person in poor health who could be expected to become disabled or hospitalized soon. For a certain period of time, therefore, persons to whom policies are issued constitute a select group whose morbidity should be better than that of the public as a whole. After a few years, this distinction

113

fades as the insured block becomes subject to new sicknesses and accidents.

The degree to which the characteristics of the initial group are better than those of the general population depends on the amount of underwriting done. If there is significant underwriting, the difference in early policy years also will be significant. If there is limited underwriting, there will be little or no difference in the early policy years. If no underwriting is done (guarantee issue), there may be some antiselection in the early policy years. In calculating the claim cost, the individual insurers estimate the effect of underwriting on the risk they insure.

The HIPAA of 1996 requires insurers in the individual market to accept (guarantee issue) certain "eligible" individuals. Generally, to be eligible for this special guarantee issue coverage, an individual must have 18 months of previous coverage—most recently group coverage; must apply within 2 months (63 days) of losing his/her group coverage; and must not be eligible for other group health coverage or government health programs.

Length of Premium Rate Guarantee Period

The length of a premium rate guarantee period offered by the insurer affects rates. This is particularly true for coverages such as medical and dental expense benefits, where cost trends show increases. For these coverages, the renewal rate guarantee period is becoming shorter. A one-year guarantee was routinely offered in past years, but the trend is toward a guarantee of six months or less.

Regulatory and Legislative Issues

In an effort to make group health insurance more accessible to a larger number of working families, several states have enacted small group reform legislation. Small employers usually are defined as those having between 25 and 50 full-time, permanent employees. Some states define certain base benefit plans that must be offered on a guaranteed-issue basis to all small employer groups. The laws allow different premium rates to be charged based on demographics, but no individual can be charged a different premium rate based on his or her own health history. Also, there are limits on what an insurance company can charge a small employer. In many states, premium rates must be within 25 percent of the index (or average) rate. Most states also limit the amount of rate increase that can be given to a small employer group.

State-mandated benefits that require insurers to cover or offer certain treatments or care by specified health professionals can result in additional claims and administrative costs for insurers. These costs are reflected in the pricing structure.

For individual insurance, most states require that an insurance company return a percentage (such as 50 percent) of the policy's expected premium income to insureds in the form of paid benefits. Also affecting individual health insurance are minimum loss ratios that have been adopted by several states. The loss ratio is the ratio of claim costs to premium income. Minimum loss ratio standards affect the premium rates that can be charged as well as the expense ratio that must be maintained to have a profitable product.

Another state regulation affecting premium rates is the degree to which an insured has the right to renew a policy. Some states require noncancellable and guaranteed renewable provisions, and the HIPAA requires guaranteed renewability of medical expense policies, which affect the degree of risk associated with the pricing structure.

Persistency

Persistency, which refers to the degree to which business stays in force, is a factor in pricing both group and individual health insurance. Persistency usually improves as the policies age. For some types of coverage, the annual persistency rate may reach 95 percent or higher by the fifth policy year.

Persistency also varies by age grouping. A group of younger policyholders (e.g., ages 20 to 29) may have poorer persistency than a group of older policyholders (e.g., ages 50 to 59). This perhaps reflects the fact that the existing policy is more valuable to older policyholders because they may have more difficulty satisfying the underwriting associated with buying a new policy.

Marketing Strategies

Price structures for similar products already available in the marketplace can have a significant effect on the premium rates an insurer develops for new or revised products. Normally, an insurer evaluates its competition carefully and studies the demographics of the desired market to design a premium structure that allows its distributors to compete effectively. For example, if the targeted market requires only a basic level of coverage for a product, an insurer's product design and premium structure reflect this condition. If an insurer intends to market a product to particular segments of the marketplace, the unique characteristics of these segments may affect the premium or product structure.

Company Objectives

An insurance company normally establishes a corporate policy that determines how it sets premium rates. A company may want to sell a great deal of a product, or it may wish to provide the product only as an accommodation to its salespeople and customers. These alternatives lead to different premium structures.

■ Rating Classes and Structures

Group Rating Classes

A key step in the development of a premium rate for group insurance coverage is establishing rating classes, which are distinguished by the degree to which the insurer uses the policyholder's own past claim experience. There are three classes: manually rated groups, fully experience-rated groups, and blended manual/experience-rated groups.

Manually Rated Groups

Manually rated groups are those whose rates are based on the insurance company's rate tables rather than on their own experience. The premium rates for these groups are the insurer's current tabular, premium rates or those in the insurer's rate manual. The premium rates in the manual are developed using combined experience from a large number of groups and reflect the expected claim experience of the group as a whole. In developing the rates for each group, there are adjustments to reflect that group's composition—age, sex, and geographic distribution. Groups whose past claims experience is not likely to be a reliable guide to future claim results are generally those in which either a few individuals have been insured under the plan or few individuals might be expected to have a claim.

Fully Experience-Rated Groups

Fully experience-rated groups have their premium based exclusively on their own past claims experience. An insurer decides to experience rate a group if it determines that the possible distortions in past claims resulting from chance fluctuations will be small, and the use of past results will enable the insurer to satisfactorily predict future claims.

The likelihood of chance fluctuations in total claims decreases as both the frequency of claim per individual and the number of individuals covered under the plan increase. Coverage such as a medical expense that has a high frequency of claims can be fully-experience rated on groups with a lower number of employees (such as 500 employees) than can total disability coverage.

Blended Manual/Experience-Rated Groups

The third premium rating class lies between manually rated and fully experience-rated groups. Even before the point at which full-experience rating is deemed appropriate, it is natural for insurers to assume that including a degree of past claims experience in the calculation process would improve the estimate of a group's future claim results. Most insurers assign a credibility percentage to actual past experience and blend it

Table 4.1
Examples of Blended Manual/Experience Rating

Method	Expected claim cost
Fully experience rated	$60
Manually rated	$70
Blended at 20% credibility (.20 × $60) + (.80 × $70)	$68
Blended at 90% credibility (.90 × $60) + (.10 × $70)	$61

with the manual or average expected claims level. When determining actual premium rates for a group, the closer the group is in size to the manually rated class, the less the credibility that will be assigned to its actual experience and the greater the reliance on the manual rate. Conversely, the closer a group is in size to the fully experience-rated class, the greater the reliance placed on its actual experience.

For example, if 20 percent credibility is assigned to the group's experience, 20 percent of the expected claim cost will be based on its actual experience while 80 percent will be based on the average or manual cost. Similarly, a group with 90 percent credibility would have 90 percent of its expected claim cost based on its own claim experience, while only 10 percent would be based on the manual cost. (Table 4.1)

Individual Premium Rate Structures

Tables of gross premium rates for individual health insurance policies are developed in several different ways. The most common methods are uniform premiums, attained-age (step-rate) premiums, and level premiums. Occasionally an insurer uses a combination of two, or even all three, of these methods, in developing the premium structure.

Uniform Premium Rates

Insurers only charge uniform premium rates for all persons, regardless of age, sex, or occupation, if the claim cost does not vary significantly

PRICING HEALTH INSURANCE PRODUCTS

among insureds of different classes, or if state insurance law requires uniform rates. Accidental death and dismemberment is an example of a coverage for which there is little difference in claim cost by age and sex.

Attained-Age Premium Rates

Attained-age premium rates increase according to the age of the insured on each renewal date. This system is appropriate if there is a significant variation in the claim cost depending on attained age. The annual claim cost may be averaged for insureds between the ages of 20 and 29, between 30 and 39, and so on. A separate gross premium is calculated for each age grouping. If the claim cost varies too much within each ten-year age bracket, five-year brackets are used. In some cases, premiums vary year-by-year.

Attained-age rating structures are commonly seen on individual medical expense policies because claim costs increase significantly between the ages of 20 and 65. The advantage of the attained-age rating structure is that premiums can more appropriately reflect increasing morbidity by age.

One disadvantage associated with an attained-age premium structure is its possible adverse effect on persistency. Insureds often find that paying the increasing premium becomes more burdensome, and eventually this may cause policy lapses.

Level Premium Rates

Many insurers prefer to establish a level premium rate for all issue ages. The level premium is made possible by charging more in the early years of the policy than is needed to pay for the benefits and the insurer's expenses. The excess premium is placed into a fund that earns interest.

Level premium rating structures are commonly seen on supplemental health policies such as hospital indemnity and specified disease policies. One major advantage of level premium products is that persistency is

119

better than on attained-age products since the premiums do not increase as the insured ages. Also, these individual products can be marketed as supplemental insurance in a group (or employer) environment and paid for by payroll deduction.

The disadvantage of the level premium structure is that pricing becomes more difficult. The average age of the insured block must be predicted for accurate claim costs to be developed. Since the product will be issued over a wide range of ages, the average age can be difficult to accurately predict.

Combination Premium Rates

In some situations, insurers use a combination or variation of these approaches. For example, there may be an attained-age approach at the younger ages followed by a level premium to age 65 and a uniform rate thereafter.

One combination rating structure that is popular is the age-at-entry structure. This structure is a combination of the attained-age and level premium structures. The age-at-entry premium structure is similar to the attained-age structure in that premiums vary by age groupings. The difference is that once the initial premium is established, it does not increase as the insured ages. The initial premium is established by using the age of the insured at the time the policy is issued. From that point forward, the premium is a level premium and takes on the characteristics of the level premium structure.

The advantage of the age-at-entry premium rate over the attained-age premium rate is that the premium does not increase with age and, as a result, persistency is better. The disadvantage is that initial premiums are higher using the age-at-entry structure since the premium will remain level.

Assuming all actuarial assumptions are correct and conditions are equal, attained-age, age-at-entry, and level premium structures would provide the same profit results. (See following page.)

Table 4.2

Effect of Different Premium Structures

	$100 Hospital indemnity benefit monthly unisex premiums				
Attained-age premiums		Age-at-entry premiums		Level premiums	
Attained ages	Monthly premium	Issue ages	Monthly premium	Issue ages	Monthly premium
20–29	$ 4.75	20–29	$ 6.60	20–74	$18.70
30–39	$ 8.40	30–39	$11.40		
40–49	$12.65	40–49	$15.85		
50–59	$17.00	50–59	$21.50		
60–64	$21.00	60–64	$38.00		
65–69	$38.20	65–69	$56.00		
70–74	$72.90	70–74	$72.90		

■ Development of Premium Rates

Actuaries can use several different techniques to develop health insurance premium rates. Whether they are pricing a group or an individual product, actuaries make assumptions about the various components that are to be included (claim cost, expenses, investment rate, profit and contingency margins, and so forth). Then, all of the various factors that may influence the premium rates are considered (for example, persistency, age/sex distributions, occupation classifications, trend). Finally, the rating class or structure is determined and pricing techniques are used to incorporate everything and produce a premium rate structure.

Group Insurance Manual Rating

An insurer customarily prepares a manual of premium rates for each coverage. The manual is composed of many factors that are combined to produce a premium sufficient to fund benefit payments and expenses. To provide flexibility in designing group benefit plans, there are provisions in the rate structure for adjusting the standard schedule of manual premium rates to reflect the benefit pattern and the composition of the group.

Calculation of Net Premium Rate

The starting point in the development of manual premium rates is the determination of the expected claim cost of each coverage, referred to as the net premium rate. This rate represents the portion of the total premium rate available for claim payments; it contains no provision for expenses or other considerations. The net premium rate represents the anticipated cost of the benefits—the product of the probability of claim (frequency) and the expected amount of claim (severity).

Conversion of Net Rate to Manual Rate

Net premium rates are converted to manual premium rates by adding factors for expenses, contribution to surplus or profit, and higher-than-anticipated claims. Finding an equitable basis of increasing the net premium to arrive at the manual premium is difficult. For example, the amounts of certain expenses, such as commissions and state premium taxes, are related to the size of the premium. Other expenses, such as those associated with processing the application, setting up records, and issuing the master contract, are essentially the same from one group to another. Still other expenses depend on the number of lives involved, which affects the costs of printing announcement booklets and certificates and establishing and maintaining records on the individual insureds.

Adjustment Factors

Health insurers generally establish a single standard rate and adjust it to reflect the specific characteristics of a group, such as age, sex, occupation, and income, that are expected to affect the cost of claims for the coverage.

To reflect the different proportion of the premium needed for expenses (and often the desired margin for contribution to surplus and higher-than-anticipated claims experience), manual premium rates usually are adjusted by a percentage reduction or increase that depends on the size of the premium before the adjustment. The premium that is used in the table of loadings and discounts usually is the total premium for all of a group's coverages. Some insurers also use the number of employees in determining the adjustment.

Most insurers design the table so that there is no percentage increase or decrease (i.e., the manual rates need no size adjustment) for cases of a certain size. For smaller cases, the table may apply percentage increases, and for larger cases, the percentage reductions increase as the premium gets larger.

Group Insurance Experience Rating

Experience-rated premiums reflect the claims and expenses for a policyholder's specific plan of benefits. Most insurers use past claims experience to develop premium rates only for groups that satisfy certain size requirements, as explained earlier in the chapter. These requirements vary from coverage to coverage and insurer to insurer.

Choice of Experience Period

The starting point in developing experience-rated premiums is determining the actual claims experience for a stipulated period of time. This is called the experience period. An insurer may select the most recent 12 months for which claims experience is available to eliminate the normal seasonal variations in medical expense claims. The choice of the most recent 12 months would ensure that each portion of the year received equal weight in the experience. By using the most recent experience, the insurer more accurately reflects any changes in the nature of the risk being insured.

The insurer may believe that the nature of the risk has remained constant over time and that greater accuracy would be obtained by combining several years of experience. The impact of any chance fluctuations in recent experience would be lessened by using a larger experience base. The insurer also may decide to assign proportionately higher weight to more recent experience and lower weight to older experience. In reviewing the claims experience of policyholders with more than one option available to employees, the risk of each option must be understood and evaluated.

Valuation of Incurred Claims

After choosing the experience period, the insurer determines the value of the policyholder's actual incurred claims during the experience period. Incurred claims for a particular period are those claims an insurer is obliged to pay because the insurance was in force during that period. The value of incurred claims usually is not directly available, since claims are not reported immediately and it may take months or even years before final payments can be made on some claims incurred during the experience period. As noted earlier in this chapter, insurers estimate the value of claims incurred but not paid during the experience period.

In addition, a portion of the claims paid during the experience period may have been incurred prior to the period. These claims must be eliminated from consideration to determine the proper value of claims incurred during the experience period. To obtain the true incurred claims for the experience period, insurers often modify the claims paid during the period as follows:

Incurred claims = Claims paid during the period – Claims paid during the period but incurred during prior periods + Estimated value of claims incurred during the period and to be paid in future periods

For example, assume the experience period for a particular group is the calendar year of 1996. Claims paid during 1996 for this group were $250,000; however, $120,000 of these claims were incurred before 1996. The actuary estimates the claim reserve at the end of 1996 to be $100,000. This reserve is for claims incurred during 1996 but not paid as of the end of 1996. The incurred claims for the experience period (1996) is $230,000 ($250,000 – $120,000 + $100,000).

Projection of Prospective Claims

Now that the value of incurred claims for the experience period has been determined, the insurer next considers the projection of the anticipated amount of claims for the prospective rate period. The projection

Table 4.3a

New Cost: Hospital Charge

New daily hospital charges ($100 × $1.10)		$110.00
Plan maximum		$100.00
Increase in number of days used		× 103%
Prior claim cost	divided by	$100.00
Increase in insurer's claim cost		3.0%

normally allows for changes in the basic risk characteristics, such as age and income of the group since the beginning of the experience period. Insurers also consider in their rate projections changes in the general business environment—especially health care costs—that might affect the level of claims.

All these factors are considered in the context of the benefits offered to a group or the plan design. The following examples demonstrate the wide variation in the insurer's claim costs for a given condition that can be traced to variations in benefit design. Both instances assume a 10 percent annual rate of increase in the cost of medical services and a 3 percent annual rate of increase in utilization, as well as no change in the medical technology for treating the condition.

The first example is a plan that reimburses the individual for room and board charges during each day of hospitalization, subject to a maximum daily benefit of $100. The hospital in the locality in question has been charging $100 per day. In this example, an increase in the hospital charge of 10 percent to $110 would have no effect on the insurer's claim cost because of the policy limitation. The only anticipated increase in claims cost would arise from increased utilization. Under these assumptions the insurer's claim costs would rise by 3 percent. (Table 4.3a)

The second example concerns a major medical plan with a $100 surgical deductible. It assumes that the average surgeon's charge for a particular procedure is $200. If this average charge and the amount eligible for reimbursement rises 10 percent to $220, and 3 percent more people

Table 4.3b

New Cost: Surgeon's Charge

New average surgeon's charges ($200 × 1.10)	$220.00
Subtract plan deductible	–$100.00
New average benefit payment	$120.00
Increase in number of operations	× 103%
New claim cost	$123.60
Prior claim cost ($200 charge – $100 deductible)	–$100.00
Increase in insurer's claim cost	23.6%

have this operation, the insurer's claims increase would be, as illustrated in Table 4.3b.

Contingency Margin

Once the projection of prospective claims is complete, it is common for an insurer to add a contingency margin (also called fluctuation margin) to protect against higher-than-anticipated claim results. This margin typically varies with the size of the group and type of coverage. As the size of the group increases, the probability of extreme fluctuations in the claims level decreases and, therefore, the required margin percentage decreases. Higher margins generally are needed in situations where the coverage insured is subject to forces that make it difficult to predict the ultimate effect, or where the base of past experience available to estimate future claims results has been modest.

The amount of margin needed for a given coverage or group also may be related to the experience refund formula applied to the group. In many cases involving experience-rated groups, an experience refund is made available if the experience during the period has been favorable. In situations where the refund depends on the experience of an individual group, higher margins may be needed to allow for the fact that monies refunded to groups with favorable experience are not available to offset losses on groups with unfavorable experience.

Load for Expected Expenses

After applying the appropriate contingency margin, the insurer loads the premium for anticipated expenses. If a significant variation is anticipated from one group to another in the area of services or other costs, the expense component of the premium rate takes such variations into account. For larger experience-rated groups, it is common to relate expenses in the development of a group's premium to the actual charges that will be made against the group in the experience-refund formula. First-year expenses, which usually are higher than renewal expenses, are spread or amortized over time and recovered from premiums received from the group or portfolio of groups in subsequent years.

Load for Profit

The premium charged a policyholder also contributes to the insurer's surplus fund. This is accomplished by loading the premium with a margin for profit. Surplus funds are designed to provide policyholders with the assurance that their claims will be honored even during times when the insurer's costs exceed income. The profit margin (or surplus charge) usually is a percentage of premium depending on the size of the group and the type of coverage. The larger the group, the lower the percentage because of the lower probability of fluctuation of future claim experience. Investment income earned on cash flow and reserves also is considered in this percentage as long as this income is not credited back to the policyholder in the experience-rating formula. The more investment income available to the insurer, the lower the specific percentage needed for profit margin. #36

Experience-Rated Calculation Methods

Insurers use various methods in developing the total amount of premium required for any particular experience-rated group. Generally, three methods are used: desired loss ratio, incurred loss ratio, and split retention. All the methods take into account each of the elements of the premium discussed in this chapter: claim costs, contingency margins, expenses, and profit margins. For simplicity, expenses and profit margins often are combined in the premium rate formula and are referred to as retention, a term that indicates the amounts to be retained by the insurer for items other than claims charged to the group. The complexity of these formulas are beyond the scope of this text. #37

Table 4.4
Example of Loss Ratio Formula

Expected annual claim cost	$39.60
Expenses and profit as a percent of premium	
Sales compensation expense	20%
Acquisition and maintenance expenses	12%
General overhead	3%
Premium taxes	2%
Profit and contingency margin	8%
Total	45%

Conversion to Unit Rates

In addition to knowing the exact amount of incurred claims, insurers need to know the number of benefit units during the period. A benefit unit is defined differently for different coverages. Long-term disability benefit units usually are $100 of monthly covered payroll, while medical benefit units usually are expressed as the number of individuals and dependents insured. After the premium rates have been determined, these rates are then applied to the benefit units to develop the premium for each coverage. The total premium payable by the policyholder is the sum of the premium for each coverage provided by the policy.

Individual Insurance Rating Methods

There are many formulas available to calculate gross premiums for individual health insurance, and a comprehensive review is beyond the scope of this text. The two most widely used ones are the loss ratio formula and the fund account formula.

Loss Ratio Formula

This formula requires two factors: the claim cost and the loss ratio. The claim cost is the expected claim cost for the period covered by the premium. The loss ratio is the ratio of the claim cost to the premium; it provides sufficient funds for expenses and profit margins. This method is identical to the desired loss ratio method used in group pricing. Table 4.4 illustrates this formula.

PRICING HEALTH INSURANCE PRODUCTS

The result is that 45 percent of the total premium will be used for expenses, profit, and contingency margins, and the remaining 55 percent is the expected loss ratio (ratio of claims to premium). The annual gross premium would be:

$$\frac{\text{Expected claim cost}}{\text{Expected loss ratio}} \quad \text{or} \quad \frac{\$39.60}{55\%} = \$72.00$$

Fund Account Formula

The purpose of the fund account formula is to determine the premium that, with interest, provides adequately for the cost of benefits and expenses. The fund account formula is more precise than the loss ratio formula.

Performance Measurements

There are several ways to measure the performance of group and individual health insurance products. One way is to examine the profit (or positive fund balance) as a percent of premium. A positive fund balance indicates that a percentage of the premium collected contributes to the surplus fund of the company.

Another way to measure the performance is to examine the break-even year. Because first-year expenses are higher than renewal expenses, the fund account may be negative for the first policy year and even the first few policy years. This creates a strain on surplus, as existing surplus must be used for several years to support the product until a profit is generated. The break-even year is the first policy year in which the accumulated fund for the policy becomes positive and stays positive for the remaining life of the policy. If a policy takes several years to break even, a portion of the company's surplus fund is used to support the product. The earlier the break-even year, the sooner the surplus can be recovered and used to support other products.

Because the company must support each product with a portion of the surplus fund, another measure of performance is the return on investment. The investment is the amount of surplus loaned by the company to support the product, and the return is the interest earned on (or the value returned for) this investment. If the company is going to lend money to support the product or invest in the product, it should expect a reasonable return on this investment from the product.

■ Experience Monitoring and Rate Review

Pricing group and individual health products does not stop with the development of the initial premium rate structure. Ongoing experience analysis and premium rate review also are important parts of the pricing process. Expected claims and expense assumptions rarely unfold with pinpoint accuracy, so they are monitored regularly. Manually rated and experience-rated group experience is reviewed during each experience period to determine renewal premium rates. Individual health products may have premium rate periods that are much longer than group products and are monitored periodically to determine if rate adjustments are necessary.

Group Insurance Rerating Considerations

Rates established at the inception of a group plan usually are guaranteed for the first 12 months if the plan is not changed during that period, although longer rate guarantee periods sometimes are granted. Premium rates for subsequent policy periods are determined as part of the rerating (or rate review) process, which may include the determination of any experience refunds for the prior periods of coverage. New rates usually are established at the end of the first policy year. Depending on the provisions of the contracts, these rates may be guaranteed for a stated time.

Experience Refunds

When the costs of providing group insurance are less than the costs anticipated in the premium rates charged, many insurers return the unneeded premium to their policyholders as an experience refund. Although similar terminology may be used to describe group insurance premium setting and experience refund determination, there are important differences between the two processes:

- The insurer's objective in setting premium rates is to provide for expected claims, expenses, margins, and profit.
- In contrast, the experience refund process is an evaluation of past results and has as an objective the adjustment of the policyholder's cost for the past periods.

Because of this difference in objectives, the prospective premium setting process may differ from the retrospective experience refund process. For example, the first-year premium rates may be based exclusively on the insurer's manual rates, and the experience refund could be based on the policyholder's actual experience. Policyholders generally find the possibility of experience refunds attractive, which enhances the insurer's chances of obtaining and retaining policyholders.

Timing of Rerating Action

Most insurers give a policyholder at least 30 days' notice before implementing a rate increase. When a large number of insureds are involved, 60 or even 90 days' notice may be given. When 30 days' notice is given, an insurer begins its rerating procedures approximately 60 to 90 days before the premium change date.

Considering the lead time required to implement a rate change, an insurer usually bases a rate increase on the first nine months of paid claims so that the increase can become effective on the first policy anniversary. In many cases, there is insufficient claims experience for the insurer to obtain a satisfactory estimate of the first year. Therefore, an insurer may choose to defer rerating action until completion of the first policy year. This procedure generally results in new premium rates that are not effective until three or four months after the first policy year. This rerating activity normally occurs at the same time as the experience refund calculation and allows the insurer to realize some administrative savings and to have a better picture of the group's emerging claim experience.

The insurer may conclude, however, that nine months of the policyholder's first-year experience indicates sufficiently unfavorable experience to require a rate increase on the first policy anniversary. In this instance, the insurer may give up the convenience and modest administrative savings to avoid potentially large losses from delaying rate increases.

Analysis of Emerging Claims Experience

Special analyses of the claims paid to a group often can be useful for identifying factors that might affect claims projection for the next rate period. These studies may indicate the need for claim control procedures or modifications in the benefits. Insurers also use information to better understand past claims results and to estimate the probable future experience of the group. For example, if claims were high during the first part of the experience period but decreased in recent months, the insurer decides whether the earlier experience shows a chance upward fluctuation or the more recent experience a chance downward fluctuation.

Cross-Subsidization Between Products

In setting premium levels for a particular group, the insurer must take account of special situations that may exist. Although most insurers attempt to charge premiums in proportion to the risks covered, margins available from a particular coverage may be used to offset a premium increase needed for another coverage. For example, a disability insurance margin in a program combined with medical care can be used to maintain a medical care premium rate below the level that would otherwise be required. Often a rate increase is not requested unless the expected claims for all coverages combined require such a step.

Plan Changes

An insurer occasionally offers the policyholder alternatives besides increased premium rates. These alternatives can either lessen or eliminate the need for higher premiums or make higher premiums more acceptable.

For example, the insurer may suggest a reduction in benefits to offset a proposed rate increase. An increase in the deductible or a change in the

PRICING HEALTH INSURANCE PRODUCTS

coinsurance percentage under a comprehensive medical plan can affect the future level of claims enough to offset a proposed rate increase. The introduction of managed care features can reduce the cost and/or utilization of services and also affect the level of future claims.

Group plans often require regular updating to maintain a reasonable relationship between the benefits provided and the expenses likely to be incurred. A needed rate increase may be more acceptable if it is combined with the addition of new benefits or updating of existing benefits.

Individual Insurance Experience Analysis

Insurers conduct a periodic experience analysis on individual health products so that timely rate changes can be made. Rate adjustments for individual health contracts must be filed with the state insurance departments. This process can take from several weeks to several months to complete. Many states require the insurer to give the insured at least 30 days notice before increasing premium rates. Individual policy rate increases reflect the experience of a block of business, not an individual's claims experience.

Incurred Claims Loss Ratios

The most appropriate way to analyze individual health experience is to analyze the incurred claims loss ratios for a particular experience period. The incurred claims loss ratio is the ratio of incurred claims during the experience period to the premium earned during that period. The claims incurred during the experience period are the sum of the claims incurred and paid during the experience period plus the outstanding claim reserve at the end of the period for claims incurred during the period but not yet paid.

Once the actual incurred claims loss ratio is determined, it can be compared to the expected loss ratio used in developing the premium rates for that period. The ratio of actual incurred claims to the expected incurred claims is called the actual-to-expected (A/E) ratio. An A/E ratio under 100 percent indicates that actual experience is better than expected; a ratio above 100 percent indicates the actual experience is worse than expected. This ratio gives the actuary a tool to determine if any rate adjustments are necessary to bring the actual claim experience back in line with the expected incurred claims.

Other factors, such as medical cost trend and inflation, are incorporated into this analysis. For example, it may be that the A/E ratio is 98 percent, but once medical cost trend and inflation are projected in for the coming rate period, the ratio could be greater than 100 percent, thus indicating the need for a rate increase to keep pace with trend and inflation.

Policy Year Experience

Some individual insurers examine experience by policy year. Policy year experience is particularly helpful in analyzing policies where the expected loss ratio is likely to increase over time. An example of this type of policy is a guaranteed renewable policy with level premiums and morbidity that increases with age.

Emerging Trends

There are many changes in the health care arena that are affecting—and will continue to affect—the pricing of health insurance products. The implementation of the Health Insurance Portability and Accountability Act of 1996 will have a significant influence on product pricing for small group and individual medical expense products, in particular. State regulations affecting pricing of these same product areas can be expected to expand both in conformance with the new federal legislation and independently. Managed care is becoming more popular, and HMOs and PPOs are gaining an increased market share. In addition, new managed care products are being introduced regularly. All of this activity makes it more difficult for insurers to price traditional health insurance.

Another trend that affects pricing is that larger insurance companies are buying blocks of major medical insurance from smaller insurers to increase their market share and revenue. Insurers that got out of the major medical market are exploring other markets to replace their lost revenue. Disability, supplemental health, and long-term care markets are being priced more competitively as new insurers enter these markets.

■ Summary

There are a number of components and factors that an actuary considers when developing premium rates for group and individual health insurance. The gross premium must consider claims, reserves, expenses, and margins. Factors such as age, sex, medical cost trend, occupation, and plan design also have an effect on the level of premium that is charged. Insurers must balance these items to develop premium rates that are not only fair and equitable to the insured, but also competitive in the marketplace and adequate to provide the company with a reasonable profit.

■ Key Terms

Acquisition expenses
Actual-to-expected (A/E) ratio
Actuary
Adequacy
Age-at-entry premium rate
Antiselection
Attained-age premium rate
Break-even year
Claim cost
Claim reserve
Contingency margin
Contribution to surplus
Credibility
Desired loss ratio
Equity

Expected claims
Experience period
Experience rating
Experience refund
Frequency
Fund account formula
General overhead expenses
Gross premium
Incurred but not reported (IBNR) claim reserve
Incurred claims
Incurred loss ratio
Investment income
Level premium rate
Loss ratio
Maintenance expenses
Manual premium rate

Morbidity
Net premium rate
Percent of premium
Persistency
Policy reserve
Premium rate
Premium taxes
Profit
Rate guarantee period
Rerating process
Retention
Return on investment
Sales compensation expenses
Severity
Transactions of the Society of Actuaries
Uniform premium rates

Chapter 5

GOVERNMENT REGULATION

137 *Introduction*
138 *History of Insurance Regulation*
140 *Sources of Regulation*
142 *State Insurance Departments*
144 *State Insurance Law*
150 *Impact of NAIC Model Laws on State Regulation*
152 *State Tax Laws*
153 *Federal Benefits Programs*
157 *Federal Actions and Laws Affecting Insurance*
163 *Financial Reporting Requirements*
168 *Industry Compliance Mechanisms*
170 *Emerging Trends*
171 *Summary*
171 *Key Terms*

■ Introduction

The insurance industry is subject to stricter regulation and supervision than most industries. That is appropriate because the essence of insurance is the payment of money by the insured in the form of premiums in exchange for the insurer's promise to pay money if a specified event occurs. The insurer must have the means of fulfilling its promises when the need arises. Government helps to protect the policyholder by making certain the insurer is solvent—that is, it has sufficient reserves to handle any payment it is likely to be called on to make in accordance with the terms of the insurance contract.

Another reason for government oversight of insurance is the technical nature of the insurance contract. Managed care contracts, for example, contain terms, concepts, and options that are important to understand because they affect the level of benefits payable under the policy. Government supervision is a means of making sure that the insurance policy is understandable and does not contain unreasonable restrictions and limitations.

Insurers generate a considerable amount of revenue and accumulate sizeable assets. Governments, particularly state governments, have seen in these revenues and assets the means of generating revenues of their own. Some of the earliest statutes relating to the insurance business were essentially tax measures.

Finally, insurance companies are financial institutions that control the investment of billions of dollars, which they place in a variety of assets. Their investment operations are subject to the same degree of supervision as those of banks, trust companies, and similar fiduciaries. The primary purpose of such investment supervision is to guarantee insurance company solvency.

This chapter discusses the history of insurance regulation and key state and federal actions and laws that affect health insurance.

■ History of Insurance Regulation

Insurance companies formed during the first half of the 19th century were either chartered by state legislatures or incorporated according to state laws. Insurance companies, therefore, came into existence through the power of the state and were subject to state authority.

Establishment of State Insurance Departments

The early insurance legislation, concerned largely with taxation, licensing, and solvency, proved too limited to do an adequate job of protecting the insurance-buying public. During the 1850s, states began to establish special departments to look after insurance matters. The first state insurance department was created in New Hampshire in 1851. Massachusetts followed in 1852 and New York in 1859. Within the next ten years, most of the states then in existence had insurance departments.

Formation of the NAIC

In 1871, the National Convention of Insurance Commissioners (later called the National Association of Insurance Commissioners, or NAIC) was formed. This organization helped to promote some degree of uniformity in the regulation of insurance by the various states and to prevent unnecessary duplication of effort by both the regulatory authorities and the insurance companies.

As a result of an investigation in 1910 of 15 different insurers writing various forms of health insurance in New York, a model law—the Standard Provisions Law—was developed and approved by the Convention in 1912. This law stipulated certain provisions that were to be included in every health insurance policy in the interest of fairness to the insured. For more information about the history of the NAIC, see Chapter 1: History of Health Insurance in *Fundamentals of Health Insurance: Part A*. See page 150 of this chapter for more about NAIC model laws.

McCarran-Ferguson Act (Public Law 15)

Starting in the mid-19th century, some insurers felt that state regulation was too burdensome. They raised the question of whether control and regulation of the insurance business should be a function of state governments or the federal government. This question was brought before the courts, including the Supreme Court, several times.

To resolve the difficulty, Congress passed the McCarran-Ferguson Act in 1945. In this statute, Congress declared that "the continued regulation and taxation by the several states of the business of insurance is in the public interest and that silence on the part of the Congress shall not be construed to impose any barrier to the regulation or taxation of such business by the several states." It also provided that the Sherman, Clayton, Federal Trade Commission, and Robinson-Patman acts (all federal antitrust laws) should apply to the insurance business only to the extent that it was not regulated by state law.

As a result of the McCarran-Ferguson Act, the NAIC, with the support of the insurance industry, worked for passage of legislation needed to bring about a more thorough and uniform system of regulation. Most states adopted fair trade practice laws to prohibit unfair methods of competition and unfair practices. Legislation also was enacted to provide a means for service of legal papers on insurers not licensed to do business in the state, thereby making the unlicensed insurers subject to the state's courts.

Although several court decisions have reaffirmed the right of the states to exercise control over the insurance industry, the McCarran-Ferguson Act explicitly leaves this control in the hands of the states only so long as the states do an adequate job. If they do not, the McCarran-Ferguson Act stands as a reminder that the federal government has the power to step in and do it for them.

In recent years, various special interest groups have pressed for repeal of the McCarran-Ferguson Act. Such repeal would clear the way for federal regulation of the insurance industry, which would have a major impact on the industry.

Growth of Regulation

Beginning in the late 1960s, there was a dramatic increase in the level of government activity in insurance in general and health insurance in particular. The reasons vary, but contributing factors include the increasing costs and the increasing complexity of medical care.

■ Sources of Regulation

The degree of control over insurance matters varies from one state to another. However, the methods used to control the insurance industry are similar and generally are separated into three categories: statutes, formal regulations, and informal regulations.

- ■ Statutes are laws enacted by either a state legislature or, in the case of federal statutes, the U.S. Congress. Most state statutes relating to insurance are found in a grouping of statutes generally referred to as the insurance code.

GOVERNMENT REGULATION

- Formal regulations are specific rules established by a state insurance department from authority conferred by statutes.
- Informal regulations include insurance department bulletins or official letters addressing certain issues or areas to be controlled, as well as guidelines adopted by some insurance departments.

All three branches of government—legislative, executive, and judicial—participate in the regulation of insurance in one way or another.

Legislative Branch

Legislative regulation consists of the body of insurance law in effect in a particular state. States vary widely in the sheer volume of insurance law on the books. The fact that a given state has just a small amount of written law does not mean that regulation is weak in that state. In many cases, legislators enact laws that provide the general framework for regulation and then authorize an administrative officer to supply the more specific rules and regulations.

Executive Branch

All states have an insurance department that usually is an administrative arm of the executive branch of the government. It not only issues rules and regulations affecting the insurance business but also is responsible for enforcing them.

Judicial Branch

The judicial branch has an effect on the insurance business in several ways. A policyholder may file suit against the insurer as a result of the insurer's actions under a particular insurance contract. In the course of deciding such a case, courts may have to interpret the meaning of a word or phrase commonly found in insurance contracts. Courts also may be called upon to decide the legality of an insurance company practice.

141

Court action may be brought by a state insurance commissioner to enforce action against an insurer or to enjoin it from certain practices. In relatively rare circumstances, an insurer may bring an action to decide the constitutionality of a statute or regulation. Even more rarely, an insurer may bring legal action—called a writ of mandamus—against the insurance commissioner that compels the insurer to take a certain action or to permit the insurance company to take a certain action.

■ State Insurance Departments

The insurance department is the state administrative agency established to implement insurance laws and, within the scope of these laws, to supervise the activities of insurance companies doing business in the state.

In most states, this is a separate department, but sometimes it is combined with the department regulating banking or all business. The head of the department generally is called the commissioner, but in some states the title is superintendent or director. Usually the commissioner is appointed by the governor with confirmation by the state senate; in a few states, the commissioner is an elected official. The commissioner's function is a dual one: to represent the public interest and to enforce the insurance laws.

Organization and Powers of the Department

The insurance department usually is vested with broad powers and has jurisdiction over many activities. It typically is organized according to the functions it performs, such as:

- licensing of insurance companies and agents;
- examination of companies;
- liquidation or rehabilitation of insurance companies in financial difficulty; and
- approval of policy forms, certificates, booklets, and rate manuals.

GOVERNMENT REGULATION

Procedures for Enforcement and Review

The state insurance department's strongest weapon is its licensing power. Every insurer and agent must have a license to do business in the state. If the insurance commissioner withholds a license, the insurer or agent cannot sell insurance in that state. It is a particularly serious matter if an insurer loses its license in its home state because then all states in which it does business will withdraw their licenses.

State insurance commissioners have the authority to examine an insurer's records and its securities and to interrogate its officers, agents, and employees. Insurance commissioners may not do this, however, without prior notice and without giving reasons to the insurer.

The state legislature also exercises control over the commissioner and the operation of the insurance department. Besides establishing the framework within which the commissioner operates, the legislature controls the department's budget.

Periodic Examinations

State insurance departments conduct periodic examinations of each insurer operating in the state to determine that its practices are satisfactory and that it is financially stable. Generally, the examination is made every three to five years. Examiners representing the insurance department visit the insurance company and review in detail the insurance company's operation and management. On occasion, the state will examine only a portion of the insurer's operation, such as its claims payment practices or managed care arrangements. Growing attention is being devoted to advertising practices.

An examination often requires a number of months—even as much as a year for large insurers. The insurer pays for the cost of the examination. Typically the major examination of an insurer is made by the insurance department of the state where it is domiciled. The insurance departments of other states accept the results of that examination and may send representatives to participate in it.

143

■ State Insurance Law

All states have laws governing insurance. The insurance laws of most states contain provisions that relate specifically to group or individual insurance.

- Laws pertaining to group health insurance indicate the kinds of groups to which such coverage can be issued and generally prescribe some of the features and provisions the group policy must include.
- Laws pertaining to individual health insurance address eligibility, issue requirements, pricing, and features and provisions the individual policy must include.

Insurance laws vary considerably by state with little consistency or uniformity, which greatly increases the complexity and volume of filings.

Organization and Licensing

The most fundamental control possessed by regulators is that of governing the organization of insurers. Before an insurance company can be formed, the organizers must obtain the insurance commissioner's approval of the proposed organization. Requirements for incorporation, certificates of intention, and bylaws are similar to those for other types of corporations.

The insurance laws of most states require licensing of domestic, foreign (domiciled out-of-state), and alien (domiciled out-of-country) insurance companies before they may do business in that state.

Insurer Solvency and Financial Condition

The primary concern of the states in regulating the insurance industry is protecting their residents against insurance company insolvency. The public must have the confidence that their insurers are able to make good on their promises when claims occur.

If an insurer becomes insolvent or is in danger of becoming so, the insurance commissioner has the power to assume control of the insurer.

GOVERNMENT REGULATION

The commissioner will make every attempt to restore the insurer to solvency or, if that is impossible, will liquidate it. In the liquidation process, the commissioner will attempt to find a solvent company to take over the in-force business of the insolvent insurer.

One of the most important factors in ensuring the solvency of an insurer is that its reserves be adequate to meet demands likely to be made on it. The following reserves are needed:

- reserves for unearned premiums;
- reserves for future payments on claims not yet completed; and
- reserves for claims incurred but not yet reported.

Insurance departments establish standards by which the adequacy of these reserves may be tested.

Permissible Investments

All states have laws governing the types of investments that insurance companies are permitted to make. These laws are designed to require diversification of investments and to restrict investments that tend to fluctuate greatly in value.

Annual Statements

To check the financial condition of insurers, the insurance commissioner of each state requires each insurer licensed by that state to report its results on a prescribed form. See the section on financial reporting requirements on page 163.

Filing Requirements

Most state laws require that the policy form issued in the state, and the insurance policy or certificate used with it, be submitted to and approved by the insurance department prior to its use. States also have rate requirements specific to group and individual products. The requirements for submitting policy forms and rates are for the protection of the persons insured.

145

FUNDAMENTALS OF HEALTH INSURANCE: PART B

State laws generally are written in a way that makes them applicable only to insurance policies in that particular state. A number of states, however, have extraterritorial laws that apply not only to policies issued in that particular state but also to policies issued in other states that cover residents of that particular state.

Determining filing language and issuing contracts that involve extraterritorial laws are complex procedures because the plan must include any benefits mandated by the state in which the plan is issued, plus any benefits required under extraterritorial laws.

Grounds for disapproval of filings vary from state to state. Three typical reasons for disapproval are:

- The policy does not conform to requirements imposed by statute or regulation.
- The policy is inconsistent, ambiguous, misleading, unfair, or inequitable.
- The benefits provided are unreasonable in relation to the premium charged. State regulatory officials want to be sure that premiums are adequate but not excessive.

Mandates

Each state has statutes specifying certain provisions and coverages that must appear in every health insurance policy issued in the state. Mandates cover a wide range of subjects and are growing rapidly in number. Some of the more common mandated benefits relate to treatments for drug addiction, alcoholism, mental health care, well-baby care, cosmetic surgery, and transplants, including autologous bone marrow transplants. Some of these mandates pertain only to group insurance, but increasingly such coverage is required in individual policies. Insurers must develop and file language for each mandate, and contracts must be amended to include them.

Each state also has statutes that require an insurer to offer a particular coverage or provision to its insureds. Insureds can choose to accept or not accept the coverage. To comply with mandated offers, insurers often develop forms that require the insured's signature indicating that he or she was advised of the coverage.

Compulsory Nonoccupational Disability Benefits Laws

Six jurisdictions—California, Hawaii, New Jersey, New York, Puerto Rico, and Rhode Island—have compulsory nonoccupational disability benefit laws. Rhode Island has a single state fund and no private plans can be written. The other five jurisdictions allow choices between the state fund and a private plan, although California's regulations effectively preclude most private plans. These plans provide for minimum and maximum weekly disability benefits.

Pricing and Rate Revision

Many states have regulations pertaining to health insurance rates. There are differences in how group and individual health insurance are treated.

Group Pricing Regulations

The laws of some states require each insurer doing business in the state to gain approval for its first-year group health insurance manual premium rates. Additionally, several states require the filing of manual premium rates with changes to an existing product or development of a new product that will be used with an existing (previously filed) form.

Some states also require an actuarial memorandum showing how rates were developed and indicating the anticipated loss ratio (claims divided by premiums).

Individual Pricing Regulations

Individual health insurance rates are not mandated, but states do require some degree of rate surveillance. Most states require individual health insurers to file with the insurance department all rates and classifications of risks. As is the case for group insurance, some states also

147

require an actuarial memorandum showing how rates were developed and a statement as to the anticipated loss ratio for the policy form in question.

Each year, individual health insurers are required to file, as a supplement to the annual statement, an accident and health policy exhibit that shows the loss ratio for each policy form being issued by the insurer. Some states have established loss ratio benchmarks that must be met before a premium increase can be approved.

Agent Licensing and Selling Methods

The licensing and conduct of agents, advertising methods, and the content of advertising material are regulated by states.

Agents must have a license to sell insurance in every state in which they expect to sell. All states require that agents either pass a written examination or complete an approved course of study. Once issued, agents' licenses usually are renewable annually, although they sometimes are issued on a perpetual basis. In either case, the state requires an annual license fee.

If a state receives complaints about the conduct of an agent, that agent may be called before the insurance department. In certain cases, they may be fined or their license may be revoked. The usual grounds for extreme measures are a violation of law, dishonest practices, twisting (using misrepresentation to cause a policyholder to replace a policy), and rebating (giving the policyholder something of value, for example, a kickback from the agent's commission).

Free Policy Examination

Related to selling methods, a policy provision required in most states for individual products is the ten-day free look, which gives the insured ten days to examine the policy and return it if dissatisfied. If the policy is returned, all premiums are refunded, and the policy is treated as if it had never been issued.

GOVERNMENT REGULATION

Claim Practices

A majority of states have statutes governing an insurer's conduct in handling claims. Prohibition of certain claim practices often is contained in a state's unfair trade practices act. The following are examples of claim prohibitions:

- misrepresenting pertinent facts or policy provisions;

- failing to act promptly in answering a claimant's correspondence in regard to the payment or denial of a claim;

- refusing to pay a claim without conducting a reasonable investigation based on all available information;

- attempting to settle a claim based on an application altered without the insured's knowledge and consent;

- failing to explain the basis for denying a claim; and

- forcing the insured to start legal action to collect an amount due.

Some states go further and spell out time limits in terms of a specific number of days in which the insurer must acknowledge a claim, furnish claim forms, answer a claimant's correspondence, and pay or deny a claim. In an increasing number of states, the insurer must pay the claimant interest on amounts that are due but not paid within a specified number of days.

Policyholder Complaints

Dealing with policyholder complaints is an important function of the state insurance departments. The first step an insurance department takes in processing a policyholder complaint is to ask the insurer to state the reasons for its position. After reviewing this material, the department can require the insurer to provide more information if it appears that the policyholder has a valid position. If a violation of law is found to have occurred, the department can impose penalties.

Impact of NAIC Model Laws on State Regulation

States are encouraged to enact NAIC model laws, rules, and regulations. Each state has the freedom to adopt all, none, or a portion of each model. NAIC model acts have found their way, in varying degrees, into the laws and regulations of all states. A description of some NAIC model acts follows.

Eligible Groups

The NAIC Model Group Health Insurance Act defines group health insurance and the kinds of eligible groups. Eligible group laws also include a number of restrictions, such as definition of the minimum percentage of eligible persons who must enroll if the group is to qualify for insurance. Most states follow this act.

Minimum Benefit Standards for Individual Insurance

The NAIC Model Individual Accident and Sickness Insurance Minimum Standards Act provides reasonable standardization and simplification of terms and coverages of individual accident and sickness insurance policies. It also describes permissible policy exclusions. The model law was designed to facilitate public understanding, to eliminate provisions that may be misleading or confusing, and to provide for full disclosure in the sale of policies. Most states follow this act.

Readability Standards

The NAIC Model Policy Language Simplification Act requires that policy forms be written in readable language, which is measured by an objective test based on the length of words and sentences. The intent of this law is to simplify the language and format used in policy contracts so that an average consumer would be able to comprehend the document. Most states have adopted this act.

GOVERNMENT REGULATION

Privacy of Information

To safeguard the confidentiality and privacy of personal information gathered and disseminated on individual citizens, a growing number of states have enacted the NAIC Model Insurance Information and Privacy Protection Model Act. Since the insurance industry is one of the major collectors and users of personal data concerning individuals, the content of this act is very important. This model act establishes standards for the collection, use, and disclosure of information gathered in connection with insurance transactions.

Advertising

The NAIC's Model Advertising Rules require that all advertising relating to health insurance be truthful and not misleading in fact or by implication. The rules prohibit deceptive words, phrases, or illustrations. Statistics used in ads must be relevant and their sources must be identified. Exceptions, reductions, and limitations must be clearly set forth, including those relating to pre-existing conditions. Advertisements must disclose policy provisions relating to renewability, cancellability, and termination.

Each insurer is required to maintain a complete file of all its advertising materials. This file is subject to inspection by the insurance department.

Prevention of Unfair Discrimination

The NAIC has adopted model regulations that, to some extent, limit the insurer's right to classify risks. Each model regulation describes certain practices that are deemed to constitute unfair discrimination within the meaning of the state's unfair trade practices act.

An unfair trade practices act prohibits any unfair discrimination between individuals of the same class who present essentially the same hazard. A number of states have prohibited discrimination or classification on the basis of one or more of the following: sex, marital status, sexual preference, deafness, blindness, visual acuity, lawful occupation,

151

or the presence of certain genetic traits (most commonly, for sickle cell and Tay-Sachs diseases).

AIDS

In 1986, the NAIC adopted guidelines outlining minimum standards for insurance application questions relating to AIDS and the underwriting of persons with AIDS. An insurer must refrain from using questions designed to elicit information about an individual's sexual orientation or preference. Information about sexual orientation is not to be used in the underwriting process and is not to influence the decision on whether an individual is considered insurable. For the most part insurers are permitted to ask questions of a strictly medical nature, such as whether an individual has been diagnosed or treated for the human immunodeficiency virus (HIV) or AIDS.

Most states allow insurers to test for exposure to HIV as long as such testing is done in a nondiscriminatory fashion. Specific restrictions are placed upon insurers who do AIDS testing, such as informed consent prior to testing, confidentiality, and the disclosure of test result information. Some states also prohibit any inquiry by insurers about prior blood tests for AIDS.

■ State Tax Laws

The business of insurance generates revenues for states through taxes.

Premium Tax

Each state imposes a premium tax on out-of-state insurers licensed to do business in that state, generally at a rate of 2 to 3 percent of insured premium. More than half of the states tax premiums of domestic companies at a somewhat lower rate. Some states do not impose any premium tax on domestic insurers. Premium taxes do not apply to self-funded plans.

Income Tax

Many states have income tax laws that parallel or are used on a percentage of the federal income tax. Medical expense insurance benefits are tax-free for group holders. Individual health insurance premiums are only partially tax-free. Employer-paid disability income benefits generally are taxable.

Other Charges

Besides premium taxes, states impose fees for:

- licensing insurers;
- the privilege of doing business in a state;
- examining and licensing agents;
- filing policy forms; and
- filing annual statements.

Federal Benefits Programs

The federal government has enacted laws that provide health, disability, or pension benefits to various designated groups. To coordinate benefits and to ascertain product markets, private insurers must be aware of the benefit provisions of such programs as well as changes that occur in them.

Social Security

The Social Security law, enacted by Congress in 1935 and amended many times since, consists of four types of benefits:

- retirement benefits for covered workers and their families;
- death benefits for the survivors of deceased covered workers;
- disability benefits to eligible persons and their eligible dependents; and

- medical care expense benefits (Medicare and Medicaid) for covered persons.

An overview of Medicare and Medicaid follows.

Medicare

Medicare was created by amendments to the Social Security Act in 1965 (Title 18), which established two health care programs for persons aged 65 or older: a hospital benefit plan (Part A) and a medical benefits plan (Part B).

Medicare benefits also are payable to persons receiving Social Security disability benefits and can begin after 29 months of disability. The Medicare program also covers persons receiving treatment for end-stage renal disease (ESRD); these benefits generally are secondary to private group health benefits during the first 18 months of treatment.

Hospital Benefit Plan (Part A)

Part A of the program is financed by an earnings tax, paid by employers, employees, and self-employed persons. It designates four kinds of providers of service, each of which is required to meet certain qualifying standards:

- **Hospital Care.** Benefits are payable subject to a deductible, followed by coinsurance, the terms of which change periodically.
- **Skilled Nursing Care.** Benefits are generally payable in an approved skilled nursing facility following a minimum 3-day hospital stay.
- **Home Health Services.** With no prior hospitalization required, a patient may receive home health care services for a limited number of days.
- **Hospice Care.** Where a doctor has certified that a patient is terminally ill, the patient may choose to receive care from a participating hospice in place of standard Medicare benefits for a terminal illness.

Part A also pays for all blood needed, following a deductible of the first three pints of blood.

Supplementary Medical Insurance (Part B)

Part B helps pay for doctors' services and medical items and services not covered under the hospital insurance program. Participation in Part B is voluntary. Benefit payments are subject to a deductible and coinsurance.

Part B requires the secretary of the Department of Health and Human Services to contract, to the extent possible, with insurers to carry out the major administrative functions of the medical benefits plan. These functions include such activities as claims processing, disbursing funds for benefits, determining compliance, and assisting in utilization review. Insurance companies, service-type plans (Blue Cross and Blue Shield Plans) and administrative service organizations undertaking these functions have been designated as fiscal intermediaries for Part A and carriers for Part B.

Provider Payment

Effective October 1, 1983, the Health Care Financing Administration (HCFA) implemented federal legislation requiring prospective payment to hospitals for inpatient care of persons under Medicare. This system uses diagnosis-related groups (DRGs) to establish per case payment levels for hospitals. DRG payments are recalculated annually and are adjusted to reflect area wage index and capital adjustment factors. Effective January 1, 1992, HCFA, again operating under federal legislation, implemented a payment system for physician services under Part B using a national uniform resource-based relative value scale (RBRVS) with payments adjusted to reflect geographic cost differences. Previously, Medicare paid hospitals on a cost reimbursement basis, with physicians receiving payment based on historical charges.

Medicare Secondary Payer (MSP)

Beginning in 1982, several federal laws were enacted or amended to make Medicare the secondary payer to certain employers' group health plans. Group health plans of employers with 20 or more employees must pay their benefits before Medicare for active employees and their dependents who are aged 65 and over.

FUNDAMENTALS OF HEALTH INSURANCE: PART B

For beneficiaries who are entitled to Medicare on the basis of disability, employers with 100 or more employees must pay their benefits before Medicare, if the beneficiary is covered under the employer's plan on the basis of current employment status. If a beneficiary is entitled to Medicare on the basis of ESRD, an employer of any size must pay its benefits before Medicare during the first 18 months of dialysis. This could be 21 months if the patient does not self-administer the dialysis.

If the beneficiary is over age 65 and is also entitled to Medicare because of ESRD, special rules apply. The plan (either Medicare or the employer's) that was the primary payer on the first day of ESRD entitlement continues in that role.

Medicaid

Title 19 of the Social Security amendments of 1965 provides government-financed medical care for the poor. The federal government shares with the states the cost of providing this care; the amount varies according to the plan adopted by the state. To qualify for federal matching funds, the state must include in its Title 19 program the following minimum services:

- inpatient and outpatient hospital services;
- laboratory or X-ray services;
- skilled nursing home services;
- physicians' services;
- home health services;
- screening and diagnosis for children under age 21; and
- family planning.

For a state to qualify for matching federal funds, medical assistance must be available for all persons qualifying in either of the assistance categories: families with dependent children or needy persons who are aged, blind, or disabled. Also, a state may include people with medical need who do not qualify for public assistance.

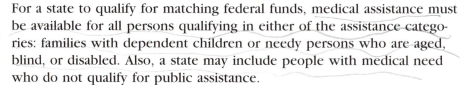

Each state may establish its own concept of medical indigence or need, considering an individual's income in excess of the level required for maintenance established by the state and the individual's medical care costs. The required types of medical care service must be provided without deductibles, coinsurance, or other charges to a patient who qualifies for public assistance. If a state extends eligibility to medically indigent individuals, who do not qualify for public assistance, any deductibles, coinsurance, or other charges to such individuals must be nominal.

Civilian Hospital and Medical Program of the Uniformed Services (CHAMPUS)

This program for dependents of military personnel on active duty was begun in 1956. It provides for extensive medical care services either in a civilian or an armed forces facility for spouses, children, and any other persons legally dependent on the service person. In 1966, the program was extended to include coverage for retired military personnel and their dependents. Since 1983, CHAMPUS has been secondary to private group insurance plans if an individual is covered under both.

■ Federal Actions and Laws Affecting Insurance

Federal regulations that affect health insurance are divided into two distinct areas: employee benefits, and employment and discrimination.

Employee Benefits

Since 1974, the federal government has become increasingly involved in health insurance and other employer-paid benefits. Legislation has been enacted in response to two major benefits-related issues:

- control over tax-exempt, employer-paid benefits; and
- extension of social policy to protect or expand benefits for lower-paid workers.

Employee Retirement Income Security Act (ERISA)

In 1974, ERISA established minimum participation, vesting, funding, and termination standards for employer-sponsored pension plans. Although ERISA was directed primarily to pension plans, most group insurance plans are subject to the reporting and disclosure requirements of the law. All plans subject to the law must be established in writing and must describe the benefits provided under the plan, name the person(s) responsible for the operation of the plan, and spell out the arrangements for funding and amending the plan.

ERISA applies three general kinds of responsibility to employee welfare plans: reporting and disclosure, fiduciary matters, and claim procedure.

Reporting and disclosure. All participants in the welfare plan must be given a summary plan description. It must be worded in a manner that can be understood by the average plan participant and that is sufficiently comprehensive to inform the participants and beneficiaries of their rights and obligations under the plan. If the plan covers more than 100 lives, the administrator of the plan must file the summary plan description with the Department of Labor.

Fiduciary responsibility. ERISA requires that every employee welfare plan name one or more fiduciaries who jointly or separately have authority to control and manage the operation and administration of the plan. A fiduciary is required to act solely in the interest of the participants and beneficiaries of the plan.

Claim procedure. ERISA requires that every employee benefit plan will:

- provide adequate notice to any participant whose claim for benefits under the plan has been denied, setting forth the specific reasons for such denial; and

- afford a reasonable opportunity to any participant whose claim for benefits has been denied for a full and fair review by the fiduciary of the decision denying the claim.

Preemption. The law also contains a provision regarding its preemption of state laws covering employee benefit plans. There have been many legal challenges to various state laws based on this preemption provision. The general trend of court decisions indicates that states may not regulate employee benefit plans, the employers who maintain them, or trust funds established under them.

Consolidated Omnibus Budget Reconciliation Act (COBRA)

COBRA, which was enacted in 1985, requires employers with 20 or more employees to allow continuation of group health care coverage for 18 months, at the employee's expense, for employees (and their dependents) who leave the company for any reason other than gross misconduct. Continuation for up to 36 months is also to be made available to:

- dependents who lose coverage as a result of divorce;
- dependents who lose coverage as a result of death of the employee; and
- a dependent child ceasing to qualify as an eligible dependent.

Disabled individuals may be able to extend the continuation of coverage from 18 months to 29 months if they meet certain criteria.

Health Insurance Portability and Accountability Act

The HIPAA of 1996 is the first major health insurance legislation enacted at the federal level. The act expands access to health insurance through the following key provisions:

- Requires individual health insurers to provide coverage to people who lost their group coverage because they changed or lost their jobs, providing they had maintained continued coverage for at least 18 months;
- Limits the pre-existing condition exclusion to no more than 12 months for group insurance (If an insured switches group health plans, insurers must credit prior coverage, month for month, against any new pre-existing condition limits.);

- Requires all insurers serving the small group market (2 to 50 employees) to accept every small employer that applies for coverage and to accept every individual in the group who applies when he/she first becomes eligible; and
- Increases the health insurance tax deduction for self-employed persons from 30 percent to 40 percent in 1997, up to 45 percent in 1998, and up to 80 percent on 2006.

See the references throughout *Fundamentals of Health Insurance: Part A* and *Part B* for more details on provisions of this law.

Employment and Antidiscrimination Laws

Employers are subject to various federal employment and antidiscrimination laws that must be considered in benefit design, underwriting, and rating of group insurance plans.

Civil Rights Act, Title 7

Title 7 of the Civil Rights Act of 1964 makes it an unlawful employment practice for an employer to unfairly discriminate against any individual with respect to compensation, terms, conditions, or privileges of employment—including participating in an employer-sponsored group health insurance plan—because of the individual's race, color, religion, sex, or national origin.

Federal Maternity Law

Title 7 of the Civil Rights Act was amended in 1978 to require employers to treat pregnancy, for all employment-related purposes, the same as any illness. This includes the payment of disability income and medical expense benefits under fringe benefit programs. One notable exception to the law is that the employer does not have to provide medical expense benefits for abortions unless the mother's life would be endangered or there are medical complications following an abortion.

The law has been construed to mean that dependent wives must receive the same pregnancy benefits that female employees receive.

Age Discrimination in Employment Act (ADEA)

The ADEA, which was enacted in 1967, prohibits employers with 20 or more employees from discriminating in all aspects of employment, including employee benefits, against individuals aged 40 or older. The law allows for a reduction in disability benefits, provided the reduction is actuarially justified. For example, a lesser benefit may be provided for older employees if it can be demonstrated that the cost of the lesser benefit is equivalent to the cost of the higher benefits for younger employees.

Americans with Disabilities Act (ADA)

The ADA, enacted in 1990, bans discrimination against disabled people in the areas of employment, transportation, public facilities, and telecommunications. It prohibits discrimination against a qualified individual with a disability in hiring, promoting, compensating, terminating, training, and other terms, conditions, and privileges of employment. This has been interpreted to include health insurance and other benefits that may be provided or offered by an employer.

Family and Medical Leave Act (FMLA)

The FMLA, enacted in 1993, allows eligible employees to take up to 12 work weeks of unpaid leave in a 12-month period for:

- birth, adoption, or foster care placement of a child;
- a serious health condition that prevents the employee from doing the essential functions of his or her job; or
- caring for a child, spouse, or parent with a serious health condition.

Most employees are allowed to maintain health coverage while on leave and return to the same or equivalent position at the end of the leave. The FMLA applies to companies with 50 or more employees within a 75-mile radius and is intended to help employees balance work and family needs.

Other Federal Laws that Affect Health Insurance

Fair Credit Reporting Act

The Fair Credit Reporting Act of 1971 requires that consumer reporting agencies adopt reasonable procedures for meeting the needs of commerce for consumer credit, personnel, insurance, and other information in a manner that is fair and equitable to the consumer.

The act safeguards the confidentiality, accuracy, relevance, and proper utilization of such information. Its purpose is to protect consumers against the circulation of inaccurate or obsolete information.

As part of its protections, the act makes a distinction between a consumer report and an investigative consumer report.

- Consumer reports include credit information such as credit worthiness, standing, and capacity, and may or may not include the information of an investigative consumer report.

- Consumer investigative reports, referred to as inspection reports, are underwriting tools. They are used to obtain information about such matters as an applicant's occupational duties, health history, other insurance coverage, finances, driving record, and mode of living. The Fair Credit Reporting Act requires the insurer to notify the applicant that such an investigation may be made.

Health Maintenance Organization (HMO) Act

The HMO Act of 1973 gave formal federal recognition to the HMO concept. It encouraged and exerted some control over the development of the HMO movement in an attempt to improve the health care delivery system in the United States.

In 1988, amendments to the HMO Act set forth several changes that were designed to respond to the changing marketplace for employee health plans. Major changes allow:

- prospective experience rating as opposed to strict community rating in developing plan premiums;

GOVERNMENT REGULATION

- variation of employer contribution rates to reflect the cost of benefits selected by employees as well as past utilization rates by class of employees;
- HMOs to contract with non-HMO physicians for up to 10 percent of plan services; and
- the financial backing of a stable parent organization (such as an insurance company) to be taken into account in federally qualifying an HMO.

These amendments make it easier for HMOs and insurance companies to offer multiple-option plans to employers.

Financial Reporting Requirements

Insurance companies are required by law to report their financial results annually to each state in which they are licensed. Since states are concerned primarily with the solvency of an insurer and its ability to meet policyholder obligations that are often long term, state requirements reflect a conservative approach to the financial stability of an insurer.

Annual Financial Statements

The NAIC has developed a format for the annual financial statements, which is used by most states. Only minor modifications have been introduced in a few jurisdictions.

The advantages of this uniformity in reporting are twofold:

- Insurers avoid the need to produce a separate annual statement for each jurisdiction in which they operate.
- It facilitates state audits of returns, the comparison of insurers, and the compilation of industry figures.

Contents. Annual statements show in detail an insurer's:

- summary of assets, by type of asset;
- summary of liabilities, surplus, and other funds;

- summary of operations;
- analysis of operations by line of business; and
- analysis of increase in reserves during the year.

Supplementary exhibits and schedules furnish additional details that support the various entries in the five items listed above, such as premium income, investments, claims expenses, and reserves. There also is a section showing five-year historical data.

Assets. Insurer assets may be classified as admitted (assets acceptable to insurance departments) or nonadmitted (those assets not permitted by statute on the annual statement balance sheet). To be considered solvent, an insurer must have admitted assets that are at least equal to the total of its liabilities, as well as required minimum levels of surplus. Nonadmitted assets include furniture, equipment (other than admitted electronic data processing equipment valued over $50,000), and health insurance premiums more than three months past due.

Admitted assets. Admitted assets are often thought of as sound assets that can be liquidated for value. They are the assets that by statute are permitted to back the insurer's obligations. Admitted assets that are allowed on the balance sheet of the annual statement consist of both invested and noninvested assets. Invested assets include bonds, mortgage loans, stocks, and real estate.

An insurer's noninvested, admitted assets consist primarily of:

- cash on hand and on deposit;
- amounts due from other insurers because of reinsurance arrangements;
- electronic data processing equipment valued at over $50,000;
- outstanding policy loans;
- insurance premiums due and unpaid; and
- investment income due and accrued.

Liabilities and reserves. Reserves and other liabilities, key elements in the report of an insurer's results, are unique to the insurance industry. Most of an insurer's reserves and liabilities relate to policy and contract obligations, current and future, on previously written insurance policies.

Reserves represent the current value of an insurer's obligations that will not be due to its policyholders until some future date. The amount represents an estimate of the monies needed to cover defined and specific liabilities of the insurer that will come due after the annual statement date.

Regulatory authorities often set minimum standards for the valuation of liabilities based on conservative interest, mortality, and morbidity assumptions. The adequacy of group and individual health insurance reserves and other liabilities is tested carefully by the insurance departments of the states in which the insurer does business.

Summary of operations. The summary of operations provides information about an insurance company's operating income and cost of doing business. All figures in the summary of operations are shown on an accrual basis although an insurance company's general ledger is maintained on a cash basis—that is, on a basis that recognizes only the movement of money. Accrual items are those premiums, losses, or expenses that are due or payable but have not yet been actually received or paid. The summary is used to reflect the surplus increase or decrease resulting from insurance operations.

Analysis of operations by lines of business. Lines of business are classified as major lines with subclassifications or sublines. Accident and health is considered a major line of insurance. This line is subdivided into group, credit, and other, which includes all individual health.

Five-year historical data. Since 1975, the annual statement has included a set of specific figures for the current year and each of the four preceding years. The types of information reported in this section include:

- income items;
- assets (admitted and nonadmitted);
- investment data;
- reserve adjustments/adequacy of reserves;
- operating ratios (loss and expense ratios); and
- net gain from operations after federal income taxes by lines of business (statutory profit or loss).

Accident and Health Policy Experience Exhibit

The accident and health policy exhibit is a supplement to the annual statement. It is required to be filed in each state in which the insurer is licensed. It must be filed by June 30 of each year and show the experience of the previous calendar year. For each health policy form, the exhibit shows the following information:

- the first year the policy form was issued;
- the name of the policy;
- premiums earned;
- incurred claims plus increase in policy reserves, both as a dollar amount and as a percent of premiums earned;
- commissions incurred (or earned);
- rate of commission and expense allowance; and
- dividends to policyholders.

Regulatory Focus and Requirements

The annual statement serves as the primary source of information for an insurance company's federal income tax return. The Internal Revenue Service requires that a copy of the annual statement be filed with the tax return.

Management also uses the annual statement in its planning and review process. The annual statement contains a wealth of income and cash-flow information by line of business. The information can give management a clear indication of the progress of the insurance company and the direction in which its business is going.

The most important determination, from both a regulatory and a corporate point of view, is the ability of the company, based on assets available, to meet its contractual obligations plus all other known liabilities and unforeseen contingencies.

Adjusted Statements

Most stock insurance companies are required to prepare two separate statements, one on a statutory basis for the state insurance departments and one on a generally accepted accounting principles (GAAP) basis for stockholders. Mutual companies are not required to prepare GAAP statements since they do not fall under Securities and Exchange Commission jurisdiction. Some, however, prepare them for internal purposes.

Statutory accounting is primarily concerned with solvency. It requires the use of conservative assumptions to ensure that the assets will be sufficient to meet all obligations. GAAP accounting, on the other hand, attempts to give a true picture of the insurance company's progress and its value as a continuing operation and is more along the lines of the reporting done by other businesses.

A significant difference between statutory and GAAP accounting is found in the treatment of acquisition costs—the expense of putting new business on the books. Statutory accounting does not permit the deferral of acquisition costs. These costs are charged as an expense against the income of the year in which they are incurred. In GAAP accounting, costs incurred in the production of new business are capitalized—that is, they are shown in the balance sheet as an asset and charged against premiums received during all the years the business is in force.

Some examples of specific acquisition expenses, part of which may be deferred in GAAP accounting, are:

- first-year commissions paid;
- the cost of medical examinations and inspection reports; and
- the cost of issuing policies and establishing records.

Industry Compliance Mechanisms

Compliance is a term used to refer to an insurer's activities devoted to complying with state and federal laws and regulations. The compliance process varies by company, but the following basic objectives of compliance are essentially the same for all companies:

- to stay abreast of the regulatory environment relevant to the company;
- to adapt to new statutes and regulations; and
- to respond to court decisions that have an impact on health insurance, such as changes in contract language, claim-handling procedures, and underwriting rules.

The Compliance Mechanism

Although the objectives may be the same, insurers have devised several approaches for achieving those objectives.

Compliance Division

Some insurance companies have a compliance division, which is assigned the responsibility of making sure the company is in compliance with state and/or federal laws and regulations. Typically, compliance divisions are found in the larger companies that operate in many states and have a varied product line and whose products are subject to a large degree of flexibility and variability.

Compliance Committee or Staff

Another approach is an internal compliance committee composed of representatives of the various operating areas involved in the sale, issuance, and maintenance of policies. The committee generally meets on a regular basis to discuss new statutes, regulations, or court decisions and to formulate a response.

Many insurers hire a person or staff of persons for the specific purpose of monitoring the regulatory environment, evaluating the relative importance of issues, formulating recommendations for action, and monitoring follow-through by the operation areas.

Legal Department

An insurance company's legal department also plays a role in monitoring or commenting on new regulations. In some companies, the regulatory monitoring function is performed by the legal department. In other companies, the legal department is called upon to render opinions only in those situations where the meaning of a statute or regulation is not clear.

Consequences of Noncompliance

All states impose penalties or fines for the issuance of policies in violation of state statutes. If a policy contains a prohibited provision or does not contain a required provision, its issuance may constitute a violation of the insurance laws requiring prior approval of all policy forms issued.

The level of penalty for such violations varies from state to state. Fines of $500 and more for each violation of the insurance laws are not uncommon. Moreover, each policy issued in violation of the insurance laws could constitute a separate violation. In group contracts, for example, some states will apply a fine, such as $500, to each person covered under each policy found to be in violation of state requirements.

Although such monetary penalties may become quite large, they are by no means the only price an insurance company may pay for noncompliance. Whenever an insurer is fined because of noncompliance in a given state, that information is broadcast to the other states, heightening the possibility that other states will scrutinize the insurer's filings more closely or initiate a market conduct exam.

State insurance departments are empowered to go beyond scrutiny and imposition of monetary penalties. Under extreme circumstances an insurance commissioner can revoke an insurer's license to do business in a state. Obviously, such license revocation could be economically devastating. Although the power of revocation is rarely used, its threat is nonetheless very real.

The Role of Industry Associations

National industry associations such as the Health Insurance Association of America (HIAA) play a vital role in the compliance process. These associations monitor legislation and regulation at the state and federal levels and publish bulletins on pending and enacted legislation and on proposed regulations. In addition, association contacts with state and federal regulators and knowledge of industrywide positions and trends can be helpful to individual and group insurers.

■ Emerging Trends

Failure of the Congress to enact wide-scale health care reform demonstrated that the nation is not ready for the federal government to assume responsibility for health care. The concern for health care reform, however, has not gone away. Issues such as access and affordability continue to be high on the list of priorities throughout the country.

A growing number of states are seeking Medicaid waivers from the federal government. This approach permits states to use health care networks and apply managed care concepts with the intent of better managing Medicaid costs.

States continue to pass legislation that is directed at various aspects of managed care. For example, any willing provider laws require managed care plans to accept any provider who is willing and able to meet the network's terms and conditions, and freedom of choice bills require managed care plans to allow enrollees to use the services of any health care provider they choose. Anti-managed care legislation could weaken a insurer's ability to control costs.

Since 1990, almost all states have enacted small group market reforms to improve access to health insurance, in particular for organizations or employees of organizations considered to be at high risk. An increasing

GOVERNMENT REGULATION

number of small employers with healthier insurance risks are seeking ways to avoid being subject to state small group laws. They are self-insuring or joining group association plans that are exempt from such laws. Conversely, HMO offerings to small groups are increasing.

Reforming the market for individually purchased insurance requires careful balancing between increased accessibility and affordability. If a broad guarantee issue requirement were imposed on individual health insurance, people who have existing medical problems would be more likely than those who are healthy to avail themselves of the opportunity to buy it. As a result, the average cost for people in the individual insurance pool would rise, driving up premiums for all those who already have coverage. It could make individual coverage unaffordable for many people. The impact of the "narrower" guarantee issue requirement (to "eligible" individuals who have recently lost their group insurance) is an open question and a matter of great speculation.

The distinctive characteristics of the group and individual insurance markets demand that regulatory and legislative reforms be tailored specifically to each.

■ Summary

Regulation of health insurance is essential to protect consumer interests and ensure insurance company solvency. It is important that regulation be thoughtful, balanced, and well-conceived if it is to truly serve the public.

■ Key Terms

Acquisition costs
Admitted assets
Advertising rules
Age Discrimination in Employment Act (ADEA)
Agents
Americans with Disabilities Act (ADA)
Annual financial statement
Antidiscrimination laws
Assets
Civilian Hospital and Medical Program of the Uniformed Services (CHAMPUS)

171

Compulsory nonoccupational disability benefits laws
Employee Retirement Income Security Act of 1974 (ERISA)
Extraterritorial laws
Fair Credit Reporting Act
Family and Medical Leave Act (FMLA)
Formal regulations
Generally accepted accounting principles (GAAP)
Health Maintenance Organization (HMO) Act
Informal regulations
Insurance commissioner
Insurance department
Liabilities
Licensing
Loss ratio
Major lines of insurance
Mandates
McCarran-Ferguson Act
Medicaid
Medicare
Medicare secondary payer (MSP)
NAIC model acts
National Association of Insurance Commissioners (NAIC)
Nonadmitted asset
Policy form
Policyholder complaints
Premium tax
Privacy of information
Readability
Reserves
Social Security
Solvency
State premium taxes
Statute
Statutory accounting
Surplus
Unfair trade practices act

Chapter 6

FRAUD AND ABUSE

173 *Introduction*
174 *Fraud versus Abuse*
174 *Provider Fraud and Abuse*
180 *Insured Fraud and Abuse*
185 *Frequency of Fraud*
187 *Detecting and Preventing Fraud*
192 *Legal Deterrents to Fraud*
194 *Insurance Industry Activities*
195 *Ethical Issues*
199 *Emerging Trends*
200 *Summary*
200 *Key Terms*

■ Introduction

Health care fraud and abuse are serious problems that have a significant effect on the private and public health care sectors. According to a May 1992 report to Congress by the General Accounting Office, health care fraud and abuse cost the nation as much as 10 percent of the money it spends on health care annually. For health insurers, fraudulent activities lead to increased premium costs no matter what type of coverage is involved—individual policies, group plans, or managed care.

Health insurance fraud can be perpetrated by medical providers, insureds, or a combination of both. In some cases, employees of insurance companies have conspired with providers or insureds to cheat their companies.

This chapter discusses types of health insurance fraud and abuse, who commits the acts, and ways in which these practices can be curbed or prevented. It also explores related ethical and moral issues that the insurance industry faces.

Fraud versus Abuse

The various schemes, questionable practices, speculation, and outright corrupt dealings described is this chapter fit into one of two categories: fraud or abuse. The distinction lies in intent. (Table 6.1)

Fraud

Health care fraud is subject to a number of statutory and common law definitions. Persons who commit fraud must be shown to possess knowledge that they know a representation they make is false. The National Health Care Anti-Fraud Association's (NHCAA) definition is as follows:

> Health care fraud is an intentional deception or misrepresentation that the individual or entity makes, knowing that the misrepresentation could result in some unauthorized benefit to the individual, or the entity or to some other party.

Abuse

Health care abuse is a commonly used term, but it has not been defined precisely. Insurers generally use it to mean any activity that unjustly robs the health care system but does not meet the statutory definition of fraud. The missing element to prove fraud often is intent. In health care abuse, an insured or provider may obtain money or health care services to which they are not entitled but without the requisite intent to deceive. Unless intent can be proven, no criminal or civil action is available to pursue the perpetrator.

Provider Fraud and Abuse

Most providers practice good medicine. Some providers, however, engage in fraudulent practices. Some of these fraudulent practices involve questionable medical practices, such as overutilization of services. Others involves billing schemes, such as inflating charges or billing for services that were not even given.

Table 6.1
Fraud versus Abuse

Examples more likely to involve fraud*
  billing for services not rendered;
  bogus foreign claims;
  altered bills or forms;
  overinsurance/insurance speculation;
  disability claims; and
  staged motor vehicle accidents.

Examples more likely to involve abuse*
  excessive diagnostic testing;
  overutilization of services;
  use of unproven treatment;
  unbundling;
  upcoding;
  inflated charges; and
  no out-of-pocket expense.

* These examples are discussed in the following section.

Questionable Medical Practices

The practice of medicine allows physicians and other providers leeway in deciding what type of treatments or services to offer their patients. Unfortunately, some medical providers go beyond their professional authority and overprescribe needed treatment. They cannot justify all of the services rendered as necessary when questioned. In some cases, the treatments prescribed are not yet proven. All of these actions fall under the heading of questionable medical practices.

Excessive Diagnostic Testing

Doctors and clinics have fairly standardized guidelines regarding which tests or treatments are appropriate for certain medical conditions. Testing beyond the norm should be justified case-by-case. If there are complications or unusual circumstances, additional testing may be warranted. Sometimes providers do more testing than is needed because of fear of malpractice claims against them if their patients assert that not enough was done to diagnose or treat the condition.

Some providers routinely order more testing than is absolutely necessary. These tests can generate more revenue for the provider. An example is a provider who requires customary first-visit charges of $2,000 for lab tests, X-rays, and physical exam for every new patient without regard to diagnosis or symptoms. Excessive diagnostic testing is viewed as questionable only when it has become a habit or standard on the part of a provider, not when isolated patients are overtested.

Insurance companies are beginning to question testing that appears excessive and are making arrangements with utilization review firms to evaluate the necessity, appropriateness, and efficiency of the use of medical services on a prospective, concurrent, or retrospective basis. Utilization review has served to reduce the prevalence of excessive diagnostic testing.

Overutilization of Services

Just as there are guidelines for routine testing, there also are reasonable standards for the utilization of treatments or medical services. Some providers have attempted to overutilize medical treatments with the sole intent of financial gain for themselves.

One of the more common overutilization problems involves length of stay in the hospital. Statistics are available for average lengths of stay for surgical and medical confinements. Providers who extend stays without good reason may have financial motives rather than medical needs in mind. There also are cases where physical therapy or chiropractic care are given much longer than necessary or beyond the optimal recovery period.

Insurers are beginning to monitor providers to be certain that only the most reasonable amount of care be given. Cases that go outside those bounds without adequate documentation should be questioned.

Unproven Treatment

For medical science to progress, new treatments and medicines must be developed and tested. There are well-established stages of clinical trials that are required before final approval is given by government authorities that the new treatments are safe and effective.

FRAUD AND ABUSE

Some remedies are not approved by regulatory authorities but are used and recommended by providers anyway. Unproven treatment and cures often are called alternative or experimental. Some can be harmful to patients and can lead to side effects or complications.

Unproven therapies have some common characteristics:

- They lack sufficient documentation about safety and effectiveness against specific diseases and conditions.
- They generally are not taught in U.S. medical schools.
- They are not reimbursable by health insurance benefit programs.

It is appropriate to deny payment if claims are made for these therapies; however, insurers are sometimes unable to identify treatments that are experimental and might inadvertently reimburse for the services. The funds paid for these extra costs can be considered a form of provider abuse since they represent payments that would not have been made if reasonable and proven medical care had been given.

Examples of unproven treatment include:

- acupuncture to treat depression and osteoarthritis;
- hypnosis for low back pain;
- biofeedback for diabetes;
- electric treatments for tumors; and
- imagery for asthma.

Billing Schemes

There are a set of practices attributed to providers called billing schemes. These involve situations in which providers manipulate or inflate charges to reflect amounts they do not deserve. In some cases, bills are submitted for services that were not even rendered. Sometimes these situations are honest mistakes made by physicians' office employees. In other cases, the billings are intentional and constitute blatant provider fraud.

177

There are billing guidelines and protocols for medical providers. Various agencies periodically publish and revise references that providers use for billing. One of the more common references for group and individual health insurance claims is the *Physicians' Current Procedural Terminology,* published by the American Medical Association. This reference lists five-digit codes for all common medical and surgical procedures and a detailed description of services covered under each code.

Unbundling of Charges

When a procedure consists of several components, there often is one comprehensive code and charge for it. This is called a global code to imply that it covers all parts of the service. Unbundling happens when a provider uses several limited codes and charges instead of the global code and fee. In these cases, the total fees for the unbundled codes can exceed the global fee.

A typical example involves surgery for a total abdominal hysterectomy. There is one code to cover all components of a total abdominal hysterectomy, yet some surgeons may unbundle the code and make separate charges for removal of ovaries, removal of fallopian tubes, removal of the appendix, and removal of the uterus. It is likely that the total fees for the unbundled procedures will exceed the global fee for a total abdominal hysterectomy.

Upcoding

When a provider codes and charges for a service that represents more treatment than was actually given, it is called upcoding. For example, a fee may be charged for a comprehensive physical exam when only a limited physical was performed. Another example is charging for an extensive office visit when only a routine visit was provided. Other cases involve charging for a comprehensive series of laboratory tests when only a few may have been performed.

In all the cases cited above, a larger fee is billed than should have been. This is contrary to billing and protocol guidelines.

Inflated Charges

Sometimes a surgeon does several procedures during one operative session. For example, a surgeon could do a liver biopsy, remove the gallbladder, and destroy adhesions through the same incision. Billing guidelines for providers dictate whether full or partial fees should be charged for each part of a surgery. When providers do not follow billing guidelines, the bill is referred to as inflated.

Other examples of inflated charges are billing for bilateral surgery for both sides of a foot or both feet, for example, when only a unilateral operation (on one side or one foot) was performed and charging for a full operating room setup and supplies when only specialized and lesser equipment was used.

No Out-of-Pocket Expenses

Some physicians, dentists, podiatrists, chiropractors, hospitals, diagnostic centers, and other providers advertise that they will waive deductibles and coinsurance payments if patients use their services. Some even offer free exams or consultations. A variation of no out-of-pocket expenses is when a physician's office tells a patient it will accept whatever insurance pays and the insured will have no balance to pay.

The practice of waiving deductibles and copayments is not usually appropriate, and some states require disclosure of the practice. It is, however, one of the more important red flags in the monitoring of fraudulent practices. Many of the providers employing this practice couple it with one or more of the methods described in this chapter. For example, to offset the costs of offering these incentives, some providers bill for services not rendered, give unnecessary or unproven tests or treatments, inflate fees, or otherwise charge for services not appropriate or necessary. Another concern for insurers is whether patients with insurance are charged higher fees than those who do not have insurance.

Billing for Services Not Rendered

Because of automation, many provider bills are generated in some type of standardized format. Common services are bundled together under a fee code. This approach was designed to enhance productivity and save time.

Occasionally, errors are made because of this standardization. A charge is assumed to be correct or appropriate, but when the case is examined more closely, certain components of the standard services were not provided.

Some providers bill for services not rendered, because they assume claim systems will not catch inappropriate or nonrendered services on standardized claim forms or billings. Newer claim systems can audit or screen bills to determine if charges are appropriate for the case. For example, a pregnancy test ordered and charged to a male's bill may go unnoticed unless the bill is screened.

Some providers package a large number of tests together under a diagnostic panel and charge a flat fee even if some tests were not administered. Only audits of other case records or screening of bills will catch these inappropriate or fraudulent billings.

■ Insured Fraud and Abuse

In 1992 the HIAA determined in a survey that 40 percent of all consumer fraud involved falsifying health insurance claims. There are numerous ways that insureds defraud insurance companies. Some of the more common techniques or schemes falling under the category of insured fraud are bogus claims filed abroad, disability claims, altered bills and forms, collecting from two insurance companies for the same services, and staged motor vehicle accidents.

Foreign Claims

It is estimated that as many as 80 percent of all claims filed by persons in foreign countries against U.S. insurers contain a fraudulent component. Some countries have become notorious for helping people to commit fraud and even have kits or classes for those wishing to file bogus claims. Fake forms, seals, and rubber stamp signatures are readily available in some countries. Forged birth and death certificates also are sold abroad.

Fraudulent foreign claims often have one or more of the following characteristics that set them apart from meritorious claims.

- Accidents or illnesses usually treated on an outpatient basis result in lengthy hospital confinements, especially in Africa or the Middle East, where it is often difficult to get medical records.
- Common diagnoses are hepatitis or motor vehicle accidents with injuries.
- Claim papers are written in a foreign language, and expenses are expressed in a foreign currency. Exchange rates are included with claim papers to expedite settlement.
- Bills are shown as already paid in cash.
- Bills have official-looking seals or stamps of medical providers.
- Bills may contain spelling errors of medical terms.

Disability Claims

Because the nature of disability is often subjective, claims for disability are among the most difficult to manage from an insurer standpoint. They are also the easiest for insureds to exaggerate or feign.

There are several reasons why disability income claims are prone to fraud:

- **Attitude of Entitlement.** Some insureds believe they are entitled to benefits because they have paid premiums for years. They feel the insurance company owes them something, and a fraudulent claim is seen as an easy way to collect repayment.
- **Economic Conditions**. Because of the restructuring going on in many companies, job layoffs are common. During periods of unemployment, people with disability income policies may resort to filing nonmeritorious claims to sustain income sources. There also are cases

of insureds filing claims while they are gainfully employed to supplement income because they are living beyond their economic means. More white-collar workers have engaged in these practices in recent years.

- **Policy Wording.** The definition of disability in many policies is not clear and may not adequately describe duties or aspects of work a claimant is unable to perform. An insured may press the issue, even hiring legal counsel to provide interpretations of definitions that are favorable to the insured. Policy writers are realizing that definitions must be written to include conditions of employment, alternative occupations, and types of duties a claimant cannot perform.

There are many tools available to assist insurers in detecting fraudulent disability claims. However, these resources are expensive and add to the overall cost of doing business for the insurers. Some ways to manage or uncover fraudulent disability claims are:

- surveillance activities performed by the insured or private vendor firms;
- individual medical exams conducted by unbiased physicians;
- disability case management services to fully assess needs and authenticity of the disability; and
- ongoing requests for medical records and reports from physicians involved with the claimant.

Fraudulent disability cases may require large outputs of dollars before enough documentation is obtained for the insurer to deny the claim or discontinue benefit payments in ongoing claims.

Altered Bills and Forms

Altering or forging bills or medical forms is a common form of fraud by insureds. Included in the scope of this activity are actual bills for services that are changed, generation of completely false original bills, or forging of signatures on bills or medical reports.

This type of claim fraud easily can go unnoticed because claim workers usually are more interested in assessing the validity of charges and determining if benefits are payable.

FRAUD AND ABUSE

There are some common indicators that alteration or fabrication may be present:

- the signature of the employee or provider is missing from forms;
- photocopies of bills or forms are submitted in lieu of originals;
- unassigned benefits;
- several type fonts on the same document;
- services performed are inconsistent with the diagnosis; and
- physicians' bills that show many visits, but no prescription bills or other related expenses are submitted.

Tools available to spot altered bills and forms are discussed later in this chapter.

Overinsurance/Insurance Speculation

Overinsurance occurs when a person is covered under two or more health care plans and may collect total benefits that exceed actual losses. Most overinsurance is in the medical care expense coverages, but disability coverages are becoming a matter of concern. Certain circumstances may lead to unintentional overinsurance:

- Both husband and wife are employed and eligible for group coverage and cover each other as a dependent.
- A person is employed in two jobs, both of which provide group health insurance coverage.
- A person covered by an employer may also have professional association group coverage.

These situations are effectively dealt with by coordination of benefits provisions.

When people buy insurance and do not report it to other carriers, insurance-for-profit schemes are likely to be occurring. Schemes where the intent is to accumulate policies in order to submit claims under each policy for the same loss, with the expectation of making a substantial profit are referred to as insurance speculation.

183

Insurance speculation often is discovered only after one or more companies notice other policies listed on bills or other records. Sometimes inquiries by a company to a provider may reveal claims filed with other insurers. In many cases, a speculator will have made significant profits before being detected.

A recent development involves persons purchasing many hospital supplement policies that pay benefits directly to the insured when confined. These claims rarely are questioned because benefits are paid to an insured for discretionary use and are not assigned or designed to reimburse providers.

Staged Motor Vehicle Accidents

Automobiles have been used with great success to commit health care fraud. Accidents have been staged, or they have been well described on paper without having actually occurred. Compensation from medical bills paid as a result of these accidents has contributed to the ongoing problem of fraud.

These cases usually involve corrupt attorneys and medical providers who work with individuals called cappers. The cappers refer patients or clients to the providers or attorneys for a fee. The attorneys often head up a ring of people to plot the staged accident. There are basically two types of staged accidents:

Actual accidents. Fraud ring participants use two cars to cause an unsuspecting third party to rear-end one of the vehicles. The car that is hit has several occupants, all of whom may claim injuries. In many cases, the unsuspecting third-party driver is ticketed for following too closely. Once insurance benefits are paid to those supposedly injured, those involved in setting up the case are reimbursed. This scheme is called swoop and squat.

Paper accidents. There are several types of paper accidents. Cars already damaged or that have been damaged intentionally are used. Two or more car owners may conspire to report an accident. One driver claims fault or liability. Persons who orchestrate these cases sell the case to a provider and/or an attorney who pursue insurance proceeds. Those involved in the paper accident are paid by the attorneys, who collect and keep insurance payouts. Soft tissue injuries are most commonly claimed since they do not show up on X-ray. Many clinics where these people supposedly are treated submit bills for services that were never rendered.

Almost all the funds to run these fraudulent operations come from insurance companies that unknowingly pay for false bills. The sums are paid into a trust fund in a lawyer's office and used to pay off those involved in the schemes.

There are some common characteristics of all of these claims, which may alert the insurance company to the questionable nature of the claim:

- Claims for medical insurance are filed first, before any auto damage claims.
- The same medical providers may be used for many auto accident claims.
- A common occurrence is a hit-and-run or one-car accident.
- Treatment is sought one or two days after an accident for subjective injuries such as neck or back sprain.
- Police reports are filed at stations rather than at the scene of the accident.
- If there is hospital confinement, stays exceed the norm for injuries received.

Frequency of Fraud

Recent surveys revealed that 17 percent of the public thinks it is acceptable to participate in fraud rings or to stay out of work longer than necessary after an illness or accident; and 8 percent say they know people who have falsified an insurance document.

The general public's view of defrauding insurance companies has remained surprisingly accepting in comparison with its view of other

Table 6.2

Fraud against Health Insurance Companies, by Type

	1989	1992
Provider fraud	93%	65%
Insured fraud	7%	35%

SOURCE: Health Insurance Association of America

crimes. This is in spite of efforts by state and federal agencies to publicize and shore up antifraud activities and publicize punishments or fines.

Perhaps the biggest deterrent to health care fraud is insurers' efforts to develop antifraud programs and units. There has been tremendous growth of this effort since 1985. According to the HIAA, insurance companies investigated 19,600 cases of fraud in 1989. By 1992, that number had risen to 26,755. The number of cases referred to law enforcement and resulting in criminal convictions also has increased significantly in recent years.

Provider fraud continues to be the more common type of fraud; insured fraud is a distant second. However, provider fraud is declining while insured fraud is increasing. This is due in large part to insurer efforts to detect provider fraud through software, systems, and more extensive auditing practices. (Table 6.2)

The two most common types of provider fraud are submitting fraudulent diagnoses or dates of treatment and billing for services not rendered. The most common insured fraud is falsifying claims.

Antifraud programs have recovered some overpayments made by insurers. More importantly, they have prevented payments from being made that might otherwise have been processed. HIAA surveys estimate a net savings from antifraud activities of $100 million in 1992. Antifraud efforts should continue to result in significant savings, given the large amount of payout still being made under fraudulent circumstances.

FRAUD AND ABUSE

■ Detecting and Preventing Fraud

Detecting fraud requires the joint efforts of insurers and insureds as well as the cooperation of medical providers. Insurers have strengthened the training of their employees on the issues of fraud. Insureds have become more aware of fraudulent schemes and practices through insurer and governmental education and awareness programs.

Insurers have established specific programs, such as altered bill detection, medical records review, and fraud units, to help detect and discourage fraudulent practices. There also are outside services that insurers use to help in fraud detection and prevention efforts.

Insurer Efforts

Insurance companies have come to realize that they must take the initiative to curb fraud. Certain practices or procedures have become almost standard as a way for insurers to deal with suspected fraud. A few of the more common claim investigative methods are described below.

Altered Bill Detection

It is easy to identify some bills that have been altered. Those having typewriter strikeovers, liquid paper corrections, different colored inks, or nonmatching font styles are obvious. However, some alterations are performed by people who are very proficient in this practice. They may be part of a ring functioning to defraud insurance companies and may be paid for their services.

Unless a claim person is astute and has the time to examine every bill received, some of these alterations go unnoticed. A cost-benefit decision must be made by the insurers as to how much attention can be paid to this activity.

Equipment is available that may help to evaluate suspected altered bills. One machine used by the federal government and some insurance companies is a video spectral comparator. This machine uses various wavelengths of light to see through papers and inks to determine if alterations are present. The original document must be analyzed; photocopies will not show any alterations.

Medical Records Review

If a claims person questions whether treatment was given at all or if services rendered were fewer than billed, the best place to begin an investigative process is with the medical records. These records usually will reveal the nature, type, and duration of treatment prescribed or administered.

Insurers can question providers if medical records do not match billed services. In many cases, providers will either correct bills or withdraw claims if the insurer points out the inconsistencies.

Other Insurance Records

For cases where insurance speculation is suspected, insurance companies obtain records from other insurers to determine the extent of the overinsurance. Valid authorizations are needed to request and obtain this information.

Other insurance often first becomes known when an insurance company sees a notation on a bill or records submitted from a provider. Auto accident claims also tend to be revealed if other medical carriers are involved. Once there is a hint of other coverage, insurers will more readily exchange important and relevant information to determine if there are other than above-board reasons for multiple coverage.

General Insurer Initiatives

Insurance companies have become more proactive in their efforts to deter fraud in health insurance claims. Some of their more generalized efforts include establishing fraud units, training employees about fraud, auditing claims, and law enforcement.

Special investigative unit. Many insurers have a special investigative unit within their companies. This unit is their principal mechanism for

FRAUD AND ABUSE

the investigation of suspicious claims. The staff in a special investigative unit obtain necessary records, make appropriate calls, and coordinate with federal and state agencies to uncover nonmeritorious claims and perpetrators of fraud.

Fraud detection training. Companies have added training on health claim fraud to their regular continuing education programs for claim workers in order to broaden the scope of the claim workers' knowledge of fraud schemes or practices. Employees can incorporate this information into their daily claim adjudication duties.

Preauditing and postauditing claims. Many insurers conduct regular audits on representative samples of their claims. Some companies find it beneficial to screen claims as they are received for red flags that may indicate one of the fraudulent practices described in this chapter. Postaudits may reveal missed signs of defrauding activity that can be later used as training cases to illustrate clues to be alert to in future claim handling. In addition, postaudits may allow action to be initiated to recover funds paid through fraudulent misrepresentation.

Reporting to law enforcement agencies. In recent years insurers have increased the number of fraud cases they report to law enforcement agencies. The Federal Bureau of Investigation (FBI) and other federal and state governmental agencies have become more active in prosecuting individual perpetrators of fraud. In addition, several insurance companies have supported the formation of independent bureaus that specialize in the dissemination and collection of information on fraudulent activity. Examples include the NHCAA and the National Insurance Crime Bureau (NICB).

Vendor Efforts

It is not always economically feasible for health insurance companies to develop specialized personnel or units to do all types of investigative fraud work. There are many different kinds of vendors that insurers use for help with suspected fraud cases.

189

Surveillance Vendors

While some insurers conduct their own surveillance activities, vendors specializing in this service provide a full range of surveillance. The investigator may simply observe and track the activities of a person thought to be engaged in fraud. For example, a diary of activities may help if the insured claims to have been confined or at a doctor's office when in fact the investigator noted otherwise.

Electronic surveillance involves the use of equipment such as a video recorder to record information for later use. For example, insureds claiming disability have been videotaped or photographed engaging in strenuous activities; such documentation aids the insurer in building a case to terminate benefits.

Foreign Investigators

Because a high percentage of foreign claims turns out to be fraudulent, insurance companies tend to investigate these claims closely. Most insurers do not have foreign offices and must rely on special foreign investigative vendors that specialize in this service. Many of these vendors are U.S. based, with investigators available in foreign countries.

Questions that foreign investigators often focus on are:

- Do the hospitals and doctors named in the claim actually exist?
- Are bills authentic?
- Are the providers appropriately licensed?
- If an auto accident is involved, are police records available and authentic?

Foreign investigations may take weeks or months to complete, especially if the work involves medical facilities in remote locations.

Computer Support Databases

Access to public information and data continues to grow both in volume and ease. Database providers have made access to needed data simple, quick, and accurate. Insurers have been quick to take advantage of

FRAUD AND ABUSE

these services in conjunction with the investigation of suspected fraudulent claims. Information is also available on CD-ROM.

Many databases provide index or tip information only. Investigators will need to physically review actual files or documents to develop complete information.

The following are a few examples of databases available to insurers to aid in the development of fraudulent cases.

- The National Insurance Crime Bureau (NICB), the Property Insurance Loss Register (PILR), and the Central Index Bureau (CIB) contain information relevant to insurance investigators. In addition to insurance policy numbers, claim history, and other identifying information, these databases may note past convictions or suspicion of fraudulent activity.
- The National Mover's Index provides access to three years of U.S. postal records and addresses on any one person.
- The Department of Motor Vehicles (DMV) may be useful in staged accident fraud cases to determine past history of drivers or passengers.
- The Index System is a database of claim and policy information on mostly property insurance. Health insurers may benefit from identifying other insurance policies or claims for accidents where bodily injuries occurred that resulted in the use of health benefits.

In addition, federal court records, state marriage and death records, and voter registration records are public and could be searched by insurers for needed information.

Software programs have been specifically designed to audit claims falling under the category of unbundling schemes. Vendors have worked in conjunction with medical experts and agencies to program appropriate billing codes into software packages. Claim persons can enter billings into this program to determine if guidelines have been followed. In cases where they have not, the insurer may deny payment or challenge a provider to correctly rebill for services rendered.

Table 6.3
Federal Government Fraud Control, by Agency

Federal government agency	Area of fraud control
Office of Inspector General, Department of Health and Human Services	Medicare and Medicaid
Office of Inspector General, Department of Veterans Affairs	Veterans' affairs fraud
Office of Inspector General, Office of Personnel Management	Federal employee health care
Office of Crime Enforcement, Food and Drug Administration	Food, Drug, and Cosmetic Act fraud
U.S. Postal Inspection Service	Private health insurance fraud

■ Legal Deterrents to Fraud

The federal government and state governments work closely with insurance companies to deter fraud of all types. The joint efforts of health insurers working with government has led to an effective reduction of fraudulent activity. While the problems are far from solved, progress is encouraging.

Federal Agencies

The FBI serves as an umbrella over many small federal agencies responsible for combating fraud in health care. (Table 6.3) The FBI is the only federal agency with full authority to investigate all health care fraud offenses. The agency's authority includes victims of crimes (including private insurance companies) as well as large business entities. The FBI has joint authority with many other agencies in conducting health care fraud investigations.

There are many possible penalties that can be imposed if a party is found guilty of committing health care fraud. Monetary fines, prison sentences, restitution of funds, and revocation of professional licenses are a few. The Department of Health and Human Services publishes a list of sanctions taken against providers that commit Medicare or Medicaid fraud. This public document is readily available to insurance companies.

New Federal Law

In August 1996, the HIPAA of 1996 (Public Law 104-191), also known as the Kassebaum-Kennedy Health Insurance Reform Legislation, was enacted. The Act's enactment demonstrated that Congress reached agreement on an extensive new set of health care anti-fraud provisions, including the establishment of a new federal crime of health care fraud for both public and private health plans.

A summary of the key anti-fraud provisions of Public Law 104-191 is outlined below.

- Establishes a program to coordinate federal, state, and local law enforcement programs to control fraud in health plans.
- Establishes a national health care fraud and abuse data collection program for reporting final adverse actions against health care providers, suppliers, or practitioners. Each government agency and health plan is required to report any final adverse action (not including settlements in which no findings of liability have been made) taken against a health care provider, supplier, or practitioner.
- Amends the U.S. Code by adding the federal offense of health care fraud in any health care benefit program, which includes public and private plans.

State Agencies

The NAIC led the movement to create fraud bureaus or agencies in states. These bureaus serve as a reporting point for insurance companies about information on suspicious claims. Immunity is granted to insurers against lawsuits for libel or slander if they choose to report suspicious individuals.

State fraud bureaus investigate cases of potential fraud and involve local and federal authorities when needed. Not all states have fraud bureaus, but the number that do is growing. Those bureaus in existence have assisted with antifraud training and education of law enforcement agencies, individual insurance claim personnel, members of the media, judges, and prosecutors.

The NAIC also has been active in drafting model legislation intended to assist in the efforts against fraud. This legislation is considered by both the federal government and states when civil and criminal penalties are reviewed and modified for fraudulent acts.

State and local law enforcement agencies are involved in antifraud activities through their frequent assistance to federal and state agencies. In addition, local agencies have become more involved in the prevention of fraudulent activity by conducting programs that educate the public about insurance fraud. Agencies use seminars, media advertisements, and personal testimonials in those efforts.

■ Insurance Industry Activities

Because the insurance industry bears the brunt of insurance fraud by paying benefits not owed, groups of insurers have banded together to work on this problem. They also have enlisted the support and assistance of associations that support the insurance industry in day-to-day matters. Three of the most prominent industry associations supporting efforts to detect and prevent health care fraud and abuse are the National Health Care Anti-Fraud Association, the Health Insurance Association of America, and the International Claim Association.

National Health Care Anti-Fraud Association (NHCAA)

The NHCAA was founded in 1985 by several private health insurers and federal and state law enforcement officials. It is an issue-based organization of private and public sector individuals and organizations and focuses on the detection, investigation, and prosecution of health care fraud.

The NHCAA conducts national seminars on the most effective methods of combating health care fraud. Special emphasis is placed on education and detection, investigation, prosecution, and prevention of fraud. Training workshops are featured at the NHCAA's annual meeting.

An information-sharing network is available to members to aid in the investigation of fraud cases. Assistance to law enforcement agencies in their investigation and prosecution of health care fraud also is provided.

Health Insurance Association of America (HIAA)

The HIAA has several proactive efforts on fraud and abuse underway with insurance companies. Position papers representing the association's and the industry's views on fraud have been written and distributed by HIAA staff.

The HIAA's Joint Subcommittee on Fraud and Abuse develops, implements, and oversees the association's programs on health insurance fraud and abuse. Specifically, the committee's goals are to:

- increase public awareness of fraud and abuse through educational programs;
- use lobbying resources to strengthen laws pertaining to health care fraud; and
- encourage stronger fraud and abuse detection and prevention activities by state medical and professional boards.

The HIAA also serves on various federal task forces studying health care abuse and fraud and testifies at congressional hearings about issues and legislation affecting health care fraud efforts. The HIAA Insurance Education curriculum includes a course on health care fraud.

International Claim Association (ICA)

The ICA's Fraud and Claim Abuse Committee was established to educate, inform, and encourage insurers to step up antifraud efforts. The ICA holds an annual conference where fraud issues are discussed and debated. Association publications distributed by the ICA feature original articles on fraud and abuse written by employees of member companies of the organization.

■ Ethical Issues

Outside the realm of true fraudulent acts or purposeful abuse on the part of medical providers or insureds, a whole body of related issues has emerged that falls under the heading of ethical issues. These issues focus on the responsibilities of insurers, providers, and insureds and their decisions about how health care is covered, provided, or used. The impact of these ethical practices can have a significant effect on costs and coverage issues for insurers.

Insurer Responsibilities

Insurers have a responsibility to fully explain and represent coverages they offer. Advertisements, brochures, and verbal explanations must honestly and accurately reflect which services or charges are covered and which ones are not.

Misleading Marketing

There are cases where insurers have been guilty of misleading clients into believing products or policies provide benefits that they do not. In other cases, products have been sold with extremely complex and difficult language that an average person cannot interpret or understand. These practices have led to public relations concerns for insurance companies.

Covering Experimental Treatments

Insurers have been criticized for some positions they have taken regarding experimental yet potentially life-saving procedures. Medicine and treatments are under development or being tested for years before they are approved by governmental authorities for use among the general population. Until that time, these procedures and therapies are commonly termed experimental. All organ transplants at one time were considered experimental. Many organ transplants now are considered routine and are covered by insurance companies.

Insurers have long held the belief that they should not pay for experimental treatments. In most cases, these treatments are extremely expensive, although costs may decline after the treatment is out of the research stage. Premium rates are not structured to factor in payments for experimental treatments.

In spite of their stance and reasoning, insurers have been sued because they have denied coverage for experimental treatment. Patients have stated that such a treatment is their last or only chance, or they have pointed to cases where a patient has lived only because of a certain treatment.

Insurance companies must walk a fine line between paying for treatment a patient could not otherwise afford and holding fast to what they feel is an ethical responsibility to all policyholders to control costs and pay for proven treatment only. As medical science creates more alternative treatments, these issues will continue to draw publicity and opposing opinions.

Nonrenewal of Coverage

Some individual health insurance policies are written so that the company may choose not to renew the coverage for certain stated reasons. One of these reasons could be the continuing deterioration of an insured's health.

This renewal provision has caused great controversy and is being used less and less by insurance companies. Unless a claimant is doing something to purposefully contribute to his or her continuing health deterioration, insurers are reluctant to cancel coverage. Canceling coverage is viewed as ethically irresponsible on the part of insurance companies. Claimants feel they have no real control over the state of their personal health and should not be penalized for circumstances they cannot control.

Provider Responsibilities

Ethical issues for providers involve the level of care delivered in a managed care setting, the use of life-prolonging technologies, and the practice of defensive medicine.

Managed Care Developments

In some managed care arrangements, providers receive a set sum to cover all services to be provided per patient over a period of time. They do not receive more money if more services are required. Because of these arrangements, certain types of unethical practices unique to the system have emerged, including:

- denying patients access to services to increase profits;
- limiting office hours;
- not making outside referrals in order to keep the dollars in the managed care group; and
- inflating the number of office visits or treatment dates to negotiate higher capitation rates.

Quality of Life

Medical technology has advanced to the stage where people with debilitating health conditions can be kept alive longer. The ethical question is whether the quality of their life is compromised. Of particular concern are cases where life is prolonged for a terminally ill patient with an extremely poor quality of life. Providers traditionally have seen it as their role to prolong life to its natural end. However, many people have signed living wills that clearly state their wishes with regard to the level of care they are to receive—or not receive—if they are not expected to survive. In spite of these legal documents, some providers still have a difficult time following wishes of patients. This ethical dilemma is yet another issue that involves the spending of health care dollars in ways that some would argue is abusive or wasteful.

Malpractice

The United States is a litigious society, and patients are suing medical providers for malpractice in increasing numbers. Some cases involve allegations that not enough care was given or not enough tests were administered to identify completely a diagnosis or condition. Providers have become sensitized to these suits and now must carefully consider the extent and nature of treatment they recommend. Many doctors have resorted to overtesting to protect themselves if malpractice allegations are made. This is practice is called defensive medicine. The ethical dilemma is whether the dollars spent to protect providers can be justified. Are these dollars being spent wisely? Could they be better spent on other patients?

These questions are not answered easily. Trends in society, along with refined guidelines for appropriate care on the part of providers, may ease the problem.

Insured Responsibilities

The ethical issues facing insureds largely focus on how they utilize the health care system. For example, some people go to the doctor for every minor ailment or illness. Others, meanwhile, do not seek medical attention even when they should, and they may suffer illnesses that could have been prevented or minimized.

The place where treatment is sought also is a fundamental factor in an insured's contribution to managing expenses. Some people seek treatment at a hospital emergency room for very minor medical problems when they could just as well be treated at a less-costly specialized outpatient facility.

Insureds also must be assertive and question treatment recommendations if they feel that certain tests or therapies are unnecessary. They should be advocates for themselves. Even more importantly, insureds should question billings if they suspect errors or outright fraud.

There are cases where an insurance company erroneously makes overpayments to an insured person. The patient has an ethical and moral responsibility to refund such overpayments to the insurance company.

■ Emerging Trends

Health insurance claims traditionally were processed manually, which gave claim examiners the opportunity to scrutinize paper claims to detect erasures, white-outs, or other modifications of forms that can be rudimentary attempts at perpetrating fraud. As the health insurance industry moves from submitting claims on paper to submitting claims electronically, insurers are losing the capability to detect fraud by reviewing paper claims.

Insurers and other third-party payers need increasingly sophisticated automated systems to detect and investigate fraud. Such systems should be able to accommodate substantial amounts of data, conduct extensive database searches, and address complex, subtle, and costly fraud schemes. Considering the large dollar amounts at risk, it is critical that automated fraud-detection tools be used widely by the industry.

There are many players involved in the process of fraud detection. Insurers are strengthening their resistance to paying for unreasonable or questionable treatment. The government is increasing its efforts to uncover and prosecute those who commit fraudulent acts. Provider groups are monitoring their practices more diligently. And more vendors are entering the market to assist with investigations of abuse and fraud in billings.

■ Summary

Health care fraud is very costly to the insurance industry, and ultimately to the consumer. Fraudulent acts include outright fraud as well as abuses of the health care system. At the same time that methods of committing fraud have become more creative, the methods used to monitor and control questionable practices have become more sophisticated. It appears that the battle is being won in terms of discouraging providers and insureds from committing fraudulent acts on a health claim. However, only vigilant enforcement and cooperation of insurers, governmental agencies, and medical providers will ensure the continuing reduction of these illegal practices.

■ Key Terms

Abuse	Billing schemes	Disability claims
Altered bills	Central Index Bureau (CIB)	Excessive diagnostic testing
Alternative therapies		

Experimental treatment
Federal Bureau of Investigation (FBI)
Foreign claims
Fraud
Fraud detection training
Health insurance
Health Insurance Association of America (HIAA)
Health insurance fraud and abuse
Index System
Inflated charges
Insured fraud and abuse
International Claim Association (ICA)
Medical records review
National Association of Insurance Commissioners (NAIC)
National Health Care Anti-Fraud Association (NHCAA)
National Insurance Crime Bureau (NICB)
No out-of-pocket expense
Overinsurance/insurance speculation
Overutilization of services
Property Insurance Loss Register (PILR)
Provider fraud and abuse
Questionable medical practices
Special investigative units
Staged motor vehicle accidents
Surveillance
Unbundling of charges
Unproven treatment
Upcoding

Appendix A
UNFAIR LIFE, ACCIDENT AND HEALTH CLAIMS SETTLEMENT PRACTICES MODEL REGULATION

(Model Regulation Service—July 1991)

From the NAIC *Model Laws, Regulations and Guidelines.* Reprinted with the permission of the National Association of Insurance Commissioners.

Table of Contents

Section 1.	Authority
Section 2.	Purpose
Section 3.	Definitions
Section 4.	Claims Practices
Section 5.	File and Record Documentation

Section 1.   Authority

This regulation is adopted under the authority of the Unfair Claims Settlement Practices Act.

Section 2.   Purpose

The purpose of this regulation is to set forth minimum standards for the investigation and disposition of life, accident and health claims arising under policies or certificates issued pursuant to State law. It is not intended to cover claims involving workers' compensation insurance. The various provisions of this regulation are intended to define procedures and practices which constitute unfair claims practices. Nothing herein shall be construed to create or imply a private cause of action for violation of this regulation. This is merely a clarification of original intent and does not indicate of any change of position.

Drafting Note: Any jurisdiction choosing to provide for a private cause of action should consider a different statutory scheme. This regulation is inherently inconsistent with a private cause of action. The NAIC has separately promulgated an Unfair Property/Casualty Claims Settlement Practices Model Regulation.

Section 3.   Definitions

All definitions contained in the Unfair Claims Settlement Practices Act (or Unfair Trade Practices Model Act) are hereby incorporated by reference. As otherwise used in this regulation:

    A. "Agent" means any individual, corporation, association, partnership or other legal entity authorized to represent an insurer with respect to a claim;

    B. "Beneficiary" means the party entitled to receive the proceeds or benefits occurring under the policy in lieu of the insured;

    C. "Claim file" means any retrievable electronic file, paper file or combination of both;

D. "Claimant" means an insured, the beneficiary or legal representative of the insured, including a member of the insured's immediate family designated by the insured, making a claim under a policy;

E. "Days" means calendar days;

F. "Documentation" includes, but is not limited to, all pertinent communications, transactions, notes, work papers, claim forms, bills and explanation of benefits forms relative to the claim;

G. "Investigation" means all activities of an insurer directly or indirectly related to the determination of liabilities under coverages afforded by an insurance policy or insurance contract;

H. "Limited insurance representative" means an individual, partnership or corporation who is authorized by the Commissioner to solicit or negotiate certificates or policies for a particular line of insurance which the Commissioner may by regulation deem essential for the transaction of business in this State and which does not require the professional competency demanded for an insurance agent's or insurance broker's license.

I. "Notification of claim" means any notification, whether in writing or other means acceptable under the terms of an insurance policy to an insurer or its agent, by a claimant, which reasonably apprises the insurer of the facts pertinent to a claim;

J. "Proof of loss" means written proofs, such as claim forms, medical bills, medical authorizations or other reasonable evidence of the claim that is ordinarily required of all insureds or beneficiaries submitting the claims;

K. "Reasonable explanation" means information sufficient to enable the insured or beneficiary to compare the allowable benefits with policy provisions and determine whether proper payment has been made;

L. "Written communications" includes all correspondence, regardless of source or type, that is materially related to the handling of the claim.

Section 4. Claims Practices

A. Every insurer, upon receiving due notification of a claim shall, within fifteen (15) days of the notification, provide necessary claim forms, instructions and reasonable assistance so the insured can properly comply with company requirements for filing a claim.

B. Upon receipt of proof of loss from a claimant, the insurer shall begin any necessary investigation of the claim within fifteen (15) days.

C. The insurer's standards for claims processing shall be such that notice of claim or proof of loss submitted against one policy issued by that insurer shall fulfill the insured's obligation under any and all similar policies issued by that insurer and specifically identified by the insured to the insurer to the same degree that the same form would be required under any similar policy. If additional information is required to fulfill the insured's obligation under similar policies, the insurer may request the additional information. When it is apparent to the insurer that additional benefits would be payable under an insured's policy upon additional proofs of loss, the insurer shall communicate to and cooperate with the insured in determining the extent of the insurer's additional liability.

D. The insurer shall affirm or deny liability on claims within a reasonable time and shall offer payment within thirty (30) days of affirmation of liability if the amount of the claim is determined and not in dispute. If portion(s) of the claim are in dispute, the insurer shall tender payment for those portions that are not disputed within thirty (30) days.

E. With each claim payment, the insurer shall provide to the insured an Explanation of Benefits that shall include the name of the provider or services covered, dates of service, and a reasonable explanation of the computation of benefits.

APPENDIX A

F. An insurer may not impose a penalty upon any insured for noncompliance with insurer requirements for precertification unless such penalty is specifically and clearly set forth in the policy.

G. If a claim remains unresolved for thirty (30) days from the date proof of loss is received, the insurer shall provide the insured or, when applicable, the insured's beneficiary, with a reasonable written explanation for the delay. In credit, mortgage and assigned accident/health claims, the notice shall be provided to the debtor/insured or medical provider in addition to the insured. If the investigation remains incomplete, the insurer shall, forty-five (45) days from the date of initial notification and every forty-five (45) days thereafter, send to the claimant a letter setting forth the reasons additional time is needed for investigation.

H. The insurer shall acknowledge and respond within fifteen (15) days to any written communications relating to a pending claim.

I. When a claim is denied, written notice of denial shall be sent to the claimant within fifteen (15) days of the determination. The insurer shall reference the policy provision, condition or exclusion upon which the denial is based.

J. No insurer shall deny a claim upon information obtained in a telephone conversation or personal interview with any source unless the telephone conversation or personal interview is documented in the claim file.

K. Insurers offering cash settlements of first party long-term disability income claims, except in cases where there is a bona fide dispute as to the coverage for, or amount of, the disability, shall develop a present value calculation of future benefits (with probability corrections for mortality and morbidity) utilizing contingencies such as mortality, morbidity, and interest rate assumptions, etc. appropriate to the risk. A copy of the amount so calculated shall be given to the insured and signed by him/her at the time a settlement is entered into.

L. No insurer shall indicate to a first party claimant on a payment draft, check or in any accompanying letter that said payment is "final" or "a release" of any claim unless the policy limit has been paid or there has been a compromise settlement agreed to by the first party claimant and the insurer as to coverage and amount payable under the policy.

M. No insurer shall withhold any portion of any benefit payable as a result of a claim on the basis that the sum withheld is an adjustment or correction for an overpayment made on a prior claim arising under the same policy unless:

(1) The insurer has in its files clear, documented evidence of an overpayment and written authorization from the insured permitting such withholding procedure, or

(2) The insurer has in its files clear, documented evidence that:

(a) The overpayment was clearly erroneous under the provisions of the policy and if the overpayment is not the subject of a reasonable dispute as to facts.

(b) The error that resulted in the payment is not a mistake of the law.

(c) The insurer has notified the insured within six (6) months of the date of the error, except that in instances of error prompted by representations or nondisclosures of claimants or third parties, the insurer notified the insured within fifteen (15) days after the date the evidence of discovery of such error is included in its file. For the purpose of this rule, the date of the error shall be the day on which the draft for benefits is issued.

(d) Such notice stated clearly the nature of the error and the amount of the overpayment.

N. If, after an insurer rejects a claim, the claimant objects to such rejection, the insurer shall notify the claimant in writing that he/she may have the matter reviewed by the [insert state] Department of Insurance, [insert department address and telephone number].

Section 5. File and Record Documentation

Each insurer's claim files for policies or certificates are subject to examination by the Commissioner of Insurance or by his/her duly appointed designees. To aid in such examination:

A. The insurer shall maintain claim data that are accessible and retrievable for examination. An insurer shall be able to provide the claim number, line of coverage, date of loss and date of payment of the claim, date of denial or date closed without payment. This data shall be available for all open and closed files for the current year and the two (2) preceding years.

B. Detailed documentation shall be contained in each claim file in order to permit reconstruction of the insurer's activities relative to each claim.

C. Each document within the claim file shall be noted as to date received, date processed or date mailed.

D. For those insurers that do not maintain hard copy files, claim files must be accessible from Cathode Ray Tube (CRT) or micrographics and be capable of duplication to hard copy.

Drafting Note: States are encouraged to recognize the efficiencies of electronic or other type "paperless" file systems and are encouraged to accommodate all reasonable application of such systems.

Legislative History (all references are to the Proceedings of the NAIC).

1990 Proc. II 7, 13-14, 160, 185-187 (adopted).
1991 Proc. I 9, 16, 192-193, 212-214 (amended and reprinted).

This document replaces a model named "Unfair Claims Settlement Practices Model Regulation."

1976 Proc. II 15, 17 342, 365, 367-370 (adopted).
1980 Proc. II 22, 26, 906, 930, 936 (amended).
1981 Proc. I 47, 51, 255, 258, 263 (amended).

Appendix B
UNFAIR TRADE PRACTICES ACT

(Model Regulation Service—January 1993)

From the NAIC *Model Laws, Regulations and Guidelines.* Reprinted with the permission of the National Association of Insurance Commissioners.

Table of Contents

Section 1.	Purpose
Section 2.	Definitions
Section 3.	Unfair Trade Practices Prohibited
Section 4.	Unfair Trade Practices Defined
Section 5.	Favored Agent or Insurer; Coercion of Debtors
Section 6.	Power of Commissioner
Section 7.	Hearings, Witnesses, Appearances, Production of Books, and Service of Process
Section 8.	Cease and Desist and Penalty Orders
Section 9.	Judicial Review of Orders
Section 10.	Judicial Review by Intervenor
Section 11.	Penalty for Violation of Cease and Desist Orders
Section 12.	Regulations
Section 13.	Provisions of Act Additional to Existing Law
Section 14.	Immunity from Prosecution
Section 15.	Separability Provision

Prefatory Note: By adopting amendments to this model act in June 1990, the NAIC separated provisions dealing with unfair claims settlement into a newly adopted Unfair Claims Settlement Practices Model Act, to make clearer distinction between general unfair trade practices and more specific unfair claim settlement issues and to focus on market conduct practices and market conduct regulation. By doing so, the NAIC is not recommending that states repeal existing acts, but states may modify them for the purpose of capturing the substantive changes. However, for those states wishing to completely rewrite their comprehensive approach to unfair claims practices, this separation of unfair claims from unfair trade practices is recommended.

Section 1. Purpose

The purpose of this Act is to regulate trade practices in the business of insurance in accordance with the intent of Congress as expressed in the Act of Congress of March 9, 1945 (Public Law 15, 79th Congress), by defining, or providing for the determination of, all such practices in this state that constitute unfair methods of competition or unfair or deceptive acts or practices and by prohibiting the trade practices so defined or determined. Nothing herein shall be construed to create or imply a private cause of action for a violation of this Act.

Section 2. Definitions

When used in this Act:

    A. "Commissioner" means the commissioner of insurance of this state.

Drafting Note: Insert the appropriate term for the chief insurance regulatory official wherever the term "commissioner" appears.

B. "Insured" means the party named on a policy or certificate as the individual with legal rights to the benefits provided by such policy.

C. "Insurer" means any person, reciprocal exchange, interinsurer, Lloyds insurer, fraternal benefit society, and any other legal entity engaged in the business of insurance, including agents, brokers, adjusters and third-party administrators. Insurer shall also mean medical service plans, hospital service plans, health maintenance organizations, prepaid limited health care service plans, dental, optometric and other similar health service plans as defined in Sections [insert applicable section]. For purposes of this Act, these foregoing entities shall be deemed to be engaged in the business of insurance.

Drafting Note: Each state may wish to consider the advisability of defining "insurance" for purposes of this Act if its present insurance code is not satisfactory in this regard. In some cases a cross reference will be sufficient.

D. "Person" means any natural or artificial entity, including but not limited to, individuals, partnerships, associations, trusts or corporations.

E. "Policy" or "certificate" means any contract of insurance, indemnity, medical, health or hospital service, suretyship, or annuity issued, proposed for issuance, or intended for issuance by any insurer.

F. "Producer" means a person who solicits, negotiates, effects, procures, delivers, renews, continues or binds policies of insurance for risks residing, located or to be performed in this state.

Section 3.   Unfair Trade Practices Prohibited

It is an unfair trade practice for any insurer to commit any practice defined in Section 4 of this Act if:

A. It is committed flagrantly and in conscious disregard of this Act or of any rules promulgated hereunder; or

B. It has been committed with such frequency to indicate a general business practice to engage in that type of conduct.

Section 4.   Unfair Trade Practices Defined

Any of the following practices, if committed in violation of Section 3, are hereby defined as unfair trade practices in the business of insurance:

A. Misrepresentations and False Advertising of Insurance Policies. Making, issuing, circulating, or causing to be made, issued or circulated, any estimate, illustration, circular or statement, sales presentation, omission or comparison that:

(1) Misrepresents the benefits, advantages, conditions or terms of any policy; or

(2) Misrepresents the dividends or share of the surplus to be received on any policy; or

(3) Makes a false or misleading statement as to the dividends or share of surplus previously paid on any policy; or

(4) Is misleading or is a misrepresentation as to the financial condition of any insurer, or as to the legal reserve system upon which any life insurer operates; or

(5) Uses any name or title of any policy or class of policies misrepresenting the true nature thereof; or

(6) Is a misrepresentation, including any intentional misquote of premium rate, for the purpose of inducing or tending to induce the purchase, lapse, forfeiture, exchange, conversion or surrender of any policy; or

(7) Is a misrepresentation for the purpose of effecting a pledge or assignment of or effecting a loan against any policy; or

(8) Misrepresents any policy as being shares of stock.

B. False Information and Advertising Generally. Making, publishing, disseminating, circulating or placing before the public, or causing, directly or indirectly to be made, published, disseminated, circulated, or placed before the public, in a newspaper, magazine or other publication, or in the form of a notice, circular, pamphlet, letter or poster, or over any radio or television station, or in any other way, an advertisement, announcement or statement containing any assertion, representation or statement with respect to the business of insurance or with respect to any insurer in the conduct of its insurance business, which is untrue, deceptive or misleading.

C. Defamation. Making, publishing, disseminating, or circulating, directly or indirectly, or aiding, abetting or encouraging the making, publishing, disseminating or circulating of any oral or written statement or any pamphlet, circular, article or literature which is false, or maliciously critical of or derogatory to the financial condition of any insurer, and which is calculated to injure such insurer.

D. Boycott, Coercion and Intimidation. Entering into any agreement to commit, or by any concerted action committing any act of boycott, coercion or intimidation resulting in or tending to result in unreasonable restraint of, or monopoly in, the business of insurance.

E. False Statements and Entries.

(1) Knowingly filing with any supervisory or other public official, or knowingly making, publishing, disseminating, circulating or delivering to any person, or placing before the public, or knowingly causing directly or indirectly, to be made, published, disseminated, circulated, delivered to any person, or placed before the public, any false material statement of fact as to the financial condition of an insurer.

(2) Knowingly making any false entry of a material fact in any book, report or statement of any insurer or knowingly omitting to make a true entry of any material fact pertaining to the business of such insurer in any book, report or statement of such insurer, or knowingly making any false material statement to any insurance department official.

F. Stock Operations and Advisory Board Contracts. Issuing or delivering or permitting agents, officers or employees to issue or deliver, agency company stock or other capital stock, or benefit certificates or shares in any common law corporation, or securities or any special or advisory board contracts or other contracts of any kind promising returns and profits as an inducement to purchase insurance.

G. Unfair Discrimination.

(1) Making or permitting any unfair discrimination between individuals of the same class and equal expectation of life in the rates charged for any life insurance policy or annuity or in the dividends or other benefits payable thereon, or in any other of the terms and conditions of such policy.

(2) Making or permitting any unfair discrimination between individuals of the same class and of essentially the same hazard in the amount of premium, policy fees or rates charged for any accident or health insurance policy or in the benefits payable thereunder, or in any of the terms or conditions of such policy, or in any other manner.

Drafting Note: In the event that unfair discrimination in connection with accident and health coverage is treated in other statutes, this paragraph should be omitted.

(3) Making or permitting any unfair discrimination between individuals or risks of the same class and of essentially the same hazard by refusing to insure, refusing to renew, cancelling or limiting the amount of insurance coverage on a property or casualty risk solely because of the geographic location of the risk, unless such action is the result of the application of sound underwriting and actuarial principles related to actual or reasonably anticipated loss experience.

(4) Making or permitting any unfair discrimination between individuals or risks of the same class and of essentially the same hazards by refusing to insure, refusing to renew, cancelling or limiting the amount of insurance coverage on the residential property risk, or the personal property contained therein, solely because of the age of the residential property.

(5) Refusing to insure, refusing to continue to insure, or limiting the amount of coverage available to an individual because of the sex, marital status, race, religion or national origin of the individual; however, nothing in this subsection shall prohibit an insurer from taking marital status into account for the purpose of defining persons eligible for dependent benefits. Nothing in this section shall prohibit or limit the operation of fraternal benefit societies.

(6) To terminate, or to modify coverage or to refuse to issue or refuse to renew any property or casualty policy solely because the applicant or insured or any employee of either is mentally or physically impaired; provided that this subsection shall not apply to accident and health insurance sold by a casualty insurer and, provided further, that this subsection shall not be interpreted to modify any other provision of law relating to the termination, modification, issuance or renewal of any insurance policy or contract.

(7) Refusing to insure solely because another insurer has refused to write a policy, or has cancelled or has refused to renew an existing policy in which that person was the named insured. Nothing herein contained shall prevent the termination of an excess insurance policy on account of the failure of the insured to maintain any required underlying insurance.

APPENDIX B

(8) Violation of the state's rescission laws at [insert reference to appropriate code section].

Drafting Note: A state may wish to include this section if it has existing state laws covering rescission and to insert a reference to a particular code section.

H. Rebates.

(1) Except as otherwise expressly provided by law, knowingly permitting or offering to make or making any life insurance policy or annuity, or accident and health insurance or other insurance, or agreement as to such contract other than as plainly expressed in the policy issued thereon, or paying or allowing, or giving or offering to pay, allow, or give, directly or indirectly, as inducement to such policy, any rebate of premiums payable on the policy, or any special favor or advantage in the dividends or other benefits thereon, or any valuable consideration or inducement whatever not specified in the policy; or giving, or selling, or purchasing or offering to give, sell, or purchase as inducement to such policy or annuity or in connection therewith, any stocks, bonds or other securities of any insurance company or other corporation, association or partnership, or any dividends or profits accrued thereon, or anything of value whatsoever not specified in the policy.

(2) Nothing in Subsection G, or Paragraph (1) of Subsection H shall be construed as including within the definition of discrimination or rebates any of the following practices:

(a) In the case of life insurance policies or annuities, paying bonuses to policyholders or otherwise abating their premiums in whole or in part out of surplus accumulated from nonparticipating insurance, provided that any such bonuses or abatement of premiums shall be fair and equitable to policyholders and for the best interests of the company and its policyholders;

(b) In the case of life insurance policies issued on the industrial debit plan, making allowance to policyholders who have continuously for a specified period made premium payments directly to an office of the insurer in an amount that fairly represents the saving in collection expenses;

(c) Readjusting the rate of premium for a group insurance policy based on the loss or expense thereunder, at the end of the first or any subsequent policy year of insurance thereunder, which may be made retroactive only for such policy year.

Drafting Note: Each state may wish to examine its rating laws to assure that they contain sufficient provision against rebating. If they do not, this section might be expanded to cover all lines of insurance.

I. Prohibited Group Enrollments. No insurer shall offer more than one group policy of insurance through any person unless such person is licensed, at a minimum, as a limited insurance representative. However, this prohibition shall not apply to employer/employee relationships, nor to any such enrollments.

J. Failure to maintain marketing and performance records. Failure of an insurer to maintain its books, records, documents and other business records in such an order that data regarding complaints, claims, rating, underwriting and marketing are accessible and retrievable for examination by the insurance commissioner. Data for at least the current calendar year and the two (2) preceding years shall be maintained.

K. Failure to Maintain Complaint Handling Procedures. Failure of any insurer to maintain a complete record of all the complaints it received since the date of its last examination under Section [insert applicable section]. This record shall indicate the total number of complaints, their classification by line of insurance, the nature of each complaint, the disposition of each complaint, and the time it took to process each complaint. For purposes of this subsection, "complaint" shall mean any written communication primarily expressing a grievance.

L. Misrepresentation in Insurance Applications. Making false or fraudulent statements or representations on or relative to an application for a policy, for the purpose of obtaining a fee, commission, money or other benefit from any provider or individual person.

M. Unfair Financial Planning Practices. An insurance producer:

(1) Holding himself or herself out, directly or indirectly, to the public as a "financial planner," "investment adviser," "consultant," "financial counselor," or any other specialist engaged in the business of giving financial planning or advice relating to investments, insurance, real estate, tax matters or trust and estate matters when such person is in fact engaged only in the sale of policies.

Drafting Note: This provision is not intended to preclude persons who hold some form of formal recognized financial planning or consultant designation from using this designation when they are only selling insurance. This does not permit persons to charge an additional fee for services that are customarily associated with the solicitation, negotiation or servicing of policies.

(2) (a) Engaging in the business of financial planning without disclosing to the client prior to the execution of the agreement provided for in Paragraph 3, or solicitation of the sale of a product or service that

(i) He or she is also an insurance salesperson, and

(ii) That a commission for the sale of an insurance product will be received in addition to a fee for financial planning, if such is the case.

(b) The disclosure requirement under this subsection may be met by including it in any disclosure required by federal or state securities law.

(3) (a) Charging fees other than commissions for financial planning by insurance producer, unless such fees are based upon a written agreement, signed by the party to be charged in advance of the performance of the services under the agreement. A copy of the agreement must be provided to the party to be charged at the time the agreement is signed by the party.

APPENDIX B

(i) The services for which the fee is to be charged must be specifically stated in the agreement.

(ii) The amount of the fee to be charged or how it will be determined or calculated must be specifically stated in the agreement.

(iii) The agreement must state that the client is under no obligation to purchase any insurance product through the insurance agent, broker or consultant.

Drafting Note: This subsection is intended to apply only to persons engaged in personal financial planning.

(b) The insurance producer shall retain a copy of the agreement for not less than three (3) years after completion of services, and a copy shall be available to the commissioner upon request.

N. Failure to file or to certify information regarding the endorsement or sale of long-term care insurance. Failure of any insurer to:

(1) File with the insurance department the following material:

(a) The policy and certificate;

(b) A corresponding outline of coverage; and

(c) All advertisements requested by the insurance department; or

(2) Certify annually that the association has complied with the responsibilities for disclosure, advertising, compensation arrangements, or other information required by the commissioner, as set forth by regulation.

O. Failure to Provide Claims History

(1) Loss Information - Property and Casualty. Failure of a company issuing property and casualty insurance to provide the following loss information for the three (3) previous policy years to the first named insured within thirty (30) days of receipt of the first named insured's written request:

(a) On all claims, date and description of occurrence, and total amount of payments; and

(b) For any occurrence not included in Subparagraph (a) of this Paragraph (1), the date and description of occurrence.

(2) Should the first named insured be requested by a prospective insurer to provide detailed loss information in addition to that required under Paragraph (1), the first named insured may mail or deliver a written request to the insurer for the additional information. No prospective insurer shall request more detailed loss information than reasonably required to underwrite the same line or class of insurance. The insurer shall provide information under this subparagraph to the first named insured as soon as

possible, but in no event later than twenty (20) days of receipt of the written request. Notwithstanding any other provision of this section, no insurer shall be required to provide loss reserve information, and no prospective insurer may refuse to insure an applicant solely because the prospective insurer is unable to obtain loss reserve information.

(3) The commissioner may promulgate regulations to exclude the providing of the loss information as outlined in Paragraph (1) for any line or class of insurance where it can be shown that the information is not needed for that line or class of insurance, or where the provision of loss information otherwise is required by law.

Drafting Note: Loss information on workers' compensation is an example in some states of loss information otherwise required by law.

(4) Information provided under Paragraph (2) shall not be subject to discovery by any party other than the insured, the insurer, and the prospective insurer.

Drafting Note: This provision may not be required in states that have a privacy act which governs consumer access to this information. Those states considering applying this requirement to life, accident and health lines of insurance should first review their state privacy act related to issues of confidentiality of individual insured information.

P. Violating any one of Sections [insert applicable sections].

Drafting Note: Insert section numbers of any other sections of the state's insurance laws deemed desirable or necessary to include as an unfair trade practice, such as cancellation and nonrenewal laws.

Section 5. Favored Agent or Insurer; Coercion of Debtors

A. No person may require as a condition precedent to the lending of money or extension of credit, or any renewal thereof, that the person to whom such money or credit is extended or whose obligation a creditor is to acquire or finance, negotiate any policy or renewal thereof through a particular insurer or group of insurers or agent or broker or group of agents or brokers.

B. No person who lends money or extends credit may:

(1) Solicit insurance for the protection of real property, after a person indicates interest in securing a first mortgage credit extension, until such person has received a commitment in writing from the lender as to a loan or credit extension;

(2) Unreasonably reject a policy furnished by the borrower for the protection of the property securing the credit or lien. A rejection shall not be deemed unreasonable if it is based on reasonable standards, uniformly applied, relating to the extent of coverage required and the financial soundness and the services of an insurer. Such standards shall not discriminate against any particular type of insurer, nor shall such standards call for rejection of a policy because it contains coverage in addition to that required in the credit transaction;

APPENDIX B

(3) Require that any borrower, mortgagor, purchaser, insurer, broker or agent pay a separate charge, in connection with the handling of any policy required as security for a loan on real estate, or pay a separate charge to substitute the policy of one insurer for that of another. This paragraph does not include the interest that may be charged on premium loans or premium advancements in accordance with the terms of the loan or credit document;

(4) Use or disclose, without the prior written consent of the borrower, mortgagor or purchaser taken at a time other than the making of the loan or extension of credit, information relative to a policy which is required by the credit transaction, for the purpose of replacing such insurance;

(5) Require any procedures or conditions of duly licensed agents, brokers or insurers not customarily required of those agents, brokers or insurers affiliated or in any way connected with the person who lends money or extends credit.

C. Every person who lends money or extends credit and who solicits insurance on real and personal property subject to Subsection B of this section shall explain to the borrower in writing that the insurance related to such credit extension may be purchased from an insurer or agent of the borrower's choice, subject only to the lender's right to reject a given insurer or agent as provided in Subsection B(2). Compliance with disclosures as to insurance required by truth-in-lending laws or comparable state laws shall be compliance with this subsection.

This requirement for a commitment shall not apply in cases where the premium for the required insurance is to be financed as part of the loan or extension of credit involving personal property transactions.

D. The commissioner shall have the power to examine and investigate those insurance related activities of any person or insurer that the commissioner believes may be in violation of this section. Any affected person may submit to the commissioner a complaint or material pertinent to the enforcement of this section.

E. Nothing herein shall prevent a person who lends money or extends credit from placing insurance on real or personal property in the event the mortgagor, borrower or purchaser has failed to provide required insurance in accordance with the terms of the loan or credit document.

F. Nothing contained in this section shall apply to credit life or credit accident and health insurance.

Section 6. Power of Commissioner

The commissioner shall have power to examine and investigate the affairs of every insurer in this state in order to determine whether such insurer has been or is engaged in any unfair trade practice prohibited by this Act.

Section 7. Hearings, Witnesses, Appearances, Production of Books, and Service of Process

A. Whenever the commissioner shall have reason to believe that any insurer has been engaged or is engaging in this state in any unfair trade practice whether or not defined in this Act, and that a proceeding by the commissioner in respect thereto would be in the interest of the public, the commissioner shall issue and serve upon such insurer a statement of the charges in that respect and a notice of a hearing thereon to be held at a time and place fixed in the notice, which shall not be less than [insert number] days after the date of the service thereof.

B. At the time and place fixed for such hearing, the insurer shall have an opportunity to be heard and to show cause why an order should not be made by the commissioner requiring the insurer to cease and desist from the acts, methods or practices so complained of. Upon good cause shown, the commissioner shall permit any person to intervene, appear and be heard at the hearing by counsel or in person.

C. Nothing contained in this Act shall require the observance at any such hearing of formal rules of pleading or evidence.

D. The commissioner, upon such hearing, may administer oaths, examine and cross examine witnesses, receive oral and documentary evidence, and shall have the power to subpoena witnesses, compel their attendance, and require the production of books, papers, records, correspondence or other documents the commissioner deems relevant to the inquiry. The commissioner, upon such hearing, may, and upon the request of any party shall, cause to be made a stenographic record of all the evidence and all the proceedings had at such hearing. If no stenographic record is made and if a judicial review is sought, the commissioner shall prepare a statement of the evidence and proceeding for use on review. In case of a refusal of any person to comply with any subpoena issued hereunder or to testify with respect to any matter concerning which he may be lawfully interrogated, the [insert title] Court of [insert county] County or the county where such person resides, on application of the commissioner, may issue an order requiring such person to comply with the subpoena and to testify; and any failure to obey any such order of the court may be punished by the court as a contempt thereof.

E. Statements of charges, notices, orders and other processes of the commissioner under this Act may be served by anyone duly authorized by the commissioner, either in the manner provided by law for service of process in civil actions, or by registering and mailing a copy thereof to the person affected by such statement, notice, order or other process at the person's residence or principal office or place of business. The verified return by the person so serving the statement, notice, order, or other process, setting forth the manner of service, shall be proof of the same, and the return postcard receipt for the statement, notice, order or other process, registered and mailed as aforesaid, shall be proof of the service of the same.

Section 8.   Cease and Desist and Penalty Orders

If, after hearing, the commissioner finds that an insurer has engaged in an unfair trade practice, the commissioner shall reduce the findings to writing and shall issue and cause to be served upon the insurer charged with the violation, a copy of the findings in an order requiring the insurer to cease and desist from engaging in the act or practice and the commissioner may, at the commissioner's discretion order:

APPENDIX B

A. Payment of a monetary penalty of not more than $1,000 for each violation, but not to exceed an aggregate penalty of $100,000, unless the violation was committed flagrantly in a conscious disregard of this Act, in which case the penalty shall not be more than $25,000 for each violation not to exceed an aggregate penalty of $250,000; and/or

B. Suspension or revocation of the insurer's license if the insurer knew or reasonably should have known that it was in violation of this Act.

Section 9. Judicial Review of Orders

A. Any person subject to an order of the commissioner under Section 8 or Section 11 may obtain a review of such order by filing in the [insert title] Court of [insert county] County, within [insert number] days from the date of the service of such order, a written petition praying that the order of the commissioner be set aside. A copy of such petition shall be forthwith served upon the commissioner, and thereupon the commissioner forthwith shall certify and file in such court a transcript of the entire record in the proceeding, including all the evidence taken and the report and order of the commissioner. Upon filing of the petition and transcript the court shall have jurisdiction of the proceeding and of the question determined therein, shall determine whether the filing of such petition shall operate as a stay of the order of the commissioner, and shall have power to make and enter upon the pleadings, evidence and proceedings set forth in the transcript a decree modifying, affirming or reversing the order of the commissioner, in whole or in part. The findings of the commissioner as to the facts, if supported by [insert type] evidence, shall be conclusive.

Drafting Note: Insert appropriate language to accommodate to local procedure the effect given the commissioner's determination.

B. To the extent that the order of the commissioner is affirmed, the court shall thereupon issue its own order commanding obedience to the terms of such order of the commissioner. If either party shall apply to the court for leave to adduce additional evidence, and shall show to the satisfaction of the court that the additional evidence is material and that there were reasonable grounds for the failure to adduce such evidence in the proceeding before the commissioner, the court may order such additional evidence to be taken before the commissioner and to be adduced upon the hearing in such manner and upon such terms and conditions as the court may deem proper. The commissioner may modify the findings of fact, or make new findings by reason of the additional evidence so taken, and shall file such modified or new findings that are supported by [insert type] evidence with a recommendation if any, for the modification or setting aside of the original order, with the return of such additional evidence.

Drafting Note: Insert appropriate language to accommodate to local procedure the effect given the commissioner's determination. In a state where final judgment, order or decree would not be subject to review by an appellate court provision therefor should be inserted here.

C. An order issued by the commissioner under Section 8 shall become final:

(1) Upon the expiration of the time allowed for filing a petition for review if no such petition has been duly filed within such time; except that the commissioner may thereafter modify or set aside the order to the extent provided in Section 8B; or

(2) Upon the final decision of the court if the court directs that the order of the commissioner be affirmed or the petition for review dismissed.

D. No order of the commissioner under this Act or order of a court to enforce the same shall in any way relieve or absolve any person affected by such order from any liability under any other laws of this state.

Section 10.   Judicial Review by Intervenor

If after any hearing under Section 7 or Section 11, the report of the commissioner does not charge a violation of this Act, then any intervenor in the proceedings may within [insert number] days after the service of such report, cause a petition [notice of appeal] [petition for writ of certiorari] to be filed in the [insert title] Court of [insert county] County for a review of such report. Upon such review, the court shall have authority to issue appropriate orders and decrees in connection therewith, including, if the court finds that it is to the interest of the public, orders enjoining and restraining the continuance of any method of competition, act or practice which it finds, notwithstanding such report of the commissioner, constitutes a violation of this Act, and containing penalties pursuant to Section 8.

Drafting Note: The type of procedure should conform to state procedure. See also note to Section 9 concerning review by appellate courts.

Section 11.   Penalty for Violation of Cease and Desist Orders

Any insurer which violates a cease and desist order of the commissioner and while such order is in effect, may after notice and hearing and upon order of the commissioner, be subject at the discretion of the commissioner to:

A. A monetary penalty of not more than $25,000 for each and every act or violation not to exceed an aggregate of $250,000 pursuant to any such hearing; and/or

B. Suspension or revocation of the insurer's license.

Section 12.   Regulations

The commissioner may, after notice and hearing, promulgate reasonable rules, regulations and orders as are necessary or proper to carry out and effectuate the provisions of this Act. Such regulations shall be subject to review in accordance with Section [insert applicable section].

Drafting Note: Insert section number providing for review of administrative orders.

Section 13.   Provisions of Act Additional to Existing Law

The powers vested in the commissioner by this Act shall be additional to any other powers to enforce any penalties, fines or forfeitures authorized by law with respect to the methods, acts and practices hereby declared to be unfair or deceptive.

Section 14.   Immunity From Prosecution

If any person shall ask to be excused from attending and testifying or from producing any books, papers, records, correspondence or other documents at any hearing on the ground that the testimony or evidence required may tend to incriminate or subject the person to a penalty or forfeiture, and shall notwithstanding be directed to give such testimony or produce such evidence, the person shall nonetheless comply with such direction, but shall not thereafter be prosecuted or subjected to any penalty or forfeiture for or on account of any transaction, matter or thing concerning which the person may testify or produce evidence thereto, and no testimony so given or evidence produced shall be received against the person upon any criminal action, investigation or proceeding; provided, however, that no such person so testifying shall be exempt from prosecution or punishment for any perjury committed while so testifying and the testimony or evidence so given or produced shall be admissible against the person upon any criminal action, investigation or proceeding concerning such perjury, nor shall the person be exempt from the refusal, revocation or suspension of any license, permission or authority conferred, or to be conferred, pursuant to the Insurance Law of this state. Any such person may execute, acknowledge and file in the office of the commissioner a statement expressly waiving such immunity or privilege in respect to any transaction, matter or thing specified in such statement and thereupon the testimony of such person or such evidence in relation to such transaction, matter or thing may be received or produced before any judge or justice, court, tribunal, grand jury or otherwise, and if so received or produced such person shall not be entitled to any immunity or privilege on account of any testimony the person may so give or evidence so produced.

Section 15.   Separability Provision

If any provision of this Act, or the application of such provision to any person or circumstances, shall be held invalid, the remainder of the Act, and the application of such provision to person or circumstances other than those as to which it is held invalid, shall not be affected thereby.

Legislative History (all references are to the Proceedings of the NAIC).

1947 Proc. 383, 392-400, 413 (adopted).
1960 Proc. II 485-487, 509-515, 516 (reprinted).
1972 Proc. I 15, 16, 443-444, 491, 493-501 (amended and reprinted).
1977 Proc. I 26, 28, 211, 226-227 (amended).
1979 Proc. II 31, 34, 38, 39-40, 525 (amended).
1985 Proc. I 19, 39, 85-86 (amended).
1989 Proc. II 13, 21, 129-130, 132, 133-140) (amended and reprinted).
1990 Proc. I 6, 25, 122, 146 (changed name of model).
1990 Proc. II 7, 13-14, 160, 169-177 (amended and reprinted).
1991 Proc. I 9, 16, 192-193, 196-203 (amended and reprinted).
1993 Proc. I 8, 136, 242, 246-254 (amended and reprinted).
1993 Proc. 1st Quarter 3, 34, 267, 274, 276 (amended).

SUGGESTED READINGS

Academy of Actuaries. 1996. *Providing Universal Access in a Voluntary Private-Sector Market* (Febraury)

Bluhm, W.F., principal editor. 1992. *Group Insurance*. Winsted, CT: ACTEX Publishers.

Blumberg, Linda J., and Len M. Nichols. 1995. *Health Insurance Market Reforms: What They Can and Cannot Do*. Washington, DC: The Urban Institute.

Brunner, Thomas W., and Kirk J. Nahra. 1993. *Fighting Health Care Fraud: A Guide to the Benefits and Risks of Fraud Investigations*. Washington, DC: National Health Care Anti-Fraud Association.

Carlstrom, Charles T. 1994. "The Government's Role in the Health Care Industry: Past, Present, and Future," *Economic Commentary* (1 June: 1-6).

Chollet, Deborah, and Rebecca Paul. 1994. *Community Rating: Issues and Experience*. Washington, DC: Alpha Center.

Driving Down Health Care Costs: Strategies and Solutions. 1996. New York, NY: Panel Publishers. Published annually.

Fronstin, Paul. 1996. "Over 162.2 Million Nonelderly Americans Insured, 39.4 Million Uninsured, According to March 1995 CPS," *EBRI Notes* (No. 1). Washington, DC: Employee Benefit Research Institute.

Fyffe, Kathleen, et al. 1994. *Health Insurers Anti-Fraud Programs*. Washington, DC: Health Insurance Association of America.

Governent Accouting Office. 1995. *Health Insurance Regulation: Variation in Recent State Small Health Insurance Reforms.* HEHS-95-161FS (June).

Health Insurance Association of America. 1996. *Fraud: The Hidden Cost of Health Care*. Washington, DC: Health Insurance Association of America.

Health Insurance Association of America. 1997. *Fundamentals of Health Insurance: Part A*. Washington, DC: Health Insurance Association of America.

Health Insurance Association of America. 1997. *Long-Term Care: Knowing the Risk, Paying the Price*. Washington, DC: Health Insurance Association of America.

Health Insurance Association of America. 1992. *Long-Term Care: Needs, Costs, and Financing*. Washington, DC: Health Insurance Association of America.

Health Insurance Association of America. 1995. *Source Book of Health Insurance Data*. Washington, DC: Health Insurance Association of America.

Institute for Health Policy Solutions. 1995. *State Experience with Community Rating and Related Reforms*. Washington, DC: Institute for Health Policy Solutions.

Jones, Harriet E., and Dani L. Long. 1996. *Principles of Insurance: Life, Health, and Annuities*. Atlanta, GA: Life Management Institute LOMA.

Meyer, William. F. 1990. *Life and Health Insurance Law*. Cincinnati, OH: International Claim Association.

O'Grady, Francis T. 1988. *Individual Health Insurance*. Shaumburg, IL: Society of Actuaries.

Rosenbloom, Jerry S. 1996. *The Handbook of Employee Benefits Design, Funding and Administration*. 4th ed. Burr Ridge, IL: Irwin Professional Publishing.

Sadler, Jeff. 1991. *Disability Income: The Sale, The Product, The Market*. Cincinnati, OH: National Underwriter.

Sadler, Jeff. 1992. *Understanding Long-Term Care Insurance*. Amherst, MA: HRD Press, Inc.

Society of Actuaries. *Records of the Society of Actuaries*. Shaumburg, IL: Society of Actuaries. Published four times a year.

Society of Actuaries. *Transactions of the Society of Actuaries*. Shaumburg, IL: Society of Actuaries. Published annually.

Soule, Charles E. 1994. *Disability Income Insurance: The Unique Risk*. Burr Ridge, IL: Business One Irwin.

Zwanziger, Jack, and Glenn Melnick. 1996. "Can Managed Care Plans Control Health Care Costs?" *Health Affairs* (Summer): 185-199.

GLOSSARY

A

ABUSE   Stretching the truth or exaggerating the treatment of services involved in health insurance claims. May not involve misrepresentation or intention to defraud.

ACCEPTANCE   The decision made by a potential insured to enter into an insurance contract at the terms offered.

ACCIDENT   An unforeseen, unexpected, and unintended event.

ACCIDENT INSURANCE   A type of health insurance that insures against loss by accidental bodily injury.

ACCIDENTAL BODILY INJURY   An injury sustained as the result of an accident.

ACCIDENTAL DEATH AND DISMEMBERMENT INSURANCE (AD&D)   A form of health and accident insurance that provides payment to an insured's beneficiary in the event of death, or the insured in the event of specific bodily losses resulting from an accident.

ACCOUNTING   The process of recording, summarizing, and allocating all items of income and expense of the company and analyzing, verifying, and reporting the results.

ACCRUED INCOME   Income earned on a stated sum that continues to increase until payout.

ACTIVELY AT WORK   A requirement (a form of individual evidence of insurability) that an insured be at his or her usual place of employment on the date the insurance takes effect. Since this definition is impractical for dependents, plans usually require that, if a dependent is hospital confined on the date the insurance would become effective, the effective date of insurance will be deferred until release from the hospital.

ACTIVITIES OF DAILY LIVING (ADL)   Usual activities of an insured in the nonoccupational environment, such as mobility, personal hygiene, dressing, sleeping, and eating. Skills required for community or social living are also included.

ACTUARY   An accredited insurance mathematician who calculates premium rates, dividends, and reserves and prepares statistical studies and reports.

ADMINISTRATION   The handling of all functions related to the operation of the group insurance plan once it becomes effective. The claim function may or may not be included.

ADMINISTRATION MANUAL   A book of instructions provided to the policyholder by the insurer that outlines and explains the duties of the plan administrator.

ADMINISTRATIVE SERVICES ONLY (ASO) AGREEMENT   A contract for the provision of certain services to a group employer, eligible group, trustee, and so forth, by an insurer or its subsidiary. Such services often include actuarial activities, benefit plan design, claim processing, data recovery and analysis, employee benefits communication, financial advice, medical care conversions, preparation of data for reports to governmental units, and stop-loss coverage.

ADMINISTRATOR   The individual or third-party firm responsible for the administration of a group insurance program. Accounting, certificate issuance, and claims settlement may be included activities.

ADVERSE SELECTION   The tendency of those who are poorer-than-average health risks to apply for or maintain insurance coverage. Also called antiselection.

AGENCY SYSTEM   A method of selling insurance that uses persons under contract to an insurance company to act as agents for that company.

AGENT   An insurance company representative licensed by the state who solicits, negotiates, or effects contracts of insurance and services the policyholder for the insurer.

ALEATORY CONTRACT   A contract in which one of the parties may recover a substantially larger value than the value lost, depending on the occurrence of a future contingency.

GLOSSARY

ALL-CAUSE DEDUCTIBLE A policy provision under which the deductible amount is met by the accumulation of all eligible expenses for any variety of covered claims.

ALLOCATED BENEFITS Benefits for which the maximum amount payable for specific services is itemized in the contract.

ALTERED BILLS Bills for medical services that have been changed or modified in some way, forged, or are false in their entirety.

AMBULATORY CARE Medical services provided on an outpatient (nonhospitalized) basis. Services may include diagnosis, treatment, surgery, and rehabilitation.

AMBULATORY SURGICAL CENTERS A place where certain medical services can be performed on a same-day, outpatient basis.

AMENDMENT A formal document changing the provisions of an insurance policy.

ANNOUNCEMENT MATERIAL Written communications used to solicit, enroll, and explain a group insurance program.

ANNUAL STATEMENT The end-of-year report, as of December 31, of an insurer to a state insurance department showing assets and liabilities, receipts and disbursements, and other financial data.

APPLICATION Statement of relevant facts signed by an individual who is seeking insurance or by a prospective group policyholder; the application is the basis for the insurer's decision to issue a policy. The application usually is incorporated into the policy.

APPROPRIATENESS OF CARE The term used to describe the proper setting—an acute care hospital, an extended care facility, and so forth—for delivery of medical care that best responds to a patient's diagnosis.

APPROVAL (a) When used in connection with the filing of policy and certificate forms and rates with a state insurance department, approval signifies the legal acceptance of the forms by the state's representative; (b) when used in connection with underwriting, approval signifies the insurer's acceptance of the risk as set forth in the application (as originally made or as modified by the insurer); (c) approval also signifies the acceptance of an offer from an applicant or policyholder in the form of a contract for new insurance, reinstatement of a terminated policy, request for a policy loan, or other event by an officer of the company.

ASSIGNMENT OF BENEFITS   A provision in a health benefits claim form by which the insured directs the insurance company to pay any benefits directly to the provider of care on whose charge the claim is based.

ASSURANCE   Term synonymous with "insurance," more commonly used in Canada and Great Britain.

AUTOMATIC REINSURANCE   An agreement between a ceding insurer and a reinsurer that the insurer must cede and the reinsurer must accept all risks within certain explicitly defined limits.

B

BASE PLAN   Any basic medical care plan that provides limited first-dollar hospital, surgical, or medical benefits, as contrasted with major medical benefit plans that provide comprehensive hospital, surgical, and medical benefits.

BASIC COVERAGE   Refers to base plan benefits over which major medical benefits may be superimposed.

BENEFICIARY   The person or persons designated by a policyholder to receive insurance policy proceeds.

BENEFIT   The amount payable by the insurer to a claimant, assignee, or beneficiary when the insured suffers a loss covered by the policy.

BENEFIT PERIOD   The period of time for which benefits are payable under an insurance contract.

BENEFIT PROVISION   The promises made by the insurer, explained in detail in the contract.

BENEFIT WAITING PERIOD   The period of time that must elapse before benefits are payable under a group insurance contract.

BILLING SCHEMES   The manipulation of medical bills and charges to reflect amounts not justified by treatment or services rendered.

BLUE CROSS A nonprofit membership corporation providing protection against the costs of hospital care in a limited geographic area.

BLUE SHIELD A nonprofit membership corporation providing protection against the costs of surgery and other items of medical care in a limited geographic area.

BROKER A state-licensed person who places business with several insurers and who represents the insurance buyer rather than the insurance company, even though paid commissions by the insurer.

BUSINESS INTEREST INSURANCE Coverage that provides the cash for the purchase of the business interest of a partner or stockholder who becomes disabled. Also called a disability buyout.

C

CAFETERIA PLAN Another term used for a flexible benefit plan that allows employees to choose benefits from a number of different options.

CANCELLABLE CONTRACT A contract of health insurance that may be canceled during the policy term by the insurer.

CAPACITY TO CONTRACT To form a valid contract, both parties must have the ability to understand its terms. Without this ability there can be no meeting of the minds.

CAPITATION A method of payment for health services in which a physician or hospital is paid a fixed amount for each person served, regardless of the actual number or nature of services provided to each person.

CARRIER A term sometimes used to identify the party (insurer) to the group contract that agrees to underwrite (carry the risk) and provide certain types of coverage and service.

CARVE-OUT The term used to describe certain services offered by a managed care organization but singled out for individual management, usually with a capitation arrangement. Examples of carve-out service are management of chronic diseases, mental health services, and prescription drugs. Also called a specialty managed care arrangement.

CASE   The term used to refer to the entire group plan of a policyholder.

CASE MANAGEMENT   Planned approach to manage service or treatment to an individual with a serious medical problem. Its dual goal is to contain costs and promote more effective intervention to meet patient needs. Also called large case management.

CASE SUMMARY CARD   A form distributed by an insurer's home office that summarizes vital information concerning a new case or a change in an existing case.

CEDE   Activity of an insurer under a reinsurance treaty.

CEDING INSURER   The insurer that insures part of a financial risk with another insurer, called the reinsurer.

CENTER OF EXCELLENCE   A term referring to selected health care facilities that specialize and have demonstrated success in the performance of certain highly complex medical procedures.

CERTIFICATE HOLDER   The insured person under a group plan who has been issued a certificate of insurance.

CERTIFICATE OF INSURANCE   The document delivered to an individual that summarizes the benefits and principal provisions of a group insurance contract. May be distributed in booklet form.

CHECK DEPOSIT BILLING   A system, commonly referred to as preauthorized check, that allows the insurer to draw checks on the policyholder's bank account for premiums due.

CLAIM   A demand to the insurer by, or on behalf of, the insured person for the payment of benefits under a policy.

CLAIMANT   The insured or beneficiary exercising the right to receive benefits.

CLAIM COST CONTROL   Efforts made by an insurer both inside and outside its own organization to contain and direct claim payments so that health insurance premium dollars are used as efficiently as possible.

CLAIM RESERVES   Funds retained by an insurer to settle incurred but unpaid claims that may also include reserves for potential claim fluctuation.

CLASS The category into which insureds are placed to determine the amount of coverage for which they are eligible under the policy.

COINSURANCE The arrangement by which the insurer and the insured share a percentage of covered losses after the deductible is met.

COMMISSION The part of an insurance premium an insurer pays an agent or broker for services in procuring and servicing insurance.

COMPLAINT REGISTER A state insurance department list that includes the identification, handling, and disposition of consumer complaints. It may be utilized by states for enforcing unfair trade practices statutes.

COMPLIANCE In insurance, the act of conforming to or observing regulatory requirements.

COMPREHENSIVE MEDICAL EXPENSE INSURANCE A form of health insurance that provides, in one policy, protection for both basic hospital expense and major medical expense coverage.

CONDITIONAL CONTRACT A binding agreement under which the insured's acceptance is considered conditional throughout an initial set time period, and during which the insured may nullify the contract and receive a refund of the premiums.

CONDITIONAL RECEIPT A receipt given for the premium submitted with an application for insurance. Terms regarding the effective date of coverage usually are defined in the receipt.

CONSUMERISM A movement for protection of the consumer against inferior products or misleading advertising.

CONTESTABILITY The insurer's ability to investigate possible misrepresentation in an insurance application and challenge the policy's validity.

CONTESTABLE PERIOD That time allowed an insurer after a policy is issued to investigate possible misrepresentation in the application and contest the policy's validity. (See "Rescission".)

CONTRACT A binding agreement between two or more parties. A contract of insurance is a written document called the policy.

CONTRACT OF ADHESION A contract drafted by one party and accepted or rejected by the other, with no opportunity to negotiate its terms.

CONTRACT RATE The premium rate for a group insurance coverage that is specified in a master policy.

CONTRIBUTION That part of the insurance premium paid by either the policyholder or the insured or both.

CONVERSION PRIVILEGE The right given to an insured person under a group insurance contract to change coverage, without evidence of medical insurability, to an individual policy upon termination of the group coverage.

COORDINATION OF BENEFITS (COB) A method of integrating benefits payable under more than one group health insurance plan so that the insured's benefits from all sources do not exceed 100 percent of allowable medical expenses.

CORRIDOR DEDUCTIBLE A deductible used with supplemental major medical plans. It acts as a corridor between the basic plan and the medical plan. Medical expenses that exceed the amounts covered in the basic plan are covered in the supplemental major medical plan after the corridor deductible is satisfied.

COST CONTAINMENT Efforts by medical providers, insurance companies, insureds, or other interested groups to control health care costs.

COST-OF-LIVING ADJUSTMENT (COLA) A policy provision that periodically increases benefit payouts to compensate for the effects of inflation during a lengthy disability.

COST SHARING (COINSURANCE) Policy provisions that require insureds to pay, through deductibles and coinsurance, a portion of their health insurance expenses.

COST SHIFTING Transfer of health care provider costs that are not reimbursed by one payer to other payers. Many of these costs are shifted to and absorbed by private health insurance.

COVERAGE A major classification of benefits provided by a policy (e.g., short-term disability, major medical), or the amount of insurance or benefit stated in the policy for which an insured is eligible.

COVERED CHARGES Charges for medical care or supplies, which, if incurred by an insured or other covered person, create a liability for the insurer under the terms of a group policy.

COVERED EXPENSES Those specified health care expenses that an insurer will consider for payment under the terms of a health insurance policy.

COVERED PERSON Any person entitled to benefits under a policy (insured or covered dependent).

CREDIBILITY The weight assigned to a group's past claim experience in order to determine future expected claims for premium-setting purposes, or to determine claim charges for experience refund purposes for that group. Usually expressed as a percentage between 0 percent and 100 percent.

CREDIT HEALTH INSURANCE A form of health insurance on a borrower, usually under an installment purchase agreement. The benefits cover the obligations of the borrower and are payable to the creditor. This insurance is commonly used with automobile loans.

D

DAILY BENEFIT A specified daily maximum amount payable for room and board charges under a hospital or major medical benefits policy.

DECREASE IN COVERAGE Any type of change that reduces the risk assumed by the insurer.

DEDUCTIBLE The amount of covered expenses that must be incurred and paid by the insured before benefits become payable by the insurer.

DEEMER CLAUSE A statute that allows a policy form, filed with a state insurance department, to be "deemed approved" after a certain length of time unless the commissioner has given notice of disapproval.

DEFENSIVE MEDICINE Physician use of extensive laboratory tests, increased hospital admissions, and extended hospital stays for the principal purpose of reducing the possibility of malpractice suits by patients or providing a good legal defense in the event of such lawsuits.

DELINQUENT PREMIUM A premium due to the insurer that has not been paid by the end of the grace period.

DEPENDENT An insured's spouse (wife or husband), not legally separated from the insured, and unmarried child(ren) who meet certain eligibility requirements and who are not otherwise insured under the same group policy. The precise definition of a dependent varies by insurer.

DEPOSIT PREMIUM The premium deposit paid by a prospective policyholder when an application is made for an insurance policy. It is usually at least equal to the first month's estimated premium and is applied toward the actual premium when billed.

DIAGNOSIS-RELATED GROUP (DRG) A system of categorizing inpatient medical services and assigning specific reimbursement fees to each category.

DIRECT BILLING The type of billing that involves sending a premium statement to the insured as advance notification that the premium is due.

DIRECT CLAIM PAYMENT A method of paying claims whereby the insured individuals deal directly with the insurance company.

DIRECT WRITER An insurer that deals directly with prospective policyholders, without the participation of agents or brokers.

DISABILITY A physical or mental condition that makes an insured incapable of performing one or more duties of his or her own occupation or, for total disability, of any occupation.

DISABILITY BENEFIT A payment that arises because of the total and/or permanent disability of an insured; a provision added to a policy that provides for a waiver of premium in case of total and permanent disability.

DISABILITY INCOME INSURANCE A form of health insurance that provides periodic payments when the insured is unable to work as a result of illness, disease, or injury.

DISCHARGE PLANNING A managed health care process directed at limiting the duration of inpatient care to that which is medically necessary and systematically facilitating transfer of a patient to a more cost-effective care facility.

DISMEMBERMENT   The accidental loss of limb or sight.

DISTRIBUTION   The separation of all insureds (prospective or in force) under a group insurance plan by age, sex, location, income, dependency status, and benefit class for the purpose of computing gross premium rates.

DOMESTIC COMPANY   An insurer doing business in the state in which it is incorporated.

DOMICILE   The legal residence of an individual or the jurisdiction in which a corporation maintains its center of corporate affairs.

DRAFT BOOK CLAIM PAYMENT   A method of claim settlement whereby the insurer authorizes the policyholder to settle claims and to issue payment on behalf of the insurer.

DUPLICATE COVERAGE   Coverage of an insured under two or more policies for the same potential loss.

E

EFFECTIVE DATE   The date that insurance coverage goes into effect.

ELIGIBILITY   The provisions of the group policy that state the requirements members of the group and/or their dependents must satisfy to become insured.

ELIGIBILITY DATE   The date on which a member of an insured group may apply for insurance.

ELIGIBILITY PERIOD   The time following the eligibility date (usually 31 days) during which a member of an insured group may apply for insurance without evidence of insurability.

ELIGIBILITY REQUIREMENTS   Underwriting requirements the applicant must satisfy in order to become insured.

ELIGIBLE EMPLOYEES   Those employees who have met the eligibility requirements for insurance set forth in the group policy.

ELIGIBLE GROUP   A group of persons permitted, under state insurance laws and insurer underwriting practices, to be insured under a group policy; usually includes individual employer groups, multiple employer groups, labor union groups, and certain association groups.

ELIGIBLE MEDICAL EXPENSE A term describing the various types of expense the policy covers. The provision that describes these expenses commonly contains limitations applicable to certain of these expenses.

ELIMINATION PERIOD A specified number of days at the beginning of each period of disability during which no disability income benefits are paid.

EMPLOYEE BENEFITS CONSULTANT A person or firm specializing in the design, sale, and service of employee benefit plans, usually representing the policyholder in placing insurance coverage with an insurer or assisting the employer in changing or enhancing a benefit program. Compensation is provided either by commissions from the insurer or by the policyholder on a fee-for-service basis.

ENROLLMENT (SOLICITATION) The process of explaining the proposed group insurance plan to eligible persons and assisting them in the proper completion of their enrollment cards.

ENROLLMENT CARD A document signed by an eligible person as notice of desire to participate in the group insurance plan. For a contributory plan, this card also provides an employer with authorization to deduct contributions from an employee's pay. If group life and accidental death and dismemberment coverage are involved, the card usually includes the beneficiary's name and relationship.

EQUITY The value of an individual or business in excess of liabilities.

EVIDENCE OF INSURABILITY Any statement or proof of a person's physical condition and/or other factual information affecting acceptability for insurance.

EXCESSIVE DIAGNOSTIC TESTING The ordering of medical tests beyond that considered reasonable to diagnose or treat a condition.

EXCLUSIONS (EXCEPTIONS) Specified conditions or circumstances, listed in the policy, for which the policy will not provide benefits.

EXCLUSIVE PROVIDER ORGANIZATION (EPO) Form of managed care in which participants are reimbursed for care received only from affiliated providers.

EXECUTION CLAUSE   The signature of the insurer on the insurance policy signifying that the insurer has entered into the contract and will be bound by its terms.

EXPENSE LOADING   That portion of a group insurance premium required to cover acquisition and administration costs.

EXPENSE RATIO   A percentage showing the relationship of expenses to earned premiums.

EXPERIENCE RATING   The process of determining the premium rate for a group risk based wholly or partially on that risk's experience.

EXPERIENCE REFUND   The amount of premium returned by an insurer to a group policyholder when the financial experience of the particular group (or the experience refund class to which the group belongs) has been more favorable than anticipated in the premiums collected from the group.

EXPERIMENTAL TREATMENT   A method or mode of treatment not approved by medical regulatory authorities.

F

FACILITY OF PAYMENT   A contractual provision that the insurer may, under stated conditions, pay insurance benefits to persons other than the insured, the designated beneficiary, or the estate of the insured.

FACULTATIVE REINSURANCE   A type of reinsurance in which the reinsurer can accept or reject any risk presented by an insurance company seeking reinsurance.

FEE-FOR-SERVICE   A method of charging whereby a physician or other practitioner bills for each visit or service rendered.

FEE SCHEDULE   Maximum dollar or unit allowances for health services that apply under a specific contract.

FILING   The submission of a proposed policy form for approval to the insurance department of the jurisdiction where it will be issued.

FIRST-DOLLAR COVERAGE   A hospital or surgical policy with no deductible amount.

FLEXIBLE BENEFITS Employee benefit coverage offered by an employer that allows employees to select type and amount of benefits from among a menu of benefits the employer offers. Also called cafeteria plans.

FOREIGN INSURER The term a state uses to identify an insurer operating in a state other than the one in which it is incorporated.

FRANCHISE INSURANCE Individual insurance contracts issued to members of a specific group (such as employees of a common employer or members of an association) under a group-like arrangement in which the employer or association collects and remits premiums and the insurer waives its right to cancel or modify any policy unless done for all persons in the group.

FRATERNAL INSURANCE A cooperative type of insurance provided by social organizations for their members. The social group may pay premiums into a fund and withdraw monies to pay claims upon the death of one of its members.

FRAUD An intentional act or misrepresentation that results in some type of loss to another.

FUND ACCOUNT An accounting method that uses a specific formula for determining premium rates.

FUTURE INCREASE OPTION A provision found in some policies that allows an insured to purchase additional disability income insurance at specified future dates regardless of the insured's physical condition.

G

GENERAL AGENTS Agents under contract to an insurer who provide their own office facilities and clerical and supervisory personnel, and who are compensated primarily by an overriding commission.

GENERALLY ACCEPTED ACCOUNTING PRINCIPLES (GAAP) Principles of accounting and business results reporting developed by the American Institute of Public Accountants.

GRACE PERIOD A specified time (usually 31 days) following the premium due date during which the insurance remains in force and a policyholder may pay the premium without penalty.

GROSS PREMIUM   The contracted premium before applying any discounts.

GROUP CASE   Expression used to refer collectively to the entire group plan of a policyholder.

GROUP CONTRACT   A contract of health insurance made with an employer or other entity that covers a group of persons as a single unit. The entity is the policyholder.

GROUP INSURANCE   An arrangement for insuring a number of people under a single master insurance policy.

GROUP POLICYHOLDER   The legal entity to which the master policy is issued.

GROUP REPRESENTATIVE   A salaried employee of the insurer whose principal tasks are to assist agents and brokers in developing and soliciting prospects for group insurance and to install and service group contracts.

GUARANTEED INSURABILITY OPTION   (See "Future Increase Option".)

GUARANTEED ISSUE   Amounts of insurance coverage offered on a one-time basis, not requiring the insured to provide evidence of insurability.

GUARANTEED RENEWABLE POLICY   A contract under which an insured has the right, commonly up to a certain age, to continue the policy in force by the timely payment of premiums. However, the insurer reserves the right to change premium rates by policy class.

H

HAZARD   The measure of risk assumed by an insurer. It can involve physical, moral, or financial elements.

HEALTH INSURANCE   Coverage that provides for the payments of benefits as a result of sickness or injury. Includes insurance for losses from accident, medical expense, disability, or accidental death and dismemberment.

HEALTH MAINTENANCE ORGANIZATION (HMO) An organization that provides for a wide range of comprehensive health care services for a specified group at a fixed periodic prepayment.

HIGH-LOW COMMISSION SCALE A commission scale providing for the payment of a high first-year commission and lower renewal commissions.

HOME HEALTH CARE A comprehensive, medically necessary range of health services provided by a recognized provider organization to a patient at home.

HOME OFFICE ADMINISTRATION The method of insurance plan administration in which the insurer maintains the basic records for the persons covered.

HOSPICE A mode of care provided to terminally ill patients and their families that emphasizes patient comfort rather than cure and addresses emotional needs, such as coping with pain and death.

HOSPITAL BILLING AUDITS Independent examination of hospital bills by a third party to determine if services and supplies charged to the patient were actually delivered and if the price charged was correct.

HOSPITAL EXPENSE INSURANCE A form of health insurance that provides specific benefits for hospital services, including daily room and board and surgery, during a hospital confinement.

HOSPITAL INDEMNITY INSURANCE A form of health insurance that provides a stipulated daily, weekly, or monthly payment to an insured during hospital confinement, without regard to the actual expense of the confinement.

I

IDENTIFICATION CARD A form provided to insureds that identifies them as members of a particular insurance plan and may provide basic information about their coverage. Although such cards do not guarantee eligibility for medical care benefits at any given time, they provide procedures for providers to follow to verify that a patient has health coverage.

IN FORCE The total volume of insurance on the lives of covered employees at any given time (measured in terms of cases, lives, amount [volume] of insurance, or premium).

INCONTESTABILITY Result of incontestable clause defined below.

INCONTESTABLE CLAUSE The provision in a group life and/or health insurance policy that prevents the insurance company from disputing the validity of certain coverage under specific insurance conditions after the policy has been in effect for a certain time (usually two years).

INCREASE IN COVERAGE An addition in benefits that becomes effective for an insured or a group of insureds as a result of a specific change in class, due to a wage or salary increase, occupational promotion, or negotiated enhancements to the benefits program.

INCURRED BUT NOT PAID CLAIMS Claims that have not been paid as of some specified date (may include both reported and unreported claims).

INCURRED BUT NOT REPORTED (IBNR) CLAIMS Claims that have not been reported to the insurer as of some specified date.

INCURRED CLAIMS An amount equal to the claims paid during the policy year plus the change of the claim reserves as of the end of the policy year. The change in reserves represents the difference between the end of the year and beginning of the year claim reserves.

INDEMNIFY To compensate for a loss.

INDEMNITY A benefit paid by an insurance policy for an insured loss.

INDIVIDUAL INSURANCE Policies that provide protection to the policyholder and/or his or her family. Sometimes called personal insurance, as distinct from group insurance.

INDIVIDUAL PRACTICE ASSOCIATION (IPA) An association of individual physicians that provides services on a negotiated per capita rate, flat retainer fee, or negotiated fee-for-service basis. It is one model of an HMO.

INITIAL RATE A premium rate that is charged on the effective date of a new group policy.

INJURY Accidental bodily damage sustained while a particular health insurance policy is in force.

INSTALLATION The process of assisting a group policyholder to set up the administrative practices essential to the proper handling of all initial and ongoing administrative activities of the plan.

INSURABILITY Refers to the physical, moral, occupational, and financial status of a risk and its acceptability to the insurer.

INSURABLE RISK The conditions that make a risk insurable are: (a) the peril insured against must produce a definite loss not under the control of the insured; (b) there must be a large number of homogeneous exposures subject to the same perils; (c) the loss must be calculable, and the cost of insuring it must be economically feasible; (d) the peril must be unlikely to affect all insureds simultaneously; and (e) the loss produced by a risk must be definite and have a potential to be financially serious.

INSURANCE A plan of risk management that, for a price, offers the insured an opportunity to share the costs of possible economic loss through an entity called an insurer.

INSURANCE COMPANY Any corporation primarily engaged in the business of furnishing insurance protection to the public.

INSURED The person and dependent(s) who are covered for insurance under a policy and to whom, or on behalf of whom, the insurer agrees to pay benefits.

INSURER The party to the insurance contract that promises to pay losses or benefits. Also, any corporation primarily engaged in the business of furnishing insurance protection to the public.

INSURING CLAUSE The clause in a policy that names the parties to a contract and states what is covered by the policy.

INTEGRATED DEDUCTIBLE A high fixed amount (e.g., $1,000) or the sum of the benefits paid under a base medical care plan, whichever is greater, that must be exceeded before supplemental major medical benefits are payable.

INTEGRATED DELIVERY SYSTEM A system of managed care that brings together all the components of health care delivery into a single entity. They are usually organized by physicians and hospitals.

INTERIM COVERAGE Initial coverage of an applicant between the date of premium prepayment and the date the insurer notifies the applicant of its underwriting decision.

INTERNATIONAL CLAIM ASSOCIATION (ICA) An organization concerned with information and education in the area of life and health claims administration.

K

KEY-EMPLOYEE DISABILITY INSURANCE Insurance designed to protect a business firm against the loss of business income resulting from the disability or death of an employee in a significant position.

L

LAPSED COVERAGE Termination of coverage provided in an insurance contract because of the nonpayment of a premium within the time period.

LATE APPLICANT An eligible person who applies for insurance after the normal 31-day open enrollment period.

LEGAL RESERVE The minimum reserve that a company must keep to meet future claims and obligations as they are calculated under the state insurance code.

LEVEL BILLING A method of billing that allows the policyholder to pay a certain set amount of premium on each due date during the policy year, based on an estimated annual premium, with an adjustment at the end of the policy year for coverage changes that have occurred during the policy year.

LEVEL COMMISSION SCALE A method of assigning commission payments that applies the same commission rates to the premium each year, regardless of the policy year.

LEVEL PREMIUM A rating structure in which the premium level remains the same throughout the life of the policy.

LIABILITY The probable cost of meeting an obligation.

LICENSE   Certification, issued by a state department of insurance, that an individual is qualified to solicit insurance applications for the period covered.

LIFETIME DISABILITY BENEFIT   A disability income provision payable for an insured's lifetime as long as the insured is totally disabled.

LIMITATION   A provision that sets a cap on specific coverage.

LIMITED POLICY   Policy that covers only specified accidents or sicknesses.

LOADING FACTOR   The amount added to the net premium rate determined for a group insurance plan to cover the possibility that losses will be greater than statistically expected because of older average age, hazardous industry, large percentage of unskilled employees, or adverse experience.

LONG-TERM CARE   A wide range of health and personal care, ranging from simple assisted living arrangements to intensive nursing home care, for elderly or disabled persons.

LONG-TERM CARE INSURANCE   A benefits plan that provides a specific dollar benefit or a percent of expenses charged for nursing home care, home health care, and adult day care if a covered person suffers a loss of functional or cognitive capacity.

LONG-TERM DISABILITY (LTD) INCOME INSURANCE   A benefits plan that helps replace earned income lost through inability to work because of disability caused by accident or illness.

LOSS   (a) The amount of insurance or benefit for which the insurer becomes liable when the event insured against occurs; (b) the happening of the event insured against.

LOSS RATIO   The ratio of claims to premiums (claims divided by premiums).

LOSS RATIO (INCURRED BASIS)   The ratio of paid claims plus change in claim reserves to earned premiums.

M

MAJOR MEDICAL EXPENSE INSURANCE   A form of health insurance that provides benefits for most types of medical expense up to a high maximum benefit. Such contracts may contain internal limits and usually are subject to deductibles and coinsurance.

MALPRACTICE   Improper care or treatment of a patient by a physician, hospital, or other provider of health care, due to carelessness, neglect, lack of professional skills, or disregard of established rules or procedures.

MANAGED CARE   The terms used to describe the coordination of financing and provision of health care to produce high-quality health care on a cost-effective basis.

MANDATED BENEFITS   Certain coverages required by state law to be included in health insurance contracts.

MANUAL PREMIUM   The premium developed for a group's coverage from the insurer's standard rate tables.

MANUAL RATE   The premium rate developed for a group's coverage from the insurer's standard rate tables, usually contained in its rate manual or underwriting manual.

MARKETING   The sum total of all corporate functions and activities directly or indirectly involved in the selling of products to the consumer.

MASS MARKETING   Technique used by insurers to approach a large number of prospects simultaneously.

MASTER POLICY (OR MASTER CONTRACT)   The policy issued to a group policyholder setting forth the provisions of the group insurance plan.

MATERIAL MISREPRESENTATION   A false or misleading statement of fact on an application for an insurance policy, which influences the insurer's decision as to the prospective insured's insurability. Such statements may serve as a basis for voiding the policy. (See "Rescission".)

MATERNITY BENEFIT   Benefits for a normal pregnancy are paid under this provision of the hospital or medical policy rather than the regular provisions that apply to sickness, since maternity is not normally considered a sickness.

MAXIMUM BENEFIT The maximum length of time for which benefits are payable during any one period of disability.

MAXIMUM DAILY HOSPITAL BENEFIT The maximum amount payable for hospital room and board per day of hospital confinement.

MEDICAID A government insurance program for persons of all ages whose income and resources are insufficient to pay for health care; Medicaid is state-administered and financed by both the states and the federal government.

MEDICAL EXAMINATION The examination given by a qualified physician to determine an applicant's insurability or whether an insured claiming disability is actually disabled.

MEDICAL EXPENSE INSURANCE A form of health insurance that provides benefits for various expenses incurred for medical care. Benefits for prevention and diagnosis, as well as for treatment, are sometimes included.

MEDICALLY NECESSARY Term used by insurers to describe medical treatment that is appropriate and rendered in accordance with generally accepted standards of medical practice.

MEDICARE A federally sponsored program that provides hospital benefits, supplementary medical care, and catastrophic coverages to persons aged 65 and older, and to some other eligibles.

MEDIGAP A term applied to private insurance products that supplement federal insurance benefits under Medicare. Also called MedSup.

MEETING OF THE MINDS The agreement and understanding on the part of both parties concerning their respective obligations and rights under a contract.

MINIMUM GROUP The fewest number of employees permitted under a state law to constitute a group for insurance purposes; the purpose of minimum group is to maintain a distinction between individual and group insurance.

MINIMUM PREMIUM PLAN A combination approach to funding an insurance plan aimed primarily at premium tax savings. The employer self-funds a fixed percent (e.g., 90 percent) of the estimated monthly claims, and the insurance company insures the excess.

MINIMUM PREMIUM RATE The lowest premium rate that an insurer may charge a policyholder during the first year the group insurance is in effect, based on its field manual premium rates.

MINIMUM STANDARDS MODEL REGULATION Promulgated by the NAIC in 1974, it sets categories for basic forms of coverage with required minimum benefit levels.

MISREPRESENTATION A false or incomplete statement of relevant fact on an application for an insurance policy. (See Material Misrepresentation.)

MONTHLY ADJUSTMENT BILLING A method of premium billing by which the policyholder is billed on each premium due date for the insurance coverage on the actual number of persons covered by the group insurance plan.

MONTHLY INDEMNITY Benefit amount paid monthly under a health insurance policy.

MORAL HAZARD Risk from any nonphysical, personal characteristic or habit of an applicant or insured that may either increase the possibility or intensify the severity of a loss.

MORBIDITY The frequency and severity of sicknesses and accidents in a well-defined class or classes of persons.

MORTALITY The death rate in a group of people as determined from prior experience.

MULTIPLE EMPLOYER GROUP Employees of two or more employers, such as trade associations of employers in the same industry or union members who work for more than one employer, covered under one master contract.

MULTIPLE EMPLOYER TRUST (MET) A legal trust established by a plan sponsor that brings together a number of small, unrelated employers for the purpose of providing group medical care coverage on an insured or a self-funded basis.

MUTUAL INSURANCE COMPANY An insurer in which the ownership and control is vested in the policyholders.

N

NATIONAL ASSOCIATION OF INSURANCE COMMISSIONERS (NAIC) A national organization of state officials who are charged with the regulation of insurance. It was formed to promote national uniformity in the regulation of insurance. It has no official power but wields tremendous influence.

NET COST In group insurance, it equals claims plus reserves plus expenses.

NET PREMIUM The amount paid or the earned premium after discounts.

NEW BUSINESS The sale of insurance coverage to a new policyholder, and extending or adding new coverage(s) to an existing policyholder.

NONCANCELLABLE POLICY A contract the insured can continue in force by the timely payment of the set premium until at least age 50 or, in the case of a policy issued after age 44, for at least five years from its date of issue. The insurer may not unilaterally change any contract provision of the in-force policy, including premium rates.

NONCONTRIBUTORY PLAN A group insurance plan under which the employer does not require employees to share in its cost.

NONDISABLING INJURY BENEFIT A benefit in some disability income policies providing payment for medical expense due to injury when medical care is necessary but the insured is not totally disabled.

NONDUPLICATION CLAUSE A policy provision that results in a stricter application of coordination of benefits principles. When an individual is covered by two or more policies, this provision excludes expenses incurred that are covered by another policy.

NONOCCUPATIONAL INSURANCE Insurance that does not provide benefits for an accident or sickness arising out of a person's employment.

NONRENEWABLE FOR STATED-REASONS-ONLY POLICY A contract of health insurance under which the insurer has the right to terminate the coverage for only those reasons specified in the contract.

NONRENEWABLE POLICY A policy issued for a single term that is designed to cover the insured during a period of short-term risk.

NOTICE OF CLAIM A written notice to the insurer by an insured claiming a covered loss.

O

OCCUPATIONAL HAZARDS Dangers inherent in the insured's occupation that expose him or her to greater than normal physical danger by their very nature.

OCCUPATIONAL RATE A variation in premium based upon occupational class, due to differences among occupations in the incidence of accidents or illness.

OFFER The initial proposal by one contracting party to another. It is one of several necessary elements of a contract in which one party makes an initial proposal. In insurance, the application is usually considered to be the offer.

OPEN ENROLLMENT A time during which uninsured employees and/or their dependents may obtain coverage under an existing group plan without presenting evidence of insurability. Differs from a resolicitation in that a minimum number of applications are not required.

OPTIONAL PROVISIONS Certain provisions of the Uniform Policy Provision Law that an insurer may include in the insurance contract.

OPTIONALLY RENEWABLE POLICY A contract of health insurance under which the insurer has the right to terminate the coverage at any policy anniversary or, in some cases, at any premium due date.

OUT-OF-POCKET EXPENSE Those medical expenses that an insured must pay that are not covered under the group contract.

OVERHEAD EXPENSE INSURANCE A form of health insurance for business owners designed to help offset continuing business expenses during an insured's total disability.

OVERINSURANCE Coverage exceeding the probable loss to which it applies.

OVERRIDING COMMISSION A commission paid to general agents or agency managers in addition to the commission paid to the soliciting agent or broker.

P

PALLIATIVE CARE Medical relief of pain rather than cure of illness.

PARTIAL DISABILITY Inability to perform one or more functions of one's regular job.

PARTIAL DISABILITY BENEFITS A disability income benefit payable when an insured is not totally disabled but is prevented from working full time and/or is prevented from performing one or more important daily occupational duties.

PARTIAL PAYMENT A payment to a claimant where it is expected that other payments will be made before the claim can be considered closed.

PARTICIPATION The number of insureds covered under the group plan in relation to the total number eligible to be covered, usually expressed as a percentage.

PENDING CLAIM A claim that has been reported but on which final action has not been taken.

PER CAUSE DEDUCTIBLE The flat amount that the insured must pay toward the eligible medical expenses resulting from each illness before the insurance company will make any benefit payments.

PERIOD OF DISABILITY The period during which an employee is prevented from performing usual occupational duties, or during which a dependent cannot perform the normal activities of a healthy person of the same age or sex.

PERMANENT AND TOTAL DISABILITY A disability that will presumably last for the insured's lifetime and prevent the insured from engaging in any occupation.

PERSISTENCY The degree to which policies stay in force through the continued payment of renewal premiums.

PERSONAL PRODUCING GENERAL AGENT (PPGA) A person who works independently, under contract to an insurer, in the marketing of an insurer's products.

PHYSICIAN'S EXPENSE Insurance coverage that provides benefits toward the cost of such services as doctor's fees—for surgical care in the hospital, at home, or in a physician's office—and X-rays or laboratory tests performed outside of a hospital. (Also called regular medical expense insurance.)

POINT-OF-SERVICE (POS) PROGRAM A health care delivery method offered as an option of an employer's indemnity program. Under such a program, employees coordinate their health care needs through a primary care physician.

POLICY The document that sets forth the contract of insurance.

POLICY ANNIVERSARY The manual date that separates the experience under a group policy for dividend and retroactive rate purposes. The period is normally 12 consecutive months.

POLICY FEE An amount sometimes charged in addition to the first premium as a fee for issuance of the policy; for example, group health conversion policies.

POLICY ISSUE The transmittal of a policy to an insured by an insurer.

POLICY NUMBER That number assigned to a group contract that contains both the account number of the policy and the policy code number.

POLICY YEAR The time that elapses between policy anniversaries, as specified in the policy.

POLICYHOLDER The legal entity to whom an insurer issues a contract.

POLICYHOLDER ADMINISTRATION (SELF-ADMINISTRATION) Situation whereby the group policyholder maintains all records and assumes responsibility regarding the insureds covered under its insurance plan, including preparing the premium statement for each payment date and submitting it with a check to the insurer. Under this method the insurance company, in most instances, has the contractual prerogative to audit the policyholder's records.

PREADMISSION TESTING The practice of having a patient undergo laboratory, radiology, and other prescreening tests and examinations prior to being admitted to a medical facility as an inpatient.

PREAUTHORIZED CHECK (See "Check Deposit Billing".)

PRECERTIFICATION A utilization management program that requires the individual or the provider to notify the insurer prior to a hospitalization or surgical procedure. The notification allows the insurer to authorize payment, as well as to recommend alternate courses of action.

PRE-EXISTING CONDITION A mental or physical problem suffered by an insured prior to the effective date of insurance coverage.

PRE-EXISTING CONDITIONS PROVISION A restriction on payments for those charges directly resulting from an accident or illness for which the insured received care or treatment within a specified period of time (e.g., three months) prior to the date of insurance.

PREFERRED PROVIDER ORGANIZATION (PPO) A managed care arrangement consisting of a group of hospitals, physicians, and other providers who have contracts with an insurer, employer, third-party administrator, or other sponsoring group to provide health care services to covered persons.

PREMIUM The amount paid to an insurer for specific insurance protection.

PREMIUM NOTICE (BILLING) The statement requesting the policyholder to pay a premium on a particular due date. The insurer may enclose a premium remittance card that should be returned with the policyholder's check.

PREMIUM PAYMENT MODE (FREQUENCY) The number of times premiums are payable in a policy year. For example, a policy on which premiums are paid monthly is said to have a monthly premium frequency.

PREMIUM RATE The price of a unit of coverage or benefit.

PREMIUM REFUND Monies returned to a policyholder, usually because of favorable experience (e.g., an experience-rating refund).

PREMIUM TAX An assessment levied by a federal or state government, usually on the net premium income collected in a particular jurisdiction by an insurer.

PRIMARY CARE First-contact and continuing health care, including basic or initial diagnosis and treatment, health supervision, management of chronic conditions, preventive health services, and appropriate referral.

PRIMARY CARE PHYSICIAN (PCP) The network physician designated by an employee (and each of his or her dependents) to serve as that employee's entry into the health care system. The PCP often is reimbursed through a different mechanism (such as capitation) than other network providers. This physician sometimes is referred to as the "gatekeeper."

PRINCIPAL SUM The amount payable in one sum in event of accidental death and, in some cases, accidental dismemberment.

PROBATIONARY PERIOD A period from the policy's effective date to a specified time, usually 15 to 30 days thereafter, during which no sickness coverage is provided.

PRODUCTION CREDIT The new business volume and/or premium written on new and existing cases that is credited to an agent, broker, or group representative.

PROGRESSIVE CARE A term identifying a method for providing the degree of health care that is medically necessary at any given stage in illness or recovery, ranging from acute care in a hospital to recuperation at home.

PROOF OF LOSS Documentary evidence required by an insurer to prove a valid claim exists, usually consisting of a claim form completed by the insured and the insured's attending physician. Medical expense insurance claims also require itemized bills.

PROPOSAL A quotation, submitted to a prospective group insurance policyholder by an insurance company primarily through an agent, broker, or group representative, that outlines the benefits available under a suggested plan and the costs to both employer and employees.

PROSPECT A potential customer or client.

PROVIDER DISCOUNTS An element of network-based managed care programs whereby financial arrangements are negotiated with providers to reduce fees for medical services rendered.

PROVISION A part of a group insurance contract that describes or explains a feature, benefit, condition, or requirement of the insurance protection afforded by the contract.

PROVISIONAL PREMIUM An estimated premium paid prior to the exact determination of the total amount due.

Q

QUALIFICATION PERIOD The period during which the insured must be totally disabled before becoming eligible for residual disability benefits.

R

RATING Determining the cost of a given unit of insurance for a given year.

READABILITY STANDARDS Requirements that insurance policies use simplified language that an average consumer would be able to understand, as measured by an objective numerical scale.

REASONABLE AND CUSTOMARY CHARGE A charge for health care that is consistent with the average rate or charge for identical or similar services in a certain geographic area.

REBATING The illegal act of giving any valuable consideration, usually a part or all of the commissions, to a prospect as an inducement to buy insurance.

RECORD CARD (REGISTER) A card used by the insurer and/or the administrator of the plan to indicate a person insured, coverages and amounts of insurance, beneficiary, and any other information necessary to successfully administer the group plan.

RECURRENT DISABILITY CLAUSE A policy provision that clarifies amounts payable if an insured is again disabled by the same condition for which benefits previously have been paid.

REHABILITATION The process and goal of restoring disabled insureds to maximum physical, mental, and vocational independence and productivity (commensurate with their limitations). A rehabilitation provision appears in some long-term disability policies; this provides for continuation of benefits or other financial assistance during the rehabilitation period.

REIMBURSEMENT An amount paid to an insured for expenses actually incurred as a result of an accident or sickness. Payment will not exceed the amount specified in the policy.

REINSTATEMENT The resumption of coverage under a policy that had lapsed.

REINSURANCE Acceptance by one insurer (the reinsurer) of all or part of the risk of loss underwritten by another insurer (the ceding insurer).

RENEWAL Continuance of coverage under a policy beyond its original term by the insurer's acceptance of the premium for a new policy term.

RENEWAL UNDERWRITING The review of the financial experience of a group case and the establishment of the renewal premium rates and terms under which the insurance may be continued.

REPLACEMENT The substitution of health insurance coverage under one policy for coverage under another policy.

REPRESENTATION A statement by insurance applicants as to some past or existing fact or circumstance. Such statements must be true to the best of the applicant's knowledge and belief, but are not warranted as exact in every detail.

RESCISSION Voiding of an insurance contract from its date of issue by the insurer because of material misrepresentation on the application for insurance. The policy is treated as never having been issued, and the sum of all premiums paid plus interest, less any claims paid, is refunded.

RESERVE A sum set aside by an insurance company as a liability to fulfill future obligations.

RESIDUAL DISABILITY A period of partial disability that immediately follows a period of total disability.

RESIDUAL DISABILITY BENEFITS A provision in an insurance policy that provides benefits in proportion to a reduction of earnings as a result of disability, as opposed to the inability to work full-time.

RETENTION That portion of the premium kept by the insurer for expenses, contingencies, and contributions to surplus (profit).

RETENTION ESTIMATE A projection of estimated expenses on a particular group insurance case.

RIDER A document that modifies or amends the insurance contract.

RISK The probable amount of loss foreseen by an insurer in issuing a contract. The term sometimes also applies to the person insured or to the hazard insured against.

RULING A judicial decision, or a decision of the Commissioner of Internal Revenue relative to a specific tax question.

S

SCHEDULE A listing of amounts payable for specified occurrences (e.g., surgical operations, laboratory tests, X-ray services, and such).

SECOND SURGICAL OPINION An attempt to verify the need for surgery by encouraging insureds to seek the advice of another physician or surgeon who will not perform the operation.

SELF-ADMINISTRATION Maintenance of all records and assumption of responsibility, by a group policyholder, for insureds covered under its insurance plan, including preparing the premium statement for each payment date and submitting it with a check to the insurer. The insurance company, in most instances, has the contractual prerogative to audit the policyholder's records.

SELF-FUNDING A medical benefit plan established by an employer or employee group (or a combination of the two) that directly assumes the functions, responsibilities, and liabilities of an insurer.

SELF-INSURANCE A program for providing group insurance with benefits financed entirely through the internal means of the policyholder, in place of purchasing coverage from commercial carriers.

SHORT-TERM DISABILITY (STD) INCOME INSURANCE Form of health insurance that provides benefits only for loss resulting from illness or disease and excludes loss resulting from accident or injury.

SICKNESS INSURANCE A form of health insurance providing benefits only for loss resulting from illness or disease, but excluding loss resulting from accident or injury.

SOCIETY OF ACTUARIES A professional organization of life, health insurance, and pension insurance mathematicians.

SOLVENCY Ability to pay all legal debts.

SPECIFICATIONS A detailed listing of the qualifying factors of a certain group of individuals (type of risk, complete census data, contributions, past experience if a transferred case), the coverages (types, amounts, schedules), and services (self-administration, draft book claims, level commissions) that an insurance company gathers in order to obtain the right to administer the program.

SPECIFIED DISEASE INSURANCE Insurance providing an unallocated benefit, subject to a maximum amount, for expenses incurred in connection with the treatment of specified diseases, such as cancer, poliomyelitis, encephalitis, and spinal meningitis. These policies are designed to supplement major medical policies.

STANDARD PROVISIONS Policy provisions setting forth certain rights and obligations of insureds and insurers under health insurance policies. Originally introduced in 1912, these provisions were replaced by the Uniform Policy Provisions Law (UPPL).

STANDARD RISK A person who, according to an insurer's underwriting standards, is entitled to purchase insurance protection without extra premium or special restriction.

STATE INSURANCE DEPARTMENT An administrative agency that implements state insurance laws and supervises (within the scope of these laws) the activities of insurers operating within the state.

STATE OF ISSUE (SITUS) The jurisdiction in which the group insurance contract is delivered or issued for delivery.

STATUTE An enactment of a legislature (state or federal) declaring, commanding, or prohibiting something.

STOCK The outstanding capital of a corporation, represented by shares in the form of ownership certificates.

STOCK INSURANCE COMPANY An insurer in which the legal ownership and control is vested in the stockholders.

STOCKHOLDER (OR SHAREHOLDER) A person, also called a shareholder, who owns shares of stock in a corporation.

SUBROGATION The substitution of the insurer in place of an insured who claims medical expenses from a third party.

SUPPLEMENTAL MEDICAL INSURANCE Health insurance policies that fill in the gaps of medical expense coverages (e.g., deductibles, coinsurance, maximum out-of-pocket expenses); provide additional benefits (e.g., dental, prescription drugs, vision care); and cover additional expenses as a result of a severe accident or illness (e.g., accident medical expenses).

SURGICAL EXPENSE INSURANCE Health insurance policies that provide benefits toward the physician's or surgeon's operating fees. Benefits may consist of scheduled amounts for each surgical procedure.

SURGICAL SCHEDULE A list of cash or unit allowances up to a maximum amount that an insurer will reimburse, based on the seriousness of the operation.

SURPLUS The amount by which the value of an insurer's assets exceeds its liabilities.

SURVEILLANCE The covert observation of an insured to determine the extent and duration of physical activity.

T

TEN-DAY "FREE LOOK" A right of the insured to examine a policy for ten days and return it for a refund of premium if not satisfied with it. A notice of this right is required to appear on the first page of health insurance policies.

THIRD-PARTY ADMINISTRATION   That method by which an outside person or firm, not a party to a contract, maintains all records regarding the persons covered under the group insurance plan and may also pay claims using the draft book system.

THIRD-PARTY PAYER   Any organization, public or private, that pays or insures health or medical expenses on behalf of beneficiaries or recipients.

TIME LIMIT   The set number of days in which a notice of claim or proof of a loss must be filed.

TOTAL DISABILITY   Generally, a disability that prevents insureds from performing all occupational duties. The exact definition varies among policies.

TRANSFERRED BUSINESS   A term used to describe a group insurance plan that is switched from one insurer to another.

TRAVEL ACCIDENT POLICIES   Limited contracts covering only accidents that occur while an insured person is traveling on business for an employer, away from the usual place of business, and only on named conveyances.

U

UNBUNDLING OF CHARGES   The practice of making separate charges for components of a surgical procedure that results in a total fee that is higher than the usual fee for the procedure as a whole.

UNDERWRITER   The term generally applies to: (a) a company that receives the premiums and accepts responsibility for the fulfillment of the policy contract; (b) the company employee who decides whether or not the company should assume a particular risk; or (c) the agent who sells the policy.

UNDERWRITING   The process by which an insurer determines whether and on what basis it will accept an application for insurance.

UNIFORM POLICY PROVISIONS LAW (UPPL) Statutory policy provisions of health insurance policies that specify some of the rights and obligations of the insured and the insurer. These provisions, with some modifications, are part of the insurance laws of all 50 states and the District of Columbia.

UNIFORM PREMIUM A rating structure in which one premium applies to all insureds, regardless of age, sex, or occupation.

UNILATERAL CONTRACT A contract that contains legally enforceable promises by only one of the parties to the contract. An insurance policy is a unilateral contract.

UNPROVEN TREATMENT A method or mode of treatment not approved by medical regulatory authorities.

UPCODING The practice of charging for a service that represents more treatment than was actually given, either in testing, office procedures, or surgical operations.

USUAL AND CUSTOMARY CHARGE (See "Reasonable and Customary Charge".)

UTILIZATION Patterns of usage for a single medical service or type of service (e.g., hospital care, prescription drugs, physician visits). Measurement of utilization of all medical services in combination usually is done in terms of dollar expenditures. Use is expressed in rates per unit of population at risk for a given period, such as number of annual admissions to a hospital per 1,000 persons over age 65.

UTILIZATION REVIEW A program with various approaches designed to reduce unnecessary hospital admissions and to control inpatient lengths of stay through use of preliminary evaluations, concurrent inpatient evaluations, or discharge planning.

WAITING PERIOD The time a person must wait from the date of entry into an eligible class or application for coverage to the date the insurance is effective.

WAIVER The voluntary surrender of a right or privilege known to exist.

WAIVER (EXCLUSION ENDORSEMENT) An agreement attached to the policy and accepted by the insured that eliminates a specified pre-existing physical condition or specified hazard from coverage under the policy.

WAIVER OF PREMIUM A provision that, under certain conditions, a person's insurance will be kept in full force by the insurer without further payment of premiums. It is used most often in the event of permanent and total disability.

WELLNESS PROGRAMS Employer programs provided to employees to lessen health risks and thus avoid more serious health problems.

WORKERS' COMPENSATION Liability insurance requiring certain employers to pay benefits and furnish medical care to employees for on-the-job injuries, and to pay benefits to dependents of employees killed by occupational accidents.

WORKERS' COMPENSATION LAW A statute imposing liability on employers to pay benefits and furnish care to employees injured and to pay benefits to dependents of employees killed in the course of and because of their employment.

WRIT OF MANDAMUS A court order commanding a regulatory officer, such as an insurance commissioner, to perform some specified act.

INDEX

Abuse, 173-201
  fraud vs, 174-175
  insured, 180-185
  provider, 174-180
  trends, 199-200
Accessibility, 171
Accident and health policy experience exhibit, 166
Accounting, 44
Acquisition expenses, 108
Actual accidents, 184
Actual-to-expected (A/E) ratio, 133
Actuary, 101
Adequacy, premium rates, 102
Adjusted statements, 167
Adjustment factors, premium rate development, 122-123
Administration
  continuing, 43-57
  expenses, controlling, 15
  forms, 42
  insurance company, 43-44
  manual, 55
  policyholder and, 43-45
  third-party, 61-62
Administrative services only (ASO), 62
Administrator, 42
Admitted assets, 164
Advertising, 151
Affordability, 171
Age-at-entry premiums, 120, 121
Age-band method, 46
Age Discrimination in Employment Act (ADEA), 161

Age distribution, premium rate and, 111-112
Agent, 42-43
  licensing, 148-149
AIDS, 152
Alcohol treatment facilities, 13
Altered bills and forms, 182-183
  detection, 187-188
Alternatives, cost-effective, 9-13
Ambulatory care, 11
Ambulatory surgery facility review, 22
American Cancer Society, 105
Americans with Disabilities Act (ADA), 161
Analysis of claim
  by claim personnel, 95-96
  experience, 96
Analysis of operations by lines of business, 165
Announcement literature, 37
Annual claim cost, 119
Annual financial statements, 163-164
Annual statements, 145
Antidiscrimination laws, 160-161
Antifraud efforts, 186
Any occupation provision, 87
Application
  processing system, 16
Application, group health insurance
  obtaining, 36
  reviewing, 38
Assets, 164
Assistant surgeon review, 21-22
Attained-age premium rates, 119, 121

263

Attitude of entitlement, 181
Auditing, 90
   hospital bill charges, 14, 96
   self-administered policyholders, 62-64
Automated repetitive payment system, 98
Automatic bank payments, 50
Automation, 41

Benefit period, establishing, 81-82
Benefit plan design, cost containment and, 5-13
Benefits
   proper payee, 80
   -related deductible, 6
Billing
   for services not rendered, 179-180, 186
   group premium, 45-48
   guidelines, 179
   individual premium, 50-51
   schemes, 177-178
Bills, altered, 182-183
Birthing centers, 11
Blended manual/experience-rated groups, 117-118
Break-even year, 129

California, 147
Cancellation, group health insurance, 50
Card-only approach, 72
Carve-outs, 28
Case management, 23-25, 30
   needs, 23-24
   process, 24
Case summary record, preparing, 38-39
Catastrophic illness or injury, 23-24
Centers of excellence, 29

Central Index Bureau (CIB), 191
Certificates, 44
Changes, 52-57
   group, 52-55
   individual, 55-57
Check, draft vs, 70
Children, additional, 54
Civil Rights Act, Title 7, 160
Civilian Hospital and Medical Program of the Uniformed Services (CHAMPUS), 157
Claim
   costs, 103-104
   documentation, 73-80
   forms, 74-75
   fraud, indications of, 90
   frequency, 106
   investigation, 88-90
   -kit approach, 71-72
   payment process, 90-91
   practices, 149
   procedure, ERISA, 158
   processing, 80-88
   processing technology, 97-98
   provisions, disability income insurance, 86
   reserves, 106-107
   services only (CSO), 62
   systems, 180
Claim administration, 67-99
   methods, 71-73
   objective, 67-68
   trends, 98-99
Claims
   auditing, 191
   expenses, 16-17
   experience, analysis of emerging, 132
   processing, 17
   valuations of incurred claims, 124
Class method, 46
Coinsurance, 6-7, 10

INDEX

Combination premium rates, 120
Commissioners, state insurance, 143
Company objectives, premium rate and, 116
Competitiveness, premium rates, 103
Complaints
　handling, 52
　policyholder, 149
Compliance, 168
　committee or staff, 168-169
　division, 168
　mechanism, 168-169
　noncompliance, 169-170
Compulsory nonoccupational disability benefits laws, 147
Computer support databases, 190-191
Concurrent review, 18-19
Confidentiality, 151
Consolidated Omnibus Budget Reconciliation Act (COBRA), 159
Consumer investigative reports, 162
Consumer price index (CPI), 1, 2
Consumer reports, 162
Contingency margin, 109-110, 126
Continued-stay review, 19-20
Controlling claim costs, 92-96
Coordination of benefits (COB), 8-9, 93-95, 183
　HMOs and, 95
　impact of, 95
Copayment, 6-7
　waived, 179
Cost containment, benefit plan design, 5-13
Cost-effective alternatives, 9-13
Cost management, 1-34
　trends, 31-32
Cost sharing, 5-7
Costs, 1-5
　causes of increases, 4
　trends, 31-32
Coverage method, 45-46

Credit health claims, 85
Cross-subsidization between products, 132
Customary charge limits, 82-83
Customer service, 92

Date of coverage
　group health insurance, 75
　individual health insurance, 75, 78
Dates, fraudulent, 186
Decreases in coverage, 57
Deductibles, 5-6
　waived, 179
Demographics, 105
Denial of claims, 91
Department of Motor Vehicles (DMV), 191
Dependent benefit changes, 53-54, 56-57
Dependent child/parents not separated or divorced, 94
Dependent child/parents separated or divorced, 94
Dependent/nondependent, 94
Diagnoses, fraudulent, 186
Diagnosis-related groups (DRGs), 155
Diagnostic testing, excessive, 175-176
Direct billing, 50
Direct submission, 71-72
Disability insurance, 113
　compulsory nonoccupational laws, 147
　see also Rehabilitation
Disability insurance claims, 181-182
　group, 83-86
　individual, 86-88
Discharge planning, 20
　programs, 20
Discounts, 122
Discrimination, 103
　laws to prevent, 160-161
　prevention of unfair, 151-152

265

Draft
   book system, 70
   check vs, 70
Drug treatment facilities, 13
Due date, 47

Economic conditions, 181–182
   premium rate and, 112–113
Education services, 30–31
Effective date of coverage, 75
Electronic claims processing, 97–98
Electronic claims submissions, 200
Electronic funds transfer (EFT), 49
Electronic surveillance, 190
Eligible charge limits, 14–15
Eligible groups, NAIC, 150
Emergency room treatment, 10
Emerging claims experience, analysis, 132
Employee
   benefits, 157
   certificate, preparing, 39–40
   contributions, 7–9
   termination, 53
Employee Retirement Income Security Act (ERISA), 158
Employment laws, 160–161
Enforcement, procedures, 143
Enrollment
   cards, 44
   employees, 37
   forms, 37–38
   new, 52–53
Entitlement, attitude of, 181
Equal installment billing, 46
Equity, premium rates, 102–103
ESRD, 156
Ethics, 195–199
Examination
   free policy, 148
   periodic, 143

Exception billing, 46
Exclusive provider organizations (EPOs), 28
Executive branch, regulations, 141
Expense of operation, 107–109
Expenses, methods of allocating 109
Experience
   data, 105
   monitoring, 130–134
   period, choice of, 123
   refund formula, 126
   refunds, 130–131
Experience-rated premiums, 123
   calculation methods, 127
Experimental treatments, covering, 196–197
Expert disability system, 98
Extended care facility review, 20–21
External audit, 64

Fair Credit Reporting Act, 162
Family and Medical Leave Act (FMLA), 161
Federal actions and laws, 157–163
Federal agencies, fraud deterrents, 192
Federal benefits programs, 153–157
Federal Bureau of Investigation (FBI), 192
Federal Maternity Law, 160
Field office claim administration, 69
Filing requirements, 145–146
Financial condition, state laws, 144–145
Financial incentive programs, 7–9
Financial reporting requirements, 163–167
Flat deductible, 6
Fluctuation margin, 126
Foreign claims, 180–181
Foreign investigators, 190
Forms, altered, 182–183

Fraud, 173-201
  abuse vs, 174-175
  control, federal agencies, 192
  cost, 173
  detection software, 98
  detection training, 189
  frequency, 185-186
  indications of, 90
  insured, 180-185, 186
  legal deterrents, 192-194
  prevention and detection, 187-193
  provider, 174-180, 186
  trends, 199-200
Free policy examination, 148
Frequency, 104
Fully experience-rated groups, 117
Fund account formula, 129

General overhead, 108
Generally accepted accounting principles (GAAP), 167
Geographic location, premium rate and, 112
Geographic variation, 103
Government regulation, 137-172
  trends, 170-171
  see also Laws; Regulation
Government role, 170
Grace period, 49, 78
Gross domestic product (GDP), 1, 3
Group insurance
  experience rating, 123-128
  manual rating, premium rate development, 121-123
  participation level, premium rate and, 113
  plan changes, 54-55
  pricing regulations, 147
  rate assessment, 55
  rating classes, 116-118
  representatives, 42-43
  rerating, 130-133
  state laws, 144
  underwriter, 108
Group model HMO, 27
Group premium
  accounting, 49
  billing, 45-48
  collection, 49-50
  payments, 48-49
Guaranteed renewable policies, 60

Hawaii, 147
Health care
  fraud and abuse data collection, 193
  reform, 32
Health Insurance Association of America (HIAA), 195
Health Insurance Claim (HCFA-1500), 75, 77
Health Insurance Portability and Accountability Act (HIPAA), 53-54, 159-160, 192-193
  pricing and, 134
Health Maintenance Organization (HMO) Act, 162-163
Health maintenance organizations (HMOs), 27
Health promotion programs, 31
Historical data, five-year, 165-166
HIV, state regulation, 152
Home health care, 12
Home health services, 154
Home office
  acquisition expenses, 108
  claim administration, 68-69
Hospice care, 13, 154
Hospital benefit plan, 154
Hospital billing audits, 14, 96
Hospital care, 154
Hospital expenses, claims, 80-81

267

Hospitalization
    inappropriate and unnecessary, 17
    length of stay, 176
Hospital supplement policies, 184

Identification card-only approach, 72
Identification cards, distributing, 40
Imaging system, 97
Immunity, 193
Income classes, premium rate and, 112
Income tax, 153
Increases
    coverage, 57
    existing policies, 56
Incurred but not reported (IBNR) claim reserve, 106
Incurred claims, 124
    loss ratios, 133-134
Independent practice association (IPA), 27
Index System, 191
Individual insurance
    disability income claims, 87-88
    experience analysis, 133-134
    policy changes, 55-57
    premium billing, 50-51
    premium collection, 51
    premium rate structures, 118-121
    pricing regulations, 147-148
    rating methods, 128-129
    state laws, 144
Individual underwriting
    premium rate and, 113-114
    premium rate guarantee period, length, 114
Industry
    associations, role of, 170
    compliance mechanisms, 168-170
Inflated charges, 179
Inflation, premium rate and, 112-113

Information cards, 40
Initial premium, 46-47
Injury, sickness vs, 87
Inpatient utilization review, 17-20
Inquiries, handling, 51-52
Installation, group policies, 42-43
Insurance companies, as financial institutions, 138
Insurance-for-profit schemes, 183
Insurance industry, antifraud activities, 194-195
Insurance records, other, 188
Insurance speculation, 183-184
Insured
    fraud, 186
    responsibilities, ethical, 199
Insurer
    actions for renewal, 58-61
    initiatives, general, 188-189
    insolvency, 144-145
    -policyholder shared administration, 43-45
    responsibilities, ethical, 196-197
    solvency, state laws, 144-145
Integrated delivery systems, 29
Interest rates, premium rate and, 113
Internal audit, 63
International Claim Association (ICA), 195
Investigative report, 89
Investment income, 110-111
Issue procedures
    group health insurance, 38-40
    individual health insurance, 41

Judicial branch, regulations, 141-142

Kassebaum-Kennedy Health Insurance Reform Legislation, 192-193

INDEX

Large amount audit, 90
Laws, 41, 140
  new federal, 192-193
  state insurance, 144-149
Legal department, 169
Legislative branch, regulations, 141
Legislation
  health insurance industry support, 32
  premium rate and, 114-115
  see also Laws; Regulation
Length of stay in hospital, 19, 176
Level billing, 46
Level of care, 19
Level premium rates, 119-120, 121
Liabilities, 165
Licensing, 148
  state laws, 144
Life-style, 30
Lines of business, analysis of operations by, 165
List billing, 46
Loadings, 122
  expected expenses, 126-127
  profit, 127
Lock-box arrangement, 48
Long-term disability (LTD)
  income claims, 84-85
  premium rate, 112
Loss ratio
  formula, 128-129
  incurred claims, 133-134

Maintenance expenses, 108
Major medical claims, 81
Major medical insurance, block buying, 134-135
Malpractice, 198-199
Managed care, 26-30
  ethics, 197-198

insurer response, 30
Managed care organizations (MCOs), 26-29
Mandates, 146-147
Manual rate, conversion of net rate to, 122
Manually rated groups, 117
Market reform, 171
Marketing
  expenses, 15-16
  misleading, 196
  strategies, premium rate and, 116
Massachusetts, 138
Master policy, preparing, 39
Maximum reimbursement levels, 7
McCarran-Ferguson Act (PL 15), 139-140
Medicaid, 156-157
  payments, 3
  waivers, 170
Medical care, trends and premium rate, 112-113
Medical consultants, 96
Medical expense claims, 80-83
Medical practices, questionable, 175-177
Medical records review, 188
Medical rehabilitation, 25
Medical savings account (MSA), 8
Medicare, 154-156
  expenditures, 3
Medicare secondary payer (MSP), 155-156
Minimum benefit standards, individual insurance, 150
Minimum loss ratios, premium rate and, 115
Misleading marketing, 196
Misrepresentation, 79, 80
Model laws *see* National Association of Insurance Commissioners

269

Morbidity
  concept of, 104
  statistics, sources of, 105
Motor vehicle accidents, staged, 184-185

Narrower guarantee, 171
National Association of Insurance Commissioners (NAIC)
  AIDS, 152
  formation, 139
  Model Advertising Rules, 151
  Model Group Health Insurance Act, 150
  Model Individual Accident and Sickness Insurance Minimum Standards Act, 150
  Model Insurance Information and Privacy Protection Model Act, 151
  model laws, state regulation and, 150-152
  Model Policy Language Simplification Act, 150
  unfair discrimination, 151-152
National Convention of Insurance Commissioners, 139
National Mover's Index, 191
National Health Care Anti-Fraud Association (NHCAA), 194
National Insurance Crime Bureau (NICB), 191
National Safety Council, 105
Net rate
  calculation, 122
  conversion to manual, 122
Network model HMO, 27
New enrollments, 52-53
New Hampshire, 138
New Jersey, 147
New York, 138, 139, 147
No out-of-pocket expenses, 179

Noncancellable policies, 61
Noncompliance, consequences of, 169-170
Nondependent/dependent, 94
Nonrenewable for stated-reasons-only policies, 60
Nonrenewal of coverage, 197
Notice of claim, 73-74
Nurse coordinator, 19
Nursing, skilled, 12

Occupation classes, premium rate and, 112
Onset of the condition, 79
On-site audit, 90
Open enrollment requirements, 65
Optionally renewable policies, 59-60
Order of benefit determination rules, 93-94
Organization, state laws, 144
Out-of-pocket expenses, 179
Outpatient
  surgery, 10-11
  utilization review, 22-23
Overinsurance, 183-184
Overutilization of services, 176
Own occupation disability provision, 87

Paid benefits, premium rate and, 115
Palliative care, 13
Paper accidents, 184-185
Part A, 154
Part B, 155
Partial disability, 87
Participation level, premium rate and, 113
Patient involvement, 24
Paying the claim, 91
Payment controls, 14-17
Penalties, 169

Pending claim reserve, 106-107
Per policy, allocation of expenses, 109
Percentage deductible, 6
Percentage of claims, allocation of expenses, 109
Percentage of premium, allocation of expenses, 109
Performance measurements, 129-130
Permissible investments, 145
Persistency, premium rate and, 115-116
Physician's care, disability income insurance, 86
Physician's examination, disability income insurance, 86
Plan changes, 132-133
Plan design, premium rate and, 111
Point-of-service (POS) plans, 28
Policy
  exclusions, disability income insurance, 86
  issue, 35-41
  reserves, 107
  review, 43
  wording, 182
  year experience, 134
Policyholder
  complaints, 149
  draft, 70
  submission, 73
Postauditing claims, 189
Preadmission
  certification, 18
  review, 20
  testing, 9-10
Preauditing claims, 189
Preauthorized checks (PACs), 48-49
Preemption, ERISA, 159
Preferred provider organizations (PPOs), 27-28

Pregnancy, 160
Preissue procedures
  group health insurance, 36-38
  individual health insurance, 41
Premium, 15
  deposit, initial, 36-37
  due date, 47
  statements, 40, 47
  tax, 152
  see also Rate
Prevention, 30-31
Pricing, 101-135, 147-148
  components, 103-111
  influencing factors, 111-116
  principles, 102-103
  trends, 134-135
Primary carrier, 8
Privacy of information, 151
Product claim department, 69
Professional expenses, claims, 81
Profit, 110
  margin for, 127
  percentage of premium, 129
Progressive care, 11
Proof of loss, 74-75
Property Insurance Loss Register (PILR), 191
Prospective claims, projection of, 124-126
Prospective outpatient certification review, 23
Prospective review, 17-22
Provider
  fraud, 186
  payment, 155
  responsibilities, ethical, 197-199
Puerto Rico, 147

Quality of life, 198

271

Random sample audit, 90
Rate
  calculating initial, 40
  calculating net rate, 122
  development, 121-130
  increase, 131
  review, 130-134
  revision, 147-148
  see also Premium
Rating classes and structures, 116-121
Readability standards, 150
Reasonable and customary charges, 14-15
Reasonableness
  charge limits, 82-83
  premium rates, 102
Record keeping, 44
Recurrent disability, 88
Regulation
  authorities, 165
  focus and requirements, 166-167
  formal, 141
  growth, 140
  history, 138-140
  informal, 141
  premium rate and, 114-115
  source, 140-142
Rehabilitation
  benefits of, 25
  disability income insurance, 86
  management, 24-25
Reimbursement, maximum levels, 7
Reinstatement
  group health insurance, 78
  individual health insurance, 78-79
Renewal, 57-61
  insurer actions, 58-61
  notice, 61
  premium rate and, 115
  underwriting, 58

Reporting to law enforcement agencies, 189
Rerating, timing, 131-132
Reserves, 106-107, 145, 165
Residual disability, 88
Resource-based relative value scale (RBRVS), 155
Retrospective review, 22
Return on investment, 129-130
Review, procedures, 143
Rhode Island, 147

Sales compensation expenses, 107
Scanning system, 97
Screening guides, 95-96
Second opinion, 21
Secondary plan's payment, determination of, 94-95
Self-administered plans, monitoring, 89
Self-administered policyholders, auditing, 62-64
Self-administration, 45
  claims, 70-71
Selling methods, 148-149
Severity, 104
Sex distribution, premium rate and, 111-112
Short-term disability income claims, 83-84
Sickness, injury vs, 87
Single claim department, 69
Skilled nursing care, 154
Skilled nursing facilities, 12, 20
Sliding deductible, 6
Social security, 153-154
Special investigative unit, 188-189
Specialized coverage, 46
Specialty managed care arrangements, 28

Staff model HMO, 27
Standard Provisions Law, 139
Standardization, 179-180
State
    agencies, fraud deterrents, 193-194
    insurance law, 144-149
    regulations, 41
    tax laws, 152-153
State insurance departments, 142-143
    establishment of, 138
    organization and powers, 142
Statements, adjusted, 167
Statistics
    credibility of, 105-106
    morbidity, 105
Status of coverage, 75, 78
Status of the policy, 78-79
Statutes, 140
Summary of operations, 165
Supplementary medical insurance, 155
Supportive care, 12
Surgical review, 21
Surveillance vendors, 190
Swoop and squat, 184

Taxes, 108
    disability benefits, 84
    state, 152-153
Telephone inquiries, 92
Terminal illness, 13
Termination, 50
Third-party administered plans, monitoring, 89
Third-party administration, claims, 71
Third-party administrators (TPAs), 61-62

Threshold corridor deductible, 6
Total disability, 88
    related to occupation, 87
Transactions of the Society of Actuaries, 105
Treatment, unproven, 176-177

Unbundling of charges, 178
Underwriting
    changes in coverage, 56
    complaints, 52
    expenses, 16
    renewal, 58
Uniform Billing UB-92 (HCFA-1450), 74-75, 76
Uniform Policy Provision Law, 78
Uniform premium rates, 118-119
Unit rates, conversion to, 128
Upcoding, 178
Utilization profile, 22
Utilization review, 17-23, 30

Validity of the policy, 79-80
Valuations of incurred claims, 124
Variable deductible, 6
Vendor efforts against fraud and abuse, 189
Video spectral comparator, 187-188
Vocational rehabilitation, 25

Waiver of coverage, 38
Weekend admissions, 10
Welfare plan, 158
Wellness programs, 31
Written communication, 92